KENTUCKY, 1861

REACTING TO THE PAST is an award-winning series of immersive role-playing games that actively engage students in their own learning. Students assume the roles of historical characters and practice critical thinking, primary source analysis, and argument, both written and spoken. Reacting games are flexible enough to be used across the curriculum, from first-year general education classes and discussion sections of lecture classes to capstone experiences, intersession courses, and honors programs.

Reacting to the Past was originally developed under the auspices of Barnard College and is sustained by the Reacting Consortium of colleges and universities. The Consortium hosts a regular series of conferences and events to support faculty and administrators.

Note to instructors: Before beginning the game you must download the Gamemaster's Materials, including an instructor's guide containing a detailed schedule of class sessions, role sheets for students, and handouts.

To download this essential resource, visit https://reactingconsortium.org/games, click on the page for this title, then click "Instructors Guide."

KENTUCKY, 1861

Loyalty, State, and Nation

Nicolas W. Proctor and Margaret Storey

REACTING
TO THE PAST

BARNARD

The University of North Carolina Press

Chapel Hill

The University of North Carolina Press has been a member of the
Green Press Initiative since 2003.

Cover illustration: *Dividing the National Map*. Library of Congress Prints and
Photographs Division, Washington, D.C.

ISBN 978-1-4696-7071-3 (pbk.: alk. paper)
ISBN 978-1-4696-7239-7 (e-book)

ABOUT THE AUTHORS

NICOLAS W. PROCTOR is professor of history at Simpson College. He received his Ph.D. in U.S. history from Emory University and is the author of *Bathed in Blood: Hunting and Mastery in the Old South*. He is also the chair of the Reacting to the Past editorial board and the author of Reacting games on the Seven Years' War on the Pennsylvania frontier, the Chicago Democratic Convention of 1968, Reconstruction in New Orleans, and the art of the Paris Exposition Universelle of 1889, as well as a handbook for Reacting game designers.

MARGARET STOREY is professor of history at DePaul University. She received her Ph.D. in U.S. history from Emory University and is the author of *Loyalty and Loss: Alabama's Unionists in the Civil War and Reconstruction*, editor of *Tried Men and True: Or, Union Life in Dixie*, and co-curator of the online exhibit *The Civil War in Art: Teaching and Learning Through Chicago Collections*.

CONTENTS

KENTUCKY, 1861

PART 1: **INTRODUCTION**

BRIEF OVERVIEW OF THE GAME

As one of the northernmost slaveholding states, Kentucky played a pivotal role in the crisis unleashed by Lincoln's election in 1860. Fairly industrialized, quite populous, economically and culturally tied to the North and South, and astride a number of rail and river arteries, Kentucky's disposition in the secession crisis was of great strategic significance. As Lincoln remarked in 1861, "I think to lose Kentucky is nearly the same as to lose the whole game."

Kentucky, 1861, deals with the series of shocks dealt to the nation throughout the "secession winter" of 1860–61, beginning with Lincoln's election and culminating in the attack on Fort Sumter. Setting the game in the Kentucky legislature instead of in Washington, D.C., allows students to wrestle with major political thinkers of the antebellum era (including John C. Calhoun, Andrew Jackson, Daniel Webster, Abraham Lincoln, William H. Seward, Frederick Douglass, and Stephen Douglas) on unfamiliar and therefore malleable ground. Among the "big ideas" in this game are questions of state sovereignty, white supremacy, immigration, and the relationship between the individual and the state.

Students' roles in the game include political leaders, newspaper editors, and militia officers. Opening with a special session of the legislature, *Kentucky, 1861*, forces students to struggle with the complex and divided loyalties of their roles. They must determine how to reconcile varied motivations, interests, and ideologies with an unprecedented and intensely combustible situation. Informed by assorted texts from the period, including speeches and political tracts, students debate the cultural, economic, and political concepts driving secession while reacting to a constantly shifting political and military situation. Through rhetoric, the press, and paramilitary action, they struggle to alter the fate of the nation.

PROLOGUE

Frankfort, December 1860

You wake having hardly slept. Who should you blame? Your first thought is the mattress—so thin that you can feel the slats beneath it—but there are other possible culprits. Perhaps it was the snoring of your unwelcome and pointy-elbowed bedmate, or the stale reek of tobacco from the spittoon in the corner. Maybe it was bedbugs. It would not be the first time you've encountered vermin in a boardinghouse bed. Weighing these possibilities, you check yourself for bites. Finding none, you sit up and identify another likely cause: your roiling gut, queasy from a late supper of cold corn bread and stewed fruit, bolted down after a long day of travelling to the capital.

You rise and splash water on your face from the washbasin. Your head clears, and suddenly the cause of last night's discomfort and unease comes back to you in a rush. It's not the whiskey toddy you drank before retiring. It's that long-armed ape from Illinois: *Abraham Lincoln!*

He is the reason you spent last night in Frankfort, twisting in an uncomfortable bed, and why, for the first time in many years, you packed a revolver in your carpetbag before leaving home for your journey to the capital. You should have spent the night in your own bed, warmed by a fire tended by one of your loyal bondsmen, but instead you are here. You and your fellow legislators have been called by the governor for a special session because those fool Yankees elected a damned Black Republican to the White House.

You look out the window and see that the town has already shaken itself awake. Wagons, horses, and a few buggies move along unpaved streets. Several dogs and pigs nose around the gutters without much enthusiasm. The cold makes people move with stiff urgency, but boxes must be loaded and barrels must be rolled. Only children dash about as storekeepers begin the day's business. You dress quickly, thankful for your long woolen coat and the thick whiskers that grace your chin and chops.

After a breakfast of hot corn bread, sausages, and coffee, you step out into the street and survey the scene. Your boardinghouse occupies a choice location in Frankfort's modest downtown. Flanked by other two-story brick storefronts, it faces Broadway, a main thoroughfare dominated by the tracks of the Louisville and Frankfort Railroad, which run directly through its center. The trains that regularly trundle through town carry passengers west to the thriving river city of Louisville or east to prideful Lexington, the de facto capital of the Bluegrass. Further west the line connects to the Louisville and Nashville Railroad, which runs south through Tennessee to connections in Alabama and Mississippi and north to Ohio and Indiana. Under construction for years, the L&N finally opened for through service to the South just last year. This gives you a little thrill of pride—it shows Kentucky moving forward. But it is also cause for concern: if North and South come to blows, as some predict they will, those rails will gain immense strategic significance. Both sides will want to control this excellent route from North to South.

In recent years, this sort of improvement encouraged an increasing number of European immigrants to settle in Kentucky. Most remain in cities along the Ohio River, but some, like the aproned and elaborately mustachioed German storekeeper smoking his pipe in a doorway across the street, landed in Frankfort.

As you return his affable nod, you reflect that your civility toward the German and Irish newcomers is not shared by many of your countrymen. Indeed, these predominately Catholic immigrants inspired the explosive growth of the anti-immigrant American Party just five years ago. The so-called Know-Nothings lacked much of a platform beyond "throw out the foreigners" but they successfully drained votes from the Whig Party, already weak from the ongoing debate over slavery. Northern Whigs who wanted to resist the expansion of slavery into Kansas alienated the Southern Whigs, who could not take an antislavery stance without committing political suicide. Whiggery was always strong in Kentucky, the home state of the Great Compromiser, Senator Henry Clay, but even here it could not resist the centrifugal stresses of debates over Western expansion and rising nativist xenophobia. Many Kentuckians continue to espouse Whig ideals in favor of the union and progress, but as an organized national political party, the Whigs have ceased to exist.

The rhetoric of the Know-Nothings was radical and nasty, and it led to violence. One of the worst riots took place in Louisville. "Bloody Monday," as it is remembered, featured gun battles and widespread arson. Twenty-two people died. Frankfort saw violence too. A few years ago, in 1857, a crowd gathered at the polls and hurled rocks and bottles to prevent immigrants from voting. Finally, U.S. District Judge Thomas B. Monroe accompanied an Irishman to the voting place. When the crowd stirred, he drew a large knife and issued a challenge. The assailants backed down, and the Irishman cast his vote. It was not a proud moment for democracy, but it surely reveals the rough-and-tumble nature of Kentucky politics. Eventually, the Know-Nothings fell apart. You recognize that a number of factors played a role in their demise, but in your mind, the actions of Judge Monroe did more to dismantle Kentucky's branch of the American Party than anything else.

As much as you disliked the Know-Nothings and their efforts to divide Americans against themselves, you consider the party that rose to replace them—the Republicans—even worse. By self-righteously denouncing slavery and playing upon sectional tensions, they threaten to tear the entire nation apart, and despite their lack of appeal throughout the South, they installed their man as president: Lincoln. At the thought of him, you spit into the gutter.

Disgusted by the turn of your thoughts, you walk west down Broadway. Your boardinghouse is well placed, especially in this cold weather, for visiting legislators like yourself, with the grounds of the state capitol only a few steps away. But you would prefer other quarters all the same: the Mansion House Hotel across the street, a substantial brick building, possesses some true amenities, including a cigar stand and a bar. In your experience, as much legislative business takes place there as in the chambers of the capitol itself. Unfortunately, you arrived in Frankfort too late to find housing there or in the similarly well-appointed Capital Hotel. Now, it seems, every bed in town is filled: even in your humble boardinghouse, you must endure an unwelcome bedmate.

Rather than heading toward the capitol, you decide to take a quick turn around town to clear your head and settle the uncomfortable stirrings of your bowels. As you cross the intersection of Frankfort's two main roads—Broadway and St. Clair—you can survey the dimensions of the town to the north, south, east, and west. With fewer than four thousand inhabitants, Frankfort is small for a state capital. Broadway only runs a few blocks in either direction, and for a main thoroughfare it is not terribly busy. Wagons and buggies poke along, the horses drawing them slowed by the winter cold. Men and women, enslaved and free, attend to their business. A few legislators amble toward the statehouse, their breath puffing little clouds before them.

As you walk, you survey the steep hills enclosing the town, your eyes settling on the hilltop that houses Frankfort's cemetery and the grave of the celebrated frontiersman Daniel Boone. The poor fellow died in Missouri, but his remains and those of his wife were brought back home by some enterprising Kentuckians. There is also a section devoted to Kentucky volunteers who fell at the battle of Buena Vista during the Mexican War. These graves prove that Kentuckians have always been enthusiastic and patriotic expansionists. What right have the Republicans to exclude Kentuckians and their property from Western territories won with the blood of Kentucky's sons?

Your eye follows the ridgeline to the state arsenal. The old arsenal—some just called it the "gun house"—stood on the capitol grounds, but after it exploded and burned down in 1836, the legislature wisely sited its replacement a half mile away. A fortress-like brick edifice, it holds most of the arms and all of the cannons of the commonwealth's volunteer militia, the Kentucky State Guard.

As you think about this storehouse of arms, you wonder, in retrospect, if it was wise to support the bill reorganizing the state militia that the legislature passed at the request of the governor back in March of this year. At the time it seemed apt. John Brown's attack on Harper's Ferry had raised a panic; legislators started seeing abolitionist agitators under every bush and therefore strengthened the post of inspector general, which the governor promptly staffed with capable Mexican War veteran Simon Bolivar Buckner. Charged with improving the quality of the Kentucky militia, Buckner now travels throughout the state drilling militia companies and disbanding those he considers unruly or incompetent. Few objected at the time, but now some wonder where his sympathies lie on the question of secession. A few suggest that he has used his authority to purge the State Guard of those who do not share his sympathies. It is true that most of the companies he ordered disbanded were well-stocked with Unionists. As a result, some members of these units continue to drill and have taken to calling themselves the "Home Guard." Worse still, some new militia units, such as the Lexington Rifles led by the bold cavalier John Hunt Morgan, openly espouse secession and hold themselves apart from the State Guard. You dread the day that they come to blows.

As you turn south, you scold yourself for such grim considerations. Surely, the situation is not so dire. As you glance back at the capitol, it strikes you as rather grand. Completed about twenty years ago and built from polished Kentucky marble, it looks like a Greek temple. The fine columns of the portico hearken back to Athens and the birth of democracy. A mere two generations ago this was a howling wilderness—battleground of the Delaware, Shawnee, and Cherokee. Now it is a model of the republican form of government. Within the capitol lies further grandeur: an excellent law library, the first of its kind west of the Appalachians. The floor-to-ceiling bookshelves creak under the wisdom of the ages and anchor the work of the legislature in the rule of law. Surely your idle thoughts of unruly rioters and rival militias are foolish ones. You and your fellow Kentuckians are civilized and reasonable men.

You stroll further south and glimpse a lone horseman emerging from the covered bridge that crosses the Kentucky River. A plume of black smoke rises from a steamboat moving steadily upstream. Behind you, a few more legislators pile out of the Mansion House and walk towards the capitol. You consider joining them, but you think you see Stephen F. Hale among them. A representative of the Deep Southern state of Alabama, he was dispatched from Montgomery to encourage Kentucky to consider the virtues of secession. You dislike his near-constant lambasting, so you decide to continue your morning constitutional and turn west, strolling out of the business district and into an area filled with houses. Smoke rises from the chimneys of houses lining the streets while families busy themselves inside.

This elicits charming thoughts of your own family and fireside, and you lapse into a pleasant reverie until you come upon the storied Wilkinson House, built by Governor James Wilkinson soon after he was dispatched westward by President Thomas Jefferson. Wilkinson laid out much of the original town of Frankfort, and many remember him for this laudable accomplishment, but you also recall his later connection to the vicious machinations of the underhanded Aaron Burr and his so-called "western conspiracy." You know the tale well. Burr, who served as Jefferson's vice president, thirsted for power. This longing led to his deadly riverside duel with Alexander Hamilton. His appeal at the polls was ruined, but his boundless ambition continued unabated.

Rather than running for office, Burr positioned himself to become a caesar for the New World. Looking to the West, he saw opportunities for conquest and sought to lead an army of volunteers down the Mississippi River to wrest the port of New Orleans from the weak hands of the Spanish. Then, he reasoned, he could pull the entire Mississippi basin, perhaps including Kentucky, into a new empire of his founding. He drew a number of ambitious men, including Governor Wilkinson, into his web. Fortunately for the young republic, suspicions grew, Wilkinson developed doubts, and the conspiracy collapsed. Burr was jailed, and for the duration of his first trial, he was imprisoned in Wilkinson House. Although he escaped conviction, Burr was ruined. You consider this a just punishment for placing personal ambition before the manifest destiny of the nation.

Happier days surrounded Wilkinson House during the visit of Washington's aide, the Marquis de Lafayette, who stayed in Frankfort during his grand tour of the United States in 1825. Everywhere he went, Lafayette found himself bombarded with balls and receptions, as the rising generation sought to honor the accomplishments of their fathers. Frankfort proved no exception.

A generation removed, this desire to echo the War of Independence persists. You suspect that the fire-eaters, Secessionists like Rhett and Yancey, are the ones to have fully embraced the "Spirit of '76." Republicans claim Lincoln as president, but he might as well be a foreign despot like King George—no one here voted for him. Even as a native son, Lincoln failed to carry a single county of Kentucky. Out of 160,590 votes cast in the commonwealth, he received a miniscule 1,366, yet the Republicans proclaim him president over every state of the union.

You weigh the accomplishments of Burr and Lafayette in your mind as you finally turn back toward the capitol. Lafayette crossed an ocean to challenge tyranny and gained immortality. Burr laid plans to steal an empire by force, but found himself undone by untrustworthy subordinates and died in obscurity. By what tricks of fate, you wonder, could their careers have been reversed? How fine is the razor's edge upon which they danced? Given the odds, Lafayette could have been hanged on a rope (or, at the very least, lost his head to Madame Guillotine) and Burr could have been the first leader of a great inland empire.

Fortunately, you decide, Providence does not allow such randomness to direct our lives. The City on a Hill shall endure! This is a special nation and Kentucky unique within it. The challenges faced by the young nation have been many, but the United States of America emerge from each conflict stronger than when they entered it, and Kentucky is often the reason why. Internal squabbles have repeatedly threatened disunion—first over nullification, then, twenty years later, over Mexico, then over Kansas—but solutions have been repeatedly brokered by Kentuckians. Foreign threats—whether Mexican, Indian, or British—have been repeatedly defeated, and Kentuckians usually lead the way to victory.

As you take the final steps back toward the capitol, these thoughts make your heart rise until you overhear a conversation between two of your colleagues. They are discussing a speech given two years ago by the president-elect. "A house divided against itself cannot stand," he told a crowd of Illinois Republicans. "I believe this government cannot endure, permanently, half *slave* and half *free*. I do not expect the Union to be *dissolved*—I do not expect the house to *fall*—but I *do* expect it will cease to be divided. It will become *all* one thing, or *all* the other." You shudder. It is madness. Madness.

If such a thing could be accomplished without bloodshed, it would have been done by now. If giants like Henry Clay and Daniel Webster and John C. Calhoun could not effect such a change, how can an untutored country bumpkin like Lincoln expect to do so? Your spirits sink again. After half a century of peace and prosperity, you have a lunatic in the White House. The Union has never faced such great peril.

WHAT IS REACTING TO THE PAST?

Reacting to the Past is an innovative classroom pedagogy that teaches history and related subjects through a series of immersive role-playing games. Students in Reacting read from specially designed game books that place them in moments of heightened historical tension. The class becomes a public body or private gathering; students assume the roles of real or fictionalized persons from the period, some of whom are members of factional alliances. Their purpose is to advance an agenda and achieve victory objectives through formal speeches, informal debate, negotiations, vote-taking, and conspiracy. After a few preparatory sessions, the game begins and the students are in charge. The instructor serves as an adviser and arbiter. The outcome of the game sometimes differs from historical events; a debriefing session sets the record straight.

HOW TO PLAY A REACTING GAME

The following is an outline of what you will encounter in Reacting and what you will be expected to do.

Game Setup

The instructor will explain the historical context of the game before it formally begins. During the setup period, you will read several different materials:

- This game book, which includes historical background, rules and features of the game, core texts, and essential documents

- A role sheet describing the historical person you will play in the game and, where applicable, the faction to which you belong

- Supplementary documents or books that provide additional information and arguments for use during the game

Read all or as much of this material as possible before the game begins and reread it throughout the game. A second and third reading while *in character* will deepen your understanding and alter your perspective. Students who have carefully read the materials and are familiar with the rules of the game will do better than those who rely on general impressions.

Game Play

Once the game begins, usually one student will be randomly chosen, elected, or identified by role to preside over the Game Sessions. The instructor will then become the Gamemaster (GM) and take a seat at the back of the room. While not directing the play of the game, the GM may do any of the following:

- Pass notes to individuals or factions

- Announce important events, some of which may be the result of students' actions, others instigated by the GM

- Perform scheduled interventions, sometimes determined by die rolls

- Interrupt proceedings that have gone off track

- Arbitrate play-related controversies

There are usually two types of roles in Reacting games: members of factions and Indeterminates, individuals who operate outside the established factions. All role sheets include an individualized description of your biography, personal responsibilities, powers, and objectives. If you are a member of a faction, you may also receive a faction advisory, which outlines the concerns and objectives of the faction as a whole. Indeterminates provide factions with obvious sources of extra support. One faction will never have the voting strength to prevail without allies; cultivating Indeterminates' loyalty is, therefore, in the interest of every faction. Collaboration and coalition-building are at the heart of every game, but Indeterminates who recognize their own power may drive a hard bargain.

The classroom may sometimes be noisy: side conversations, note-passing, and players wandering around the room are common and accepted practices in Reacting. But these activities are also disruptive and can spoil the effect of formal speeches, so players should insist upon order and quiet before they begin their addresses.

Always assume when a fellow student speaks to you in or out of class that he or she is speaking to you in role. If you need to address a classmate out of role, employ a visual sign, like crossed fingers, to indicate your changed status. It is inappropriate to trade on out-of-class relationships when asking for support or favors.

Work to balance your emotional investment in your role with the need to treat your classmates with respect. Some specific roles may require you to advocate beliefs with which you personally disagree. While such assignments may seem difficult at first, careful study of your role sheet and the readings should help you develop a greater understanding of why this person thought and acted as he or she did. In a few cases, you may even need to promote ideas that are viewed today as controversial or offensive. Again, always go back to the sources: analyze why those ideas made sense for that person in that particular time and place, and then advocate those beliefs as persuasively and effectively as you can. If you ever feel uncomfortable or uncertain about your role, feel free to speak with your instructor. Remember also that you will have an opportunity during the debriefing session to discuss the differences between your game character and your personal beliefs and values.

All of the characters in this game are racists. This may cause discomfort, but it is essential for understanding the key role that racism played in the conflict over secession. The game asks you not to recreate the rhetoric that was historically employed in these debates—in fact, this rhetoric is prohibited—but to recognize the power and ubiquity of hateful ideas.

Game Requirements

The instructor will lay out the specific requirements for the class. In general, though, a Reacting game will ask students to perform three distinct activities:

Reading and Writing. This standard academic work is carried out more purposefully in a Reacting game, as what you read is put to immediate use and what you write is meant to persuade others to act in certain ways. The reading load (including both preparation and research) may vary with each role; the writing requirement is typically a set number of pages per game. In both cases the instructor is free to make adjustments. Papers are often policy statements but can also take the form of autobiographies, poems, newspaper articles, clandestine messages, or after-game reflections, all of which may provide the basis for formal speeches.

Public Speaking and Debate. In most games every player is expected to deliver at least one formal speech (the length of the game and the size of the class will affect the number of speeches). Debate occurs after a speech is delivered. Debate is impromptu, raucous, and fast-paced and often followed by decisions determined by voting.

Strategizing. Communication among students is a pervasive feature of Reacting games. You will find yourselves writing emails, texting, attending out-of-class meetings, and gathering for meals with your classmates on a fairly regular basis. The purpose of these communications is to lay out a strategy for advancing your agenda and thwarting that of your opponents and to hatch plots that ensnare the individuals who are working against your cause.

Skill Development

A Reacting role-playing game provides students with the opportunity to develop a host of academic and life skills:

- Effective writing
- Public speaking

- Problem-solving

- Leadership

- Teamwork

- Adapting to quickly changing circumstances

- Working under pressure

- Meeting deadlines

PART 2: **HISTORICAL BACKGROUND**

CHRONOLOGY

1788	U.S. Constitution ratified
1792	Kentucky statehood
1798	Virginia and Kentucky Resolutions
1817	American Colonization Society, devoted to the colonization of freed slaves, is founded
1820	Missouri Compromise resolves tensions over Western expansion
1828	Nullification Crisis heightens sectionalism and the conflict between states' rights and federal supremacy
1833	American Anti-Slavery Society, devoted to immediate emancipation, is founded
1844	Cassius Clay founds *The True American*, Kentucky's leading abolitionist publication
1846-48	Mexican War results in the acquisition of immense territory
1850	Compromise of 1850; Kentucky approves new constitution
1854	Kansas-Nebraska Act establishes popular sovereignty as the mechanism to admit new states
1858	*Dred Scott* decision questions the freedom of all people of African descent
1858	Lincoln–Douglas debates
1859	John Brown's raid on Harper's Ferry alarms white Southerners
1860	March: Militia Act and Manumission Act pass in Kentucky November: Lincoln elected December: South Carolina secedes; Crittenden proposes his amendments
1861	January: Kentucky state legislature meets in special session

KENTUCKY AND THE CRISIS OF SECESSION

Kentucky offers a host of contradictions to students of the secession crisis. The state is economically diverse yet deeply committed to slavery, strongly Unionist yet filled with states' rights sympathizers. It laid claim to an unequalled legacy of compromise and moderation, yet remained trapped between increasingly polarized sections. Of immeasurable worth symbolically (as a slave state in the upper South) and strategically (as a critical link between North and South), Kentucky's choices in the winter of 1860–61 crucially shaped the course of the United States.[1]

As this essay and the game it introduces will reveal, studying Kentucky provides an excellent opportunity to explore ideas essential to understanding the nation's great sectional crisis as a whole. The interplay of politics, ideology, and economics; the nature and limits of personal, local, and national loyalties; the significance of slavery and slaveholding in the debates over secession and states' rights; and the importance of subregional identities to American political history all play a role in the state's history.

To best understand Kentucky's place in the sectional crisis, it is important to begin with the origins of national ideas about states' rights, state sovereignty, and secession, and the relationship between those ideas and the debate over slavery in the antebellum era.

States' Rights

Though there was general (if not unanimous) agreement among the delegates sent to Philadelphia to attend the 1787 Constitutional Convention that they needed to jettison the Articles of Confederation and craft a republican form of government, great diversity of opinion existed about the nature and extent of federal and state sovereignty.

Two camps soon emerged among the delegates. Federalists—led by James Madison, Alexander Hamilton, and George Washington, among others—argued that the new constitution should establish a government with strong central authority. A minority of delegates, the so-called "Anti-Federalists," opposed this view because they believed it would undermine the notion of a "union of states" in favor of a potentially tyrannical national government. They jealously guarded what they considered the inheritance of the Revolution: the sacrosanct right of the people, through their states, to govern themselves.[2]

The tipping point in favor of the Constitution came in 1788 with the public promise from the Federalists that a Bill of Rights would be proposed during the first Congress. That Bill of Rights enumerated select individual rights and, in the Tenth Amendment, offered strong support for the rights of states: "The powers not delegated to the United States by the Constitution, nor prohibited by it to the States, are reserved to the States respectively, or to the people."

Kentucky, 1861

ILLINOIS

INDIANA

OHIO

Cincinnati

Covington

to St. Louis

Ohio River

Mississippi River

Louisville

Frankfort

Lexington

BLUEGRASS

VA.

PENNYROYAL

KENTUCKY

CUMBERLAND PLATEAU

Paducah

Cairo

JACKSON PURCHASE

Columbus

Cumberland River

Tennessee River

Nashville

TENNESSEE

Tennessee River

N.C.

to Memphis

The Virginia and Kentucky Resolutions. Agreement on the Constitution did not, however, signal concurrence on all issues, nor a shared sense among Americans of the proper extent of federal power. A significant debate on this question developed less than ten years after ratification, when, during President John Adams's administration, the country confronted the challenge of accommodating political dissent and the growth of political parties within the new constitutional framework. In 1798, the Federalist-controlled Congress passed a series of four laws—the Alien and Sedition Acts—designed to restrain opposition to the Adams administration.

Opponents decried the laws, charging that they violated the Constitution in various ways, not least of which was the Bill of Rights protection of freedom of speech, assembly, and the press. The fourth of this series of laws, the Sedition Act, clearly targeted the political enemies of President Adams and the Federalist Congress and became the source of the greatest controversy. In protest, Thomas Jefferson and James Madison (who had, since ratification, become increasingly distrustful of his Federalist allies) secretly authored two resolutions and arranged to have them endorsed by the legislatures of Kentucky and Virginia. The **Virginia Resolution**, authored by Madison, explicitly condemned the Alien and Sedition Acts and reminded the government that the state of Virginia had, when ratifying the Constitution, "declared that, among other essential rights, 'the liberty of conscience and the press cannot be cancelled, abridged, restrained, or modified, by any authority of the United States'."[3] Perhaps even more significant, however, Madison argued that *the states* had the power to "interpose" themselves if the federal government violated the rights of the people, and that "the powers of the federal government" resulted "from the compact to which the states are parties."[4]

The **Kentucky Resolution**, authored by Jefferson, was even stronger in its assertion of states' right to "nullify" a federal law they considered unconstitutional. Like Madison, Jefferson believed that "the several states composing the United States of America are not united on the principle of unlimited submission to their general government," but had come together in a compact under the banner of the Constitution and its amendments as "a general government for special purposes." The states had "delegated to that government certain definite powers, reserving, each state to itself, the residuary mass of right to their own self-government; and that whensoever the general government assumes undelegated powers, its acts are unauthoritative, void, and of no force." The federal government, furthermore, did not have the right to set the parameters of its own powers. Instead, "as in all other cases of compact among powers having no common judge, *each party has an equal right to judge for itself, as well of infractions as of the mode and measure of redress.*"[5]

Other states were decidedly unimpressed with this articulation of states' rights. Both resolutions had ended with explicit requests for other states to sign on, but over the course of 1799, state legislatures, including those from slaveholding states, responded critically.[6] To allow Virginia to "persist" in this course, the state of

Massachusetts argued, would reduce the Constitution "to a mere cipher, to the form and pageantry of authority, without the energy of power."[7] After Jefferson became president in 1800, the acts were allowed to expire.

The Nullification Crisis. In 1828, South Carolinian **Democrat** John C. Calhoun (vice president to Andrew Jackson at the time) resurrected and recast the constitutional theories articulated by the Kentucky and Virginia resolutions in the form of the *South Carolina Exposition and Protest*.[8] The object of Calhoun's ire was the **Tariff** of 1828, which set high taxes on imported manufactured goods. Frustrated by what he saw as an anti-Southern trend in national policies, Calhoun advocated for the **nullification**, or nonenforcement, of the tariff in his home state.

Expanding on the logic of the compact theory of government as proposed in the Virginia and Kentucky resolutions, Calhoun asserted that "it would seem impossible to deny to the States the right of deciding on the infractions of their powers, and the proper remedy to be applied for their correction."[9] Rather than allowing state legislatures to nullify objectionable federal laws, Calhoun insisted that all such questions be put to conventions of delegates elected by the people for that purpose only.[10]

Though it may seem tempting to assert a clear doctrinal connection between the language of the Virginia and Kentucky resolutions and later theories of nullification and secession, it would be a mistake to conclude that the crisis of 1798 was the same as that experienced in 1830, or in 1860–61: it was not yet a conflict between North and South.[11]

Nationalists such as Senator Daniel Webster and President Andrew Jackson rejected the basis for Calhoun's argument, although Calhoun and other Southern sectionalists firmly believed that their new ideas were based in Jeffersonian republicanism. Although the tariff issue was eventually resolved through compromise, Calhoun's ideas formed the kernel of a separatist movement that gained momentum over the subsequent decades. (See Webster's "Second Reply to Hayne," pp. 81–86.)

The question that must be explored, then, is how Southern political leaders and citizens came to embrace a states' rights defense of Southern sectional interests after the nullification crisis. Particular historical developments not only prompted the new **sectionalism** but continued to resonate profoundly with antebellum Southerners anxious about protecting slavery and the Southern "institutions" it fueled. What were those developments? And how did they lead to the crisis of secession?

The Early Republic

A cardinal feature of these changes was the evolution of the new nation's economy. During this period, the people of New England and the Middle Atlantic increasingly engaged in manufacturing and commerce oriented toward

The **Democratic Party** coalesced around President Andrew Jackson. It upheld the policy of universal white male suffrage, celebrated Western expansion, and generally supported the institution of slavery.

Tariffs are taxes on imports or exports. They were the primary source of income for the federal government in the early nineteenth century.

Nullification is the legal theory that a state has the right to invalidate any federal law it deems unconstitutional.

Sectionalism refers to the conflict between North and South—the two antagonistic "sections" of the mid-nineteenth-century United States.

intrastate trade. Local economies diversified and thereby encouraged the rise of wage labor in the new industries and commercial ventures that began to spring up in urban centers.

A notable exception to this lack of economic diversity was Kentucky's singular investment in hemp, a crop marketed almost exclusively to other Southern states for use in the bagging and baling of cotton.[12]

The economies of the Southern states did not diversify to the same degree as the North: the profitability of cotton, tobacco, rice, and sugar processed by slave labor significantly hampered the development of intrastate trade and local manufacturing. Southerners invested excess capital in slaves and in improving transportation corridors to export crops from interior regions, relying much more heavily on external markets for manufactured goods.

The rise of wage labor in the North did not result in the rapid demise of slavery. As historian Ira Berlin has noted, even though by 1804 "every state north of the Chesapeake [had] enacted some plan for emancipation," in 1810, "there were still 27,000 slaves in these so-called free states" and in "New York and New Jersey, the largest slaveholding states in the North, emancipation legislation left some black people locked in bondage or other forms of servitude until the mid-nineteenth century and beyond."[13] The market revolution in the Northern states undermined slavery by hastening this **gradual emancipation**, but its death was complicated, drawn out, and highly variable.

Southern commitment to slavery deepened overall, but in some areas—particularly in the Upper South—it seemed to be on the wane. The Westward expansion of cotton culture after the War of 1812 radically altered the nature of slave society in the South: the region went from producing about three hundred thousand bales of cotton annually just after the war to four million bales per year by 1850. Boom times for slavery in the Deep South had produced this growth, but also resulted in the relative decline of slave populations in much of the Upper South. In 1790 the slave populations of Maryland and Virginia composed 32 and 39 percent of the total population, respectively. By 1860, however, Maryland's slaves represented just under 13 percent of the state's population and Virginia's, just over 30 percent.[14] In addition to the growth of their white populations, this shift was due to the increasing volume of the domestic slave trade.[15]

The domestic slave trade was one of the few wholly internal market economies developed by the South. As historian Ira Berlin has noted, "The internal slave trade became the largest enterprise in the South outside of the plantation itself, and probably the most advanced in its employment of modern transportation, finance, and publicity.... In all, the slave trade, with its hubs and regional centers, its spurs and circuits, reached into every cranny of southern society."[16] By the Civil War, at least 875,000 African Americans had been forcibly relocated to the Deep South, the vast majority of those as part of the intrastate slave trade.[17]

Gradual emancipation is the process by which slavery was eliminated in much of the North in order to protect property rights. It was usually achieved by setting a date in the future after which no one would be born into slavery.

Though Kentucky had used slaves heavily during early settlement, by the 1820s it had become a net exporter of slaves. The state's slave population represented 16 percent of the total population in 1790, increased to 20 percent by 1810, reached an antebellum high of 24 percent in 1830, and then returned to 1810 levels by 1860.[18] North of the Ohio River, the Northwest Ordinance prohibited slavery but made allowances for the capture of escaped slaves. Thus, though the states on the borders of the South used fewer slaves in plantation agriculture than those of the Deep South, a number of those states (including Kentucky) were deeply implicated in and committed to the system itself, which fostered great wealth for many.

The **Second Great Awakening** was a Protestant revival movement during the early nineteenth century that featured progressive reforms.

Manumission is the process by which slaves were legally freed by their owners.

The nation of **Liberia** was founded on the West Coast of Africa by the American Colonization Society in the early nineteenth century. The Society hoped that it would become a homeland for free blacks.

Abolitionism

Another significant change took place alongside these economic transformations in the form of a great revolution in religious ideology and practice in both the North and the South. Referred to as the **Second Great Awakening** or the Great Revival, this episode in the expansion of evangelical Protestant Christianity continued from the late 1790s through the 1830s.

This evangelical revolution also fostered new ideas both in opposition to and in favor of slavery. The first important innovation was the American Colonization Society. Founded in 1817, it aimed to end slavery slowly through **manumission** and the purchase of individual slaves while relocating newly freed slaves, as well as free blacks, out of the United States. In 1822, the Society founded the colony of **Liberia** on the coast of West Africa for this purpose.

The idea of colonization was not a new one; Thomas Jefferson had proposed a similar scheme for Virginia in 1777. His fellow Virginian James Monroe helped to found the Society along with Kentuckians Henry Clay and James Birney. The supporters of colonization were diverse—whites from both the North and the Upper South shared a general dislike of slavery and the firm conviction that whites and blacks could not live peaceably together in the event of general emancipation. Some black activists, driven by the twin impulses of separatism and missionary zeal to convert Africans to Christianity, also supported the Society, but in the end, manumission schemes simply failed to take root. Even in Kentucky, where support for colonization was strong, manumission remained rather rare. Moreover, when masters freed their slaves, only a few of these freedpeople elected to leave the United States.[19]

In much of the North, newfound evangelical fervor fostered heightened activism against a range of "social evils," including drunkenness, prostitution, nonobservance of the Sabbath, and slavery.[20] This encouraged a radical fringe of abolitionists to reject colonization and gradual emancipation in favor of the *immediate* emancipation of slaves. In 1833, the American Anti-Slavery Society was founded by, among others, white evangelicals including William Lloyd Garrison,

Adherents of "**Free Labor**" considered wage earning superior to slavery because it facilitated upward mobility and independence. This became a central tenet of the Republican Party.

Slave societies are those in which forced labor affects every aspect of the social structure.

Arthur and Lewis Tappan, and Theodore Dwight Weld. They generally encouraged mixed racial audiences at their meetings; the most radical even encouraged the participation of women speakers. Beyond rhetorical agitation, they engaged in direct abolitionist action particularly in those areas bordering the South, including participating in the Underground Railroad.[21]

Southern evangelicals applied many of the rhetorical tactics arising from the Great Revival to craft a full-throated denunciation of abolitionism and an increasingly strident and confident defense of slavery. Pursuing the perfectionism of revivalism, they rejected the interference of Northern preachers and reformers in Southern institutions and asserted the superiority of slave society to the **free labor** North. They also suggested improvements to slavery based on their understanding of Christianity. As historian Mitchell Snay has concluded, "Religion worked as an active agent translating the sectional conflict into a struggle of the highest moral significance," though, according to historian Luke Harlow, pro-slavery evangelicals were "not uncritical" in their support of the institution. Indeed, most theological defenses of slavery in the antebellum period also argued for reforming it along the lines of Christian mastery, proposing that sinful practices plagued an essentially good system[22] (see James Henley Thornwell's "A Southern Christian View of Slavery," pp. 168–74).

Slavery in Kentucky. Kentucky represents an interesting case study of the contradictions and tensions in the national debates over slavery. It also reminds us that we should always approach the question of the sectional divide over slavery with care, for generalizations can quickly break down in the details. For example, although Kentucky held slaves, it had much in common with some of the "lower North" states. Indeed, shifts in population meant that by 1860 Kentucky—like Maryland, Delaware, and Missouri—had gone from being a "**slave society**" at its first settlement to a "society with slaves."[23] And, though Kentucky's slave population was the largest as a percentage of the total population of any of these states, the citizenry's direct participation in slavery paled in comparison to the Deep South: in 1850, 28 percent of Kentucky's white families owned slaves—a rate well below those in the Deep South. Moreover, Kentucky slaveholders owned, on average, 5.4 slaves, a figure lower only in Missouri.[24] To some extent, the marginalization of slavery was due to the export of slaves to other Southern states through the domestic slave trade.[25]

The practice of slavery within Kentucky also varied considerably due to the relatively diversified economy, which

KENTUCKY'S ENSLAVED POPULATION

- 1790: 12,430

- 1800: 40,343

- 1810: 80,561

- 1820: 126,732

- 1830: 165,213

- 1840: 182,258

- 1850: 210,981

- 1860: 225,483

utilized both free and slave labor to advantage. Though the state consistently ranked first in hemp cultivation and second in tobacco production during the 1840s and 1850s, it was also deeply invested in the production of cereal crops like wheat and rye, the raising of livestock, and manufacturing—particularly steamboat building and hemp processing. These endeavors relied on slave labor only in part, if at all. The state's most bustling city, Louisville, became increasingly oriented toward manufacturing and trade, while nearby Lexington, which was far smaller, more closely tied to the plantation elite, and the center of Kentucky's domestic slave trade, seemed more "Southern." Entire swaths of the state—particularly the eastern Cumberland Plateau—had no slaves at all, though the Bluegrass, the western Jackson Purchase, and many river counties in the northwest had dense slave populations.[26]

Varieties of Antislavery. Kentucky's diversified economy, market orientation, and varied labor force were accompanied by another distinguishing feature: a consistent stream of antislavery sentiment that, though at times muted, was openly expressed from the days of frontier settlement to the secession crisis. In this regard, Kentucky and other border states stood in stark contrast to developments in the Deep South, where an increasingly strident defense of slavery became the cornerstone of society and culture.

The origins of Kentucky's antislavery sentiment lie in early settlement patterns. Many of the early antislavery settlers arriving in Kentucky were radical "emancipating" Baptists, who had left congregations in Virginia and Maryland in the late eighteenth century. They brought an egalitarian religious worldview that infused many of the new settlements.[27] Such early religious antislavery became less common during first decades of the nineteenth century, but in the 1830s, two Kentuckians began making notable contributions to the immediate abolitionist movement.

The son of a slave owner, James G. Birney served in the Kentucky state legislature before moving to northern Alabama, where he had a short-lived career as a cotton planter. He subsequently set up a law practice in Huntsville, became increasingly uneasy about slavery, and joined the American Colonization Society, ultimately taking on considerable responsibility for the organization in the Deep South. In 1833, Birney returned to Kentucky and moved in a more radical direction. Within two years he had renounced colonization, freed his slaves, split with his old friend Henry Clay over slavery, and helped to found the Kentucky Anti-Slavery Society. He attempted to start an abolitionist newspaper in 1835 but ran into stiff opposition. Locals held a meeting and wrote a letter "vehemently remonstrating with him, and pledging themselves to prevent the publication of his paper, by the most violent means, if necessary." After a mob ransacked his office, stole the printing press, and threw it into the Ohio River, Birney moved to New York and joined the American Anti-Slavery Society. This catapulted him onto the national stage, and in 1840 and 1844 he was nominated as the presidential candidate of the abolitionist **Liberty Party**.[28]

John G. Fee was even more religiously driven than Birney, and, unlike Birney, he remained in the South. Born in the Bluegrass region of Kentucky in 1817, Fee was also the son of a slave owner. Initially persuaded by the religious defense of slavery, he viewed the system as harmless and perhaps divinely sanctioned. These views began to change when he entered Cincinnati's Lane Theological Seminary in 1842, where his Northern colleagues set out to convince him of the contradictions between the Christian Gospel and the practice of slaveholding. They succeeded: Fee became an agent of the American Missionary Association, and worked to spread evangelical Christianity and antislavery doctrine, largely in Kentucky. After founding a number of antislavery churches, he also established evangelical abolitionist Berea College in 1855.[29]

Both Birney and Fee became significant leaders in the national movement against slavery, but most antislavery figures in Kentucky were considerably less radical, tending to support gradual emancipation plans like those adopted further north in the first years of the century. Rather than focusing on the plight of the slaves, they focused on the degradation of white society. For example, the great statesman, senator, and founding member of the American Colonization Society Henry Clay argued that slavery had been detrimental to the development of Kentucky's economy, society, and culture: "[It has] placed us in the rear of our neighbors, who are exempt from slavery, in the state of agriculture, the progress of manufactures, the advance of improvements, and the general prosperity of society." Baptist theologian James Pendleton developed a similar economic argument, stating that the system had transformed Kentucky into "nothing more than a colony to the industrial North."[30]

But Henry Clay and others also feared the integration of freed slaves into white society, which explains their advocacy of colonization schemes in which freed slaves would be deported to settle the new colony of Liberia on the west coast of Africa. As historian Luke Harlow argues, "[T]he primary impulse of Kentucky's white colonizationists was racial.... For colonizationists, slavery may have been wrong, but so too was an interracial society." The American Colonization Society found considerable support among Kentuckians, including slaveholding politician and Presbyterian theologian Robert J. Breckinridge (uncle of 1860 presidential candidate John C. Breckinridge) who, though concerned for the moral well-being of freed slaves, drew a line at creating a free labor interracial society. "Outright egalitarianism," as Harlow explains, "could never be achieved without racial 'amalgamation,' and he could not 'see what good was to be effected, by reducing all races of men to one homogenous mass; mixing the white, the red, the tawny, the brown, the black, all together and thus reproducing throughout the world, or in any single State, a race different in some physical appearance from all that now exist.' " Though Pendleton disputed the Biblical claims of pro-slavery theorists, he rejected the arguments of radical abolitionists even more firmly, seeing in their arguments nothing but the potential for social upheaval, particularly because, he believed, it was impossible for whites and blacks to coexist peaceably.[31]

Cassius M. Clay. Probably the most significant voice in support of gradual emancipation in Kentucky was that of Cassius M. Clay. Born in 1810 on the southeastern edge of the Bluegrass region, Clay was the son of a Revolutionary war veteran who had become one of the wealthiest men in the state. When his father died in 1828, Clay inherited all twenty-four of his slaves; of these, fourteen were to be held in trust for his own heirs, so he was unable to emancipate or sell them.[32]

Clay claimed to have harbored an instinctive dislike for slavery as a child that deepened into hatred when he arrived at Yale University in New Haven, Connecticut, in 1831 and encountered radical abolitionism in a lecture given by **William Lloyd Garrison**. As Clay explained it, he had never heard of Garrison nor witnessed any public discussions of abolitionism, so was propelled to attend the talk largely by curiosity:

> Every accessible place was crowded; but I pressed on determinedly to the front, so far as to see and hear him fully. In plain, logical, and sententious language he treated the "Divine Institution" so as to burn like a branding-iron into the most callous hide of the slaveholder and his defenders. This was a new revelation to me. I felt all the horrors of slavery; but my parents were slave-holders; all my known kindred in Kentucky were slave-holders; and I regarded it as I did other evils of humanity, as the fixed law of Nature or of God, and submitted as best I might. But Garrison dragged out the monster from all his citadels, and left him stabbed to the vitals, and dying at the feet of every logical and honest mind.

Garrison's words came to Clay "as water to a thirsty wayfarer," and at a subsequent meeting held to rebut the abolitionist's arguments, he was horrified when his fellow students offered "sophism after sophism, and false conclusion from more false assumptions followed, in chain-like succession... [and] were greeted with thundering applause." Clay remembered his anger as intense—"I never, in all my life, was so agitated in a public assemblage"—and he went home with his mind in an uproar, determined "that when I had the strength, if ever, I would give slavery a death struggle."[33]

Clay's moral outrage combined with his conviction that free labor was superior to slavery. Upon returning to Kentucky after graduating, Clay made good on his promise to fight slavery, though he was never an immediatist like Garrison. Instead, he embarked on a political career to promote a Whig agenda of infrastructure improvements and gradual emancipation of Kentucky's slaves. A fiery

The **Whig Party** formed in the early
1830s to oppose President Jackson
and his Democratic Party. They
supported economic modernization,
internal improvements, and high
tariffs. Kentucky was one of their
strongholds until the party tore itself
apart over the issue of slavery in the
mid-1850s.

character known to carry bowie knives and pistols to public meetings,
Clay regularly encountered substantial opposition to his ideas and
engaged in more than one violent defense of his honor. In 1843 he was
shot but the bullet was deflected by the scabbard of his knife, which he
quickly drew and used to stab his would-be assassin. On another occasion, he mortally wounded a man who called him a liar. His cousin, the
renowned **Whig** politician Henry Clay, successfully defended him at
trial.

Throughout the 1830s, Clay also continued to hold slaves who labored in his
sizeable grist and sawmill operations, including many that his father's will legally
permitted him to sell. Only in 1844 did he emancipate all of his slaves; shortly
thereafter, he founded a gradualist newspaper, *The True American*, in Lexington; in
its pages, he developed his economic critique of slavery, focusing particularly on
the harm done to white working men by a system designed to enrich a minority of
wealthy slaveholders. "My prospectus was moderate enough—proposing none but
constitutional methods in the overthrow of slavery," Clay later explained. But he
knew full well that his actions would result in significant backlash and, as was his
wont, prepared himself accordingly.[34]

> I selected for my office a brick building, and lined the outside doors with sheet-
> iron, to prevent it being burned. I purchased two brass four-pounder cannons at
> Cincinnati, and placed them, loaded with shot and nails, on a table breast high;
> had folding doors secured with a chain, which could open upon the mob, and
> give play to my cannon. I furnished my office with Mexican lances, and a limited
> number of guns. There were six or eight persons who stood ready to defend me.
> If defeated, they were to escape by a trap-door in the roof; and I had placed a keg
> of powder, with a match, which I could set off, and blow up the office and all my
> invaders; and this I should most certainly have done, in case of the last extremity.

By 1845, his editorials were provocative enough to convince Lexington residents that he was actively encouraging slaves to revolt. A substantial crowd of
opponents—led by another, less sympathetic, cousin—gathered to denounce Clay
in a public meeting. Ill and unable to muster much opposition, Clay folded in the
face of the onslaught. The mob invaded his office where, in a remarkable act of
restraint, they refrained from destroying the press; instead they packed it up and
shipped it across the river to Cincinnati. Clay resumed publication for a year, but
then joined the army as an officer in the Mexican War.[35]

Despite the hostility at the time toward men like Fee and Clay, gradualism
dominated the scene in Kentucky up until the late 1840s, when pro-slavery sentiment started to gather strength. The hallmark of that shift was the staunchly
pro-slavery 1849 constitutional convention to which not a single emancipationist
candidate was elected. The reasons for this shift in Kentucky's political scene can
be traced, at least in part, to events on the national stage.[36]

The Rise of Sectionalism

From the mid-1840s on, Kentucky's role in the intensifying conflict between North and South typified much of the borderland between the free North and slave South. As historian Edward Ayers has argued, "The people of the border... prided themselves on their restraint in the face of what they saw as provocation by extremists above and below them."[37] In most areas of political activity, Kentucky, as a whole, bore out this claim. Throughout the decade and a half before secession, the state struggled to maintain equilibrium as the nation was rocked by a series of splits and controversies that seemed to threaten the very fabric of politics.

Beginning with the great sectional schism of the Methodists in 1844 and the Baptists in 1845, and followed quickly by the political schisms of the Democrats and Whigs during the debates over the War with Mexico (1846–48) and westward expansion during the 1850s, Kentucky and the nation struggled to define the very nature of the American Union in the midst of highly polarized, polemical debate. What did it mean to be united? What were the rights of political minorities within a republic? On what terms would the nation extend its sovereignty over newly conquered territories in the West? Whose moral judgments about slavery should drive domestic policy? These and similar questions strained American politics to the breaking point.

Religious Schism. By the mid-1840s, neither the Methodist nor the Baptist Church could contain the divergent views of its members on the question of slavery. For the Methodists, the catalyst of destructive controversy was the endorsement by their governing body—the General Conference—of the "gag rule" passed by Congress in 1836.[38] Such a stance, of course, came into direct conflict with the ways that many Northern Methodists interpreted the highly individualistic cast of the Great Awakening; they believed that refusing to act on one's moral conscience amounted to profound hypocrisy. In protest, antislavery Methodists seceded from the Conference in 1843 and formed their own denomination, the Wesleyan Methodist Connection. This prompted the General Conference to craft policy in opposition to slaveholding by ministers. Outraged, Southern Methodists held their own conference at Louisville, Kentucky, in 1845, and rechristened themselves the Methodist Episcopal Church, South.[39]

In 1845, the Baptists similarly split over the question of slavery, though the nature of the schism was slightly different because of the distinct organizational framework of the church. (Unlike the Methodists, the Baptists had no central authority but were essentially a coalition of individual congregations.) Again, the source of conflict lay in determining whether or not leaders of the faith could hold slaves. The result was the formation of the breakaway Southern Baptist Convention, which allowed its leaders to own slaves.[40]

The **Gag Rule** was passed by Congress in 1836 in response to the growing number of petitions from abolitionist organizations. It automatically tabled (or postponed) action on all petitions related to slavery.

Abolitionist Radicalism. The sectional split of the Methodists and Baptists was anticipated a few years earlier by a divide within the abolitionist movement itself. The factions coalesced around three distinct positions. Garrisonians found it increasingly difficult to tolerate electoral politics and the American political system as a whole. Despite their nonviolent methods, they had been brutally attacked by mobs in both the North and the South. Slaveholders blunted the effects of their postal and petition campaigns with the support of national politicians in both the Whig and Democratic Parties, claiming the Constitution as the prime defender of slaveholder rights. Disgusted and disenchanted, the Garrisonians "argued that the nation's values had now been revealed to be so utterly corrupted that abolitionists must flee from proslavery churches, spurn the proslavery political process, and oppose the proslavery Federal Union with demands for Northern secession."[41]

Such radical statements alienated two camps. White immediatists explicitly rejected Garrison's notion that the political system was irretrievably corrupt. On the contrary, they believed that "voters should be exhorted to 'vote as they prayed and pray as they voted.'" Accordingly, they formed a new political organization—the Liberty Party—in 1840 and chose Kentuckian James G. Birney to head the ticket.[42]

Another faction—led by brothers Arthur and Lewis Tappan of New York and partly composed of Liberty Party supporters—formed the American and Foreign Anti-Slavery Society. Less concerned with purity than the Garrisonians, they were willing to work within the mainline evangelical churches and sought to make the immediatist message more palatable. Key to this was the rejection of the Garrisonians' increasingly vociferous advocacy of women's rights and equality.[43]

Westward Expansion. The growth of the Liberty Party and the development of sectional denominations occurred just as the nation embarked on the War with Mexico (1846–48). Probably no event was more significant for the intensification of sectionalism than this conflict, fought ostensibly to defend the western boundary of newly annexed Texas against incursions by Mexico but clearly to obtain western territory. The debate over how to govern the immense territory gained through the **Treaty of Guadalupe Hidalgo** produced decisive political schisms within the party system; those splits, occasioned by differing opinions on slavery, mirrored the division of the churches a few years earlier.

Conflict had arisen when Representative David Wilmot of Pennsylvania introduced a proviso to be attached to a military appropriations bill before the Congress in August 1846 banning slavery in any new territory obtained through the war. Wilmot's proposal represented a shocking split with President James K. Polk of Tennessee, a fellow Democrat. Polk was closely identified with the war as a longtime proponent of westward expansion and had been accused by some in Washington of provoking the conflict merely to obtain territory for slaveholders. For a Democrat to split with his president on an issue of such great import, and on grounds so volatile, provoked confusion and dramatic shifts of power. As historian Elizabeth Varon has put it, Wilmot's action "precipitated a break in the Democratic ranks and propelled Free-Soil Democrats from the North, such as David Wilmot himself, into an alliance with antislavery Whigs and abolitionists. Southerners, both Whig and Democratic, closed ranks against this emerging Free-Soil phalanx. Party discipline broke down, and the sectional fault line over slavery was laid bare."[44]

The next ten years of national politics can be seen, in a sense, as an attempt to mend that fault line. Though the proviso itself was never passed, the dynamics of party loyalty would never be the same. Before this moment, only abolitionists had argued that slaveholder influence in the government was dangerous; by the late 1840s, this idea had gained considerable currency among those less stridently antislavery, particularly in the Midwest. Actions like the gag rule had been particularly effective in helping the Liberty Party convince voters that *white* rights were under threat by slaveholders. The **Free Soil** ideas put forward by Wilmot and his fellow Democratic "Barnburners" developed this idea in a more racist direction, emphasizing the danger that slavery represented to white men's fortunes. Many Whigs—including Abraham Lincoln—found it increasingly difficult to support westward expansion when the Southern wing of their party seemed unable to answer the South's outspokenly pro-slavery Democrats.

Alarmed by Wilmot, leading pro-slavery politicians responded with the "common property doctrine," which argued that any territory acquired by the United States was the shared property of all states and that Congress could not pass laws that might infringe on any state's ability to enjoy its "right" to that property. This platform was shaped in large part by John Calhoun, and it reveals the fundamental innovation of his political philosophy: whereas Madison and Jefferson had envisioned sovereignty as belonging to the citizens of the republic, Calhoun asserted that the *states*, not the people, were the ultimate sovereigns of the United States. In such a scenario, neither the Congress nor the people who settled the territories could legislate or regulate slavery or any other property in new territories.[45] Pro-slavery was on the march.

Popular Sovereignty. The Democratic Party was thus in quite a quandary in the wake of the debate over Wilmot, for the cry of "Free Soil" had caused a growing rift within the party. In an attempt to forge a compromise, leaders crafted a policy designed to neutralize more radical tendencies. Called "popular" or "squatter" sovereignty, the policy became central to the Democratic platform in the election of 1848. It proposed that the final decision about slavery in a prospective state be made by that state's citizens as they wrote a constitution and applied for statehood. The political appeal of the policy was its great malleability: many

The **Treaty of Guadalupe Hidalgo**, which ended the Mexican War, ceded about half of the country to the United States. This forced the nation to grapple once again with the question of the expansion of slavery.

Free Soilers advocated for the exclusion of slavery from the West in order to defend the "free labor" of white settlers.

Northerners felt confident that the plan allowed settlers to outlaw slavery in the territories, while Southerners clung to the idea that slavery could establish footholds in the West.[46]

This innovation did not carry the Democrats to a presidential victory in 1848, though the Whig's victory, led by Louisiana slaveholder General Zachary Taylor, obscured that party's relative weakness. This was due in part to the fact that they could not reconcile the Northern and Southern wings of the party on the question of expansion and slavery. The breakaway "Conscience Whigs" advocated more forthright support of slavery-free territories and unalloyed opposition to what they called "the Slave Power." They demanded resistance to what they saw as the corrupting and insidious influence of slaveholders on national policy.[47]

The Compromise of 1850. In 1850, President Taylor set out to resurrect the Whig Party's fortunes and to offer succor to a divided nation by adopting a posture of studied nonpartisanship on the slavery question. Combining the old Whig idea that if there was no territory to debate there would be no strife with the Democrats' new theory of popular sovereignty, Taylor unilaterally encouraged the residents of the newly formed California and New Mexico territories to hold constitutional conventions and apply for statehood. As historian William Freehling explains, "Taylor reasoned that skipping the territorial phase, when Congress supervised areas, and rushing to the statehood phase, when Congress had no jurisdiction, would circumvent congressional controversy."[48]

Taylor badly miscalculated. Pro-slavery Southerners—the vast majority of them Democrats—were outraged, mostly because both territories were highly likely to be free states: Mexico had outlawed slavery in 1829 and, unlike in Texas where Mexican immigration policies had briefly allowed the importation of slaves from the South, neither California nor New Mexico had an established slaveholding class. Despite this, Southerners protested and threatened dire consequences should the territories be admitted as free states. The "Fire-Eater" faction went further, arguing that the time to secede from the Union had arrived.[49]

An important catalyst for this early Secessionist movement was John C. Calhoun, who urged his fellow Southerners in Congress to abandon the national parties and unite to organize a convention of delegates from every slave state, specifically to resist westward expansion on Free Soil terms. Though the Southern caucus in Congress rejected Calhoun's proposal, some leaders moved forward.[50] The resulting Nashville Convention of 1850 was not fully attended; though South Carolina sent a complete delegation, no other state mustered the same enthusiasm. Indeed, the border states (including Kentucky), as well as Louisiana and North Carolina, refused to attend at all. Nonetheless, the men who came to Nashville included significant pro-slavery thinkers such as James Henry Hammond and Robert Barnwell Rhett of South Carolina, Beverly Tucker and Edmund Ruffin of Virginia, and William Lowndes Yancey of Alabama. Fire-Eaters hoped the convention would prompt secession, but the low attendance clearly indicated lackluster support for such a move. Still, the ideas that these men propounded would form the foundation of Secessionist thought in the subsequent decade.[51] (See Hammond's "Cotton Is King," pp. 117–23 and Yancey's "Speech of Protest in the Charleston Convention," pp. 150–55.)

The **Compromise of 1850** proved the political acumen of Henry Clay and Stephen Douglas, but a few years later the peace it forged was broken by the Kansas-Nebraska Act.

Even before the Nashville Convention opened, Kentucky's Henry Clay stepped into the breach, crafting a series of compromise measures to mitigate the crisis. Over the next nine months, Clay and Senate Democrat Stephen Douglas of Illinois shepherded the various elements of the deal through Congress, passing each with considerable parliamentary skill and astute understanding of how to build cross-party alliances in support of individual elements, despite lack of support for the whole. In the end, the **Compromise of 1850** achieved the following: California was admitted as a free state; the domestic slave trade in the District of Columbia was abolished; Texas's debt was assumed by the federal government; the vast New Mexico territory was reorganized into New Mexico and Utah territories, with popular sovereignty as the implied basis for any future decisions about slavery; and a new fugitive slave act was passed to supersede the weaker statute in the Constitution of 1793.[52] (See Daniel Webster's "Seventh of March Speech," pp. 101–109, as a good example of the spirit of nationalism that carried these measures through Congress.)

Though each of these elements had been passed to placate one or another of the partisan factions in Congress, radicals from both sides offered stiff opposition. Foremost among the Southerners was Calhoun. Near death and unable to deliver a speech himself, he nonetheless sat in the chamber while James Mason of Virginia spoke the words he was too weak to say. The Union, he argued, had already succumbed to disunion in other areas: schisms in the Protestant denominations and the political parties had been harbingers of the present crisis. But "the great and primary cause," he argued, was "the fact that the equilibrium between the two sections in the Government, as it stood when the Constitution was ratified and the Government put in action, has been destroyed…. [A]s it now stands, one section has the exclusive power of controlling the Government, which leaves the other without any adequate means of protecting itself against its encroachment and oppression."[53] Calhoun asserted that neither Clay's compromise nor Taylor's machinations would solve the crisis.

The only way to stave off the secession of the South was to give her "justice—simple justice." Central to this was the repudiation of antislavery. "The North has only to will it to accomplish it," Calhoun argued, "to do justice by conceding to the South an equal right in the acquired Territory, and to do her duty by causing the stipulations relative to fugitive slaves to be faithfully fulfilled—to cease the agitation of the slave question, and to provide for the insertion of a provision in the Constitution, by an amendment, which will restore to the South in substance the power she possessed of protecting herself, before the equilibrium between the sections was destroyed by the action of this Government."[54] (For much of the political philosophy underlying this position, see Calhoun's *A Disquisition on Government*, pp. 86–101.)

Antislavery factions also objected heartily to the Compromise, especially the new Fugitive Slave Act, which represented the culmination of a decade of conflict over free states' involvement in facilitating the return of runaway slaves. Though a spate of new and revised personal liberty laws ordered local officials to stand aloof from all such recovery proceedings, the Compromise successfully nationalized the enforcement of runaway slave recovery.[55] (Abolitionist outrage comes through clearly in Frederick Douglass's "The Meaning of July Fourth for the Negro," pp. 112–17.)

Despite hostility from partisans in the North and South, Kentucky, along with the other border states, welcomed the Compromise as the most sensible means to move forward; throughout the crisis of 1850, Kentucky's political leadership remained insistently pro-Union. As Governor Crittenden asserted:

> A moment's reflection will show the ruinous consequences of disunion to the commerce of Kentucky and the other Western States. The most obvious considerations of interest combine, therefore, with all that are nobler and more generous, to make the Union not only insensible to the causes which have produced too much sensibility and irritation with her brethren of the Southern States, nor is she without her sympathies with them. But she does not permit herself to harbor one thought against the Union. She deprecates disunion as the greatest calamity; she can see NO REMEDY in it,—none, certainly, for any grievance as yet complained of or to be apprehended. Kentucky will stand by and abide by the Union to the last, and she will hope that the same kind Providence that enabled our fathers to make it will enable us to preserve it.[56]

But such devotion to the Union did not imply a lack of support for slavery, and indeed, Upper South representatives strongly advocated for a strengthened Fugitive Slave Act.[57] Certainly, these slaveholders suffered the most from the loss of slaves. In the 1840s Kentucky lost an estimated $200,000 per year in runaway slaves.[58] Moreover, the national crisis came just as Kentucky was revising its own constitution, a document that reversed the state's long-standing moderation on slavery and reopened the domestic slave trade. This retrenchment deepened concerns about runaways.

The Kansas-Nebraska Act. The Compromise of 1850 may have avoided disunion, but it did not answer the fundamental question about the nature of national policy toward slavery in the West. The first real test of the Compromise's viability in this respect came in 1854, when Senator Stephen Douglas proposed organizing yet more territory for settlement. The area in question was called Nebraska and had originally been part of the Louisiana Purchase; as it lay north of the 36° 30′ mark,

The **Missouri Compromise** of 1820 attempted to settle the status of slavery in the Louisiana Purchase by admitting Missouri as a slaveholding state and drawing a line at 36° 30′, above which slavery would be prohibited.

slavery had been prohibited in the region by virtue of the **Missouri Compromise**. For years, citizens in Illinois, Indiana, and Kentucky had urged the opening of the territory, and for just as long, Southern Congressmen had blocked these efforts in an effort to forestall the creation of more free states that might lead to a further imbalance between the sections. Douglas believed that opening the West would ensure liberty's spread across the continent. Not incidentally, it would also allow for the construction of a transcontinental railroad with an eastern terminus in Chicago. Advocacy for these measures, he reasoned, would help cement his political influence in the Midwest, which he could then leverage to gain his party's nomination for president.

As Douglas's plans became known in Washington, however, Southerners protested the creation of another free territory and refused to support the bill. In a gambit to gain passage in the next session of Congress, Douglas revised his proposal. Instead of one territory organized according to the Missouri Compromise, Douglas now called for the creation of two territories—Kansas and Nebraska—organized according to an aggressive interpretation of the Compromise of 1850, which Douglas now asserted had negated the Missouri Compromise line altogether in favor of the concept of popular sovereignty. This solution met with general approval in the South because it undid the Missouri Compromise, which Calhoun's doctrine had long asserted was unconstitutional. This also accorded well with the views of most Northern Democrats who (like Douglas) did not oppose slavery on moral grounds, seeking merely to halt the controversy and establish territorial procedures that emphasized local control and broad-based democratic government.[59]

Predictably, antislavery Northerners (including some Democrats) were outraged. Kansas-Nebraska seemed like blatant submission to the Slave Power. Senator Salmon P. Chase of Ohio had long opposed slavery, supported Free-Soil political activity, and actively defended Northern blacks from the actions of the Fugitive Slave Act of 1850. In response to the Kansas-Nebraska Act, he co-authored the "Appeal of the Independent Democrats," which articulated deep-seated suspicions about the motivations of slaveholders in supporting the dismantling of the Missouri Compromise[60]:

> Thus you see, fellow-citizens, that the first operation of the proposed permission of slavery in Nebraska will be to stay the progress of the Free States westward, and to cut off the free States of the Pacific from the free States of the Atlantic. It is hoped, doubtless, by compelling the whole commerce and the whole travel between the East and West to pass for hundreds of miles through a slave-holding region in the heart of the continent, and by the influence of a Federal Government *controlled by the slave power* to extinguish freedom and establish slavery in the States and Territories of the Pacific, and thus permanently subjugate the whole country to the yoke of a slave-holding despotism. Shall a plot against humanity and democracy so monstrous, and so dangerous to the interests of liberty throughout the world, be permitted to succeed?[61]

Chase's "Appeal" was only one of numerous formal protests from Free Soil and antislavery Americans. Some, like Chase, emphasized the threat to liberty, broadly defined, while others emphasized the plight of the slave and the immorality of slavery. This sort of reaction forced Douglas to fight hard. When he eventually prevailed, his bill passed in a largely sectional vote.[62]

The Know-Nothings and the Republicans. The debate over Kansas destroyed what remained of party unity among the Whigs and birthed two new parties with strong support in the North: the American Party (or the "Know-Nothings") and the Republican Party. This left Southern Whigs out in the cold. As historian Michael Holt explains, "Despite the desire of many southern Whigs to preserve the national organization... no credible northern wing of the party with which to make terms remained."[63]

The successors to the Whigs had very different origins. The Republican Party arose out of a wide-ranging coalition of former Whigs, antislavery and Free Soil Democrats, and many of the abolitionists associated with the Liberty Party and its successor, the Free Soil Party. Opposition to slavery varied widely among the Republicans, who nevertheless ran their first candidates in the midterm elections of 1854 inspired by Chase's "Appeal" and other anti-Nebraska activity in the Congress. As historian Elizabeth Varon explains, the "groups coalesced around their shared antipathy to the political dominance of the imperious Slave Power, as well as around a consensus that the economic progress of the North... 'epitomized the American spirit' of opportunity and self-improvement."[64] With opposition to slavery's westward expansion at the core of its identity, the Republican Party united white men around a shared support of Free Soil. The party did *not* adopt an abolitionist stance toward slavery in the South, but it did deplore the institution as immoral and asserted that the rule of law must enforce moral order as well as political stability.[65] This staunch antislavery stance doomed the organization throughout the slaveholding states. Kentucky was no exception.

The other beneficiary of Whig disintegration was the Know-Nothing, or American, Party. Rooted in highly localized, anti-immigrant, anti-Catholic, anti-liquor movements in the Northeast, the Know-Nothings were originally a secret fraternal order whose members swore to respond, when questioned about their activities, "I know nothing." Originally, they strove to restrict naturalization and eliminate the right of the foreign-born to hold political office, but their support of temperance and opposition to Catholicism garnered the endorsement of evangelical reformers. Furthermore, some supporters saw the Know-Nothings as a Unionist alternative to extremists in both sections.[66]

In Kentucky, the Know-Nothings found especially fertile ground for their efforts. Friction between native-born Protestants and German Catholic immigrants in the city of Louisville, for example, helped the party to flourish as it had in Northeastern towns. At the same time, Kentucky's increasingly dispossessed Whigs—many of them among the most elite planters and commercial leaders in the state—looked to the Know-Nothings as a new vehicle for continued influence. Without their historic leader Henry Clay (who died in 1852) and a national party organization, these men eagerly attached themselves to the new standard. As historian Ellis Merton Coulter rather caustically remarked, "It gave them the joys of a fool's paradise for a time, where they could forget the gaping sectional wounds and contemplate things with which they were only remotely connected and which constituted not the slightest problems for them." Fool's paradise or no, the Know-Nothings gained the governorship of the state in 1855, as well as numerous local seats.[67]

At first, the Know-Nothings seemed to get the best end of the bargain, especially in the cities of the Northeast, the Midwest, and parts of the Upper South, with Republican footholds confined to the upper Midwest. But by the 1856 presidential election, the Republicans had expanded their influence throughout the free states and were quickly eclipsing the Know-Nothings, who soon collapsed. This forced Kentucky's ex-Whigs to resort to simply calling themselves "the Opposition."

Bleeding Kansas. Consequently, national pro- and antislavery forces immediately began to strategize about the best way to dominate the territorial population and legislature. As there were only about eight hundred white settlers in the region at the time, the field lay wide open for settlement by any citizen who wished to influence the course of events in the West. In 1854, William Seward of New York acknowledged this fact on the floor of the Senate. "Come on then, gentlemen of the Slave States," he parried. "Since there is no escaping your challenge, I accept it in [sic] behalf of the cause of freedom. We will engage in competition for the virgin soil of Kansas, and God give the victory to the side which is stronger in numbers as it is in right."[68]

Over the next nine months, the flood of settlers into the territory confirmed Seward's suggestion that the battle for Kansas had begun. Some eight thousand white migrants rushed in, bringing 192 slaves with them. According to the first territorial census, nearly 50 percent of these settlers came from Missouri and another 7 percent from elsewhere in the South. The newest arrivals were sponsored by a range of organizations providing the means for making the journey to Kansas and the ideological justifications for doing so. A relatively small number of migrants in favor of immediate abolition received resources from the New England Emigrant Aid Company, whereas many pro-slavery settlers were encouraged by the Blue Lodges and the Self-Defensives, secret societies in Missouri hoping to ensure slavery's spread into Kansas.[69]

Within two years, the most obvious consequence of the Kansas-Nebraska Act was the establishment of hostile, armed, and highly partisan settlements in the territory. In 1855, elections for territorial legislators were tainted by fraud, abuse, and violence and resulted in a virtual sweep by pro-slavery candidates. Free-Soil settlers cried foul, wrote lengthy protests to the federal government and to eastern newspapers, formed their own legislature, and elected their own governor. In the spring of 1856, hostilities boiled over when a pro-slavery militia attacked the Free-Soil town of Lawrence, destroying property and wreaking havoc. Three days later, a group of abolitionist settlers led by John Brown—a New Englander convinced that God had given him a divine mission to end slavery—retaliated by massacring five settlers in the tiny town of Pottawatomie. None of them were actually slave-holders, but all were known supporters of the pro-slavery faction in the territory.[70]

The Caning of Sumner. Sectional rhetoric and outrage rapidly escalated across the nation, with newspaper editorials and members of Congress shrilly proclaiming their disgust for or allegiance to various factions. Things came to a head when Senator Charles Sumner of Massachusetts, a longtime abolitionist, delivered an inflammatory discourse titled "The Crime Against Kansas," in which—among other things—he charged South Carolina Senator Andrew P. Butler with having taken "the harlot, slavery," as his mistress.

Butler's protégé and cousin, South Carolina representative Preston Brooks, originally considered challenging Sumner to a duel, but his fellow South Carolina representative Lawrence M. Keitt reminded him that dueling was for equals. Consequently, when Brooks and Keitt entered the Senate chamber, Brooks walked to where Sumner sat working at his desk and began beating him with his cane, while Keitt prevented anyone from intervening. Brooks stopped once he had broken the cane over Sumner's senseless body. Brooks was briefly arrested and fined and both he and Keitt resigned their seats rather than face expulsion after being censured by Congress. Their reception at home, however, was anything but censorious. Brooks was hailed by Southerners for what they deemed a courageous defense of his cousin's—and the region's—honor. Upon returning to South Carolina, he received dozens of new canes, including one carrying the inscription "Hit him again."[71]

Northerners were outraged, decrying the Slave Power so emboldened by recent developments in the West that it encouraged violence in the halls of government.[72] In an editorial titled "The Outrage on Mr. Sumner" in the *New York Evening Post* (a determined foe of slavery's territorial extension), editor William Cullen Bryant piquantly wondered about future retaliation from his "southern masters":

> If we venture to laugh at them or question their logic, or dispute their facts, are we to be chastised as they chastise their slaves? Are we, too, slaves, slaves for life, a target for their brutal blows, when we do not comport ourselves to please them?[73]

The Election of 1856. The violence associated with Kansas fueled remarkable expansion in the Republican Party ranks. In 1856, they nominated nationally known explorer and expansionist John C. Frémont to run against Know-Nothing Millard

Fillmore and the Democrats' James Buchanan. Fillmore ran on an explicitly Unionist platform, asserting that the country's troubles lay with agitators in the North and South and that the Know-Nothings (now disassociating themselves somewhat from their nativist and anti-Catholic roots) were the heirs to a Whiggish, non-sectional moderation. Not surprisingly, the Know-Nothings received some of their greatest support in Upper South states like Kentucky.

Frémont lost, but the Republicans had finally found a clear message, the appeal of which pulled Free-Soil Know-Nothings into the fold.[74] William Seward, Salmon Chase, Abraham Lincoln, and even former slave Frederick Douglass (who, like many radical abolitionists, had previously rejected party politics) began to hone and sharpen an indictment of the "Slave Power conspiracy" and its destructive consequences for the nation. In this view, the perpetrators of the disastrous situation that faced the nation were conspirators determined to trample on the "Constitutional rights" of white men throughout the country.[75]

The Democrats, with Pennsylvanian James Buchanan at the head of the ticket, held on to the center and the principle of popular sovereignty, rebuffing the Southern rights wing of the party who clamored for a plank demanding specific protections of slavery in the territories. They also blurred the substantial ideological gap between radical abolitionists and antislavery Republicans by asserting the primacy of law and order and using John Brown's actions at Pottawatomie as an example of the lawless fanaticism that would run amok should the "**Black Republicans**" win.

Despite healthy support for Fillmore, Kentucky ultimately went for Buchanan, due most likely to native son John C. Breckinridge's vice-presidential candidacy. This marked the first time the state had gone Democratic since 1828.[76] The results of the election favored the Democrats in the short term, but sounded a worrisome note. Buchanan had carried a little less than one-third of the non-slaveholding parts of the Union. Most crucially, Democratic victories in Pennsylvania, Illinois, and Indiana had resulted from a fairly strong showing by Fillmore of the American Party. As Abraham Lincoln argued in a post-election analysis, "All of us who did not vote for Mr. Buchanan, taken together, are a majority of four hundred thousand. But, in the late contests, we were divided between Frémont and Fillmore. Can we not come together, for the future[?]"[77]

The Future of Slavery

The years that followed gave multiple opportunities for public debate over the question of slavery in the territories, which helped sharpen divisions and hone the partisan language that increasingly characterized the camps prior to the presidential election of 1860. Two of the most important developments arose largely from the ill-conceived machinations of the newly elected Democratic president, James Buchanan.

Dred Scott v. Sandford. The first of Buchanan's political blunders came at the end of Dred Scott's ten-year court battle. In the 1830s, Scott was owned by an army surgeon in Missouri. The doctor was later assigned to work in the free state of Illinois and later in free Wisconsin territory. When his owner died, Scott sued the heirs of his estate for freedom on the grounds that he had been emancipated by spending time in these free areas. The first court found in Scott's favor, a decision that was appealed and subsequently overturned by the Missouri Supreme Court in 1852. Scott then sued for his freedom again, this time in federal court and against his new owner, John Sanford (whose last name was misspelled with a "d" in the case title), on the grounds that the Constitution allowed citizens of different states to sue one another. Scott claimed again to be a citizen of Missouri, not a slave, and demanded his freedom from Sanford, a citizen of New York; Sanford disputed the claim on the grounds that Scott could not be a citizen, arguing that he was of African descent and his ancestors had been designated slaves, not citizens, when they were brought to North America. The Missouri federal court concurred with Sanford, finding Scott to be a slave, not a citizen; Scott appealed to the U.S. Supreme Court in 1856, which delivered its opinion in 1857.

It was at this juncture that considerable political influence was used to shape the outcome of the case. The chief justice of the Supreme Court, Roger B. Taney, was a Marylander by birth, a slaveholder, and a member of the Democratic Party. Four of his fellow judges were, likewise, Southern Democrats who held or had held slaves. Despite this sectional element of the Court, as historian William Freehling has pointed out, none of these men can be described fairly as extreme sectionalists; indeed, they all endorsed variations on slavery reform and were all Unionists in the 1850s. The political aspect of the case before these justices was, of course, clear from the outset. Coming as it did on the heels of the controversy over Kansas-Nebraska, Southern justices on the Court felt that they were in a position to settle the vexing question of slavery in the territories once and for all. And though the opinions from the Court generally supported the opinions of pro-slavery ideologues, it is also clear that the justices were aiming to stifle discussion of the issue as much as to advance a clear-cut agenda regarding slavery as an institution.[78]

The majority asked Chief Justice Taney to author the opinion. Taney presented a distinctly anti-black and pro-slavery interpretation of the matter before the Court, and indeed, went beyond the substance of discussion between the members of the majority.[79] First, he disagreed with Scott's claim of citizenship and, concurring with Sanford's attorneys, ruled that Scott's African ancestry itself (not his status as a slave) barred him *and all others* of African descent from citizenship. As a non-citizen, Scott therefore had no right to bring a suit in federal court. Taney aggressively countered the fact of black citizenship in various states of the Union since the founding of the republic, propounding the view that state citizenship was distinct from citizenship in the Union. As such, even if a given state accorded citizenship rights to an individual, those rights ended at the boundary of the state.[80]

Though this narrow determination regarding citizenship would have been sufficient to dismiss Scott's case, Taney next addressed whether time spent in a free territory or state conferred freedom upon a slave. Taney argued that Congress's power to regulate matters in the territories applied only to those territories in the possession of the United States at the time the Constitution was ratified. The Missouri Compromise was therefore unconstitutional, and the free soil status of any territory erroneous.[81]

Taney continued his aggressive interpretation of the limits of Congressional powers in the territories. The Constitution, he argued, only allowed for the acquisition of territories as a means to admit new states, and any rules or regulations set by Congress in the territories needed to apply to the states as well. Consequently, Congress could not limit any of the rights in the territories that were protected by the Constitution. Among these, Taney argued, was the right to property embedded in the Fifth Amendment, "which provides that no person shall be deprived of life, liberty, and property, without due process of law." Moreover, he contended, "if Congress itself cannot do this—if it is beyond the powers conferred on the Federal Government—it will be admitted, we presume, that it could not authorize a Territorial Government to exercise them. It could confer no power on any local Government, established by its authority, to violate the provisions of the Constitution."[82]

In one fell swoop, Taney declared unconstitutional almost every avenue to limited slavery in the West and, indeed, suggested that the territorial bans against slavery might also have been unconstitutional. The Free-Soil platform of the Republican Party was unconstitutional as well, and the Democrats' policy of popular sovereignty was an illegal extension of a power that Congress did not have in the first place.

Southerners hailed the decision as a masterpiece of jurisprudence. The South's leading journal, *DeBow's Review*, asserted that the decision had been made by "the gravest, the most learned, and the most august tribunal in America and perhaps the world."[83] Newspaper editors across the South seemed to "welcome relief from the moral stigma" they had perceived in Congressional efforts to halt slavery's spread; many were gleeful at what they supposed was the end of the debate and the nail in the coffin of the upstart Republicans.[84]

But, as historian Kenneth Stampp put it, "[m]oral and constitutional vindication... was not easily translated into a tangible southern advantage."[85] Whatever acquiescence to a "final settlement" the Court and President Buchanan had hoped to generate did not materialize; instead an even more serious crisis arose as many free state citizens began to doubt the political legitimacy of their government. Buchanan's meddling with the Court (at first only suspected but later confirmed) gave even greater credence to the Republican Slave Power thesis. His successful attempt to persuade fellow Pennsylvanian Justice Robert Cooper Grier to join the majority decision was later denounced by Abraham Lincoln in his "House Divided" speech (see pp. 123–27).

Newspaper editors throughout the North decried the decision as the product of a tyrannical conspiracy, and the voices of leading Free-Soil and abolitionist politicians began to converge on the problem in a way that had previously eluded them. As historian Elizabeth Varon has argued, a speech to the American Anti-Slavery Society by Frederick Douglass epitomized this melding of purpose across antislavery's varied constituency. Dismissing the Court's negation of black citizenship, Douglass spoke "of the Slave Power's 'poisoning, corrupting, and perverting the institutions of the country,' warning that 'the white man's liberty has been marked out for the same grave with the black man's.'"[86] The logical conclusion of Taney's decision, Douglass argued, was that slaveholders could take their slaves anywhere—that the Slave Power had been given access to all the free corners of the nation, regardless of state prohibitions. With *Dred Scott*, danger was no longer confined to the South or the West; the slaveholder shadow had reached the threshold of the North.[87]

Many Northern Democrats read the decision selectively, ignoring potential damage to popular sovereignty and celebrating the apparent destruction of the Missouri Compromise. Others recognized the implications of the decision and pleaded for restraint and obedience to the Supreme Court lest the Union be torn asunder. Stephen Douglas began to craft an interpretation of the decision, the Freeport Doctrine, that allowed popular sovereignty to limp along. He affirmed the constitutional right to carry slave property into the territories but noted that the decision said nothing about the terms under which slavery would function in those areas. According to this theory, self-determination in the territories remained a possibility as long as governments there refused to pass laws regulating slavery.[88]

The Lecompton Constitution. President Buchanan himself subscribed to the view that the *Dred Scott* decision shored up the legitimacy of popular sovereignty. In yet another ill-considered move, he involved himself in a unilateral effort to shape the bid for statehood in Kansas, which, as we have seen, had been torn apart by violence and rival legislatures since the summer of 1856. At a constitutional convention in the town of Lecompton, pro-slavery settlers crafted a slaveholding constitution over the objections and boycott of free-state Kansans, men who petitioned Congress to admit the state under a constitution written in Topeka many months before. The Lecompton convention clearly permitted slaveholders to retain possession of all slaves who were already in the territory, but also allowed voters to ban future imports of slaves in the referendum to come.

Free Soilers rejected the Lecompton constitution with the support of the territorial governor, Robert J. Walker, who even visited Washington to argue against it in person. In his absence, acting governor Frederick Perry Stanton allowed the Free-Soil majority of the newly elected territorial legislature to go into special session. It established new rules through which voters would be allowed to reject the entire constitution, not just future importations of slaves. Buchanan, influenced by *Dred Scott* and a swelling chorus of pro-slavery Southerners, sacked Stanton, ignored Walker, and expressed his support for the Lecompton constitution.[89]

This was a gamble, and Buchanan lost. Stephen Douglas, the architect of the Kansas-Nebraska Act, had always believed that the territories were highly unlikely to become slave states. As the champion of popular sovereignty, Douglas balked at the implications of granting Kansas statehood under the Lecompton constitution after the most recent elections, largely viewed as fair, had produced a Free-Soil territorial legislature. Consequently, Douglas split from the president and opposed both the pro-slavery Lecompton constitution and the antislavery Topeka constitution on the grounds that neither represented the will of the majority of Kansas. A series of dueling referenda in Kansas ultimately led to a compromise brokered by former Whig John Crittenden of Kentucky, which resulted in the overwhelming rejection of the Lecompton constitution in 1858.[90]

Disunion Debated

Two particularly intense rhetorical confrontations have come to epitomize the divisions in the country in the wake of *Dred Scott* and Lecompton: the Congressional sparring between Senators William H. Seward of New York and James Henry Hammond of South Carolina and a series of remarkable campaign debates between Illinois senator Stephen Douglas and his Republican challenger, Abraham Lincoln. These encounters increasingly focused on the likelihood, feasibility, and threat of disunion.

Seward v. Hammond. In the midst of the crisis in Kansas, William H. Seward, one of the fiercest critics of slavery in the Republican Party, stood on the floor of the Senate to denounce Lecompton and the president's actions in support of it. Drawing a direct parallel between the Free Soilers of Kansas and the tea-party protesters of the Revolution, Seward demanded to know if the president intended to force slavery onto a majority who opposed it. To do so, he concluded, would be to create an empire, not a confederacy. More radically, Seward characterized Southern resistance as the death throes of a system that could no longer be tolerated by the rest of the country. He rejected compromise, stating, "Free labor has at last apprehended its rights, its interests, its power, and its destiny, and is organizing itself to assume the government of the Republic." He threw down the gauntlet when he continued, "It will henceforth meet you boldly and resolutely here; it will meet you everywhere, in the Territories or out of them, wherever you may go to extend Slavery."[91] (To get a sense of the gathering radicalism of the Republicans, see Seward's later speech, "An Irrepressible Conflict," pp. 135–43.)

The next day, Senator James Henry Hammond rose to respond. In an impassioned speech, he defended the Lecompton constitution as rooted in the will of the people, ridiculed Free Soilers in Kansas as ineffective and cowardly, charged his opponents with having engineered the crisis in order to destroy the Democratic Party, and denounced Seward for advocating that the government "consecrate all the territories of the Union to free labor."[92] For every instance of fraud in Kansas, Hammond claimed equally bad faith on the part of Congress where matters important to slavery's protection were concerned. In doing so, he referenced a litany of perceived abuses, stretching back to the struggles between Hamiltonians and Jeffersonians in the early republic and continuing through the conflicts of the Jacksonian era.

Much of the Southern cotton crop was exported to the textile mills of England and France, which had few alternative sources of supply.

Finally, he rebutted Seward's assertion of the natural superiority and inevitability of free labor. First, he pointed to the South's immense contribution to national economic welfare, arguing that it would become even more significant if only the North would cease infringing on it. Threats by the North to limit slavery were thus foolish in the extreme. "What would happen if no cotton was furnished for three years?" Hammond asked. "I will not stop to depict what every one can imagine, but this is certain: England would topple headlong and carry the whole civilized world with her, save the South. No, you dare not make war on cotton. No power on earth dares to make war upon it. Cotton _is_ king."[93] Next to cotton in importance, for Hammond, lay what he considered the singularly superior social structure of the South, where slavery provided "the very mud-sill of society and of political government."

Hammond portrayed the South as justifiably proud. The region suffered none of the hypocrisy with which Hammond charged Senator Seward and his fellow Northerners, who had freed men in name only, leaving them to suffer in poverty and want, while Southerners had found a "race adapted" to labor, "elevated from the condition in which God first created them, by being made our slaves." While Northerners brought white men low under the banner of free labor, Southerners, Hammond claimed, lifted up both black and white to the highest station they could, by nature, achieve.[94] (This speech appears on pp. 117–23).

Lincoln v. Douglas. Seward and Hammond faced each other before the compromise on Lecompton was settled, but their acrimonious exchange made it clear that important men on both sides of the question openly contemplated disunion. The debates between Abraham Lincoln and Stephen Douglas, on the other hand, made another fact clear: that men of the western states, representing competing visions of **manifest destiny**, could articulate starkly different interpretations of the Constitution and the proper relationship

Manifest destiny was a widely held idea that the United States had a special mission to conquer much of North America.

between citizens, the states, and the federal government. Kansas had shifted the axis of conflict. Taken together, these arguments made it impossible to dismiss sectional agitation as the work of overzealous abolitionists and Southern Fire-Eaters.

The debates in question occurred across the state of Illinois on seven separate occasions between August and October 1858. Two themes remained prominent: slavery's relationship to the American republic and the relationship between republican government and dissent. Lincoln presented his position as one of moderation, seeking to emphasize the aggressive nature of the Slave Power conspiracy and the recklessness of Northern Democrats in acquiescing to Southern machinations. For instance, in the final debate in the southern Illinois town of Alton (where abolitionist Elijah Lovejoy was killed by a pro-slavery mob in 1837), Lincoln responded to charges by Douglas that he was an abolitionist and race equalizer by asserting that he was neither, but instead a defender of the natural law and republican principles underlying the American system.

> [T]he principle that I had insisted upon, and all the principle[s] that I have insisted upon, from the Declaration of Independence, as applicable to this discussion and this canvas, is in relation to laying the foundation of new societies. I have never sought to apply this principle to those old States where slavery exists for the purpose of abolishing slavery in those states. It is nothing but a gross perversion to assume that I have brought forth the Declaration of Independence to ask that Missouri shall free her slaves.[95]

In insisting on Free Soil in the West, Lincoln thus asserted, he was merely adhering to the founders' example, but he insisted that he had no designs on slavery in the Southern states.

Lincoln also defended himself against Douglas's charge that an earlier statement, "a house divided against itself cannot stand," amounted to advocacy of disunion. Lincoln insisted that he was highlighting the folly of the policy of popular sovereignty, which he characterized as a radical departure from the founding principles of the country. He thus disputed the contention that the founders sought to establish slavery as part of the republic.

In this response, Lincoln associated Douglas with the failures of popular sovereignty, the cupidity of Buchanan, and the revolutionary implications of Taney. He tarred his opponent with the same brush that he and the Republican Party had long used to paint the Slave Power tyrants, while at the same time presenting his own position as that of reasoned, patriotic restraint.[96] His efforts were unsuccessful as far as the Senate race in Illinois was concerned. But, as historians have noted, Lincoln won an important political victory even as he lost this battle; the debates, publicized across the country, helped the Republican Party gain a new face: that of a moderate westerner who, though antislavery, was no abolitionist. (See excerpts from the Freeport Debate, pp. 127–34, and Lincoln's earlier "House Divided" speech, pp. 123–27.)

John Brown's Raid. The problem for the Republicans, however, was that the party contained men who were decidedly more radical than Lincoln, or even Seward. And, despite the attempts of Lincoln and others to finesse this fact, 1859 brought into high relief the degree to which radical abolitionism lay beneath the surface. The central figure in the drama was John Brown, a white abolitionist who had murdered pro-slavery settlers at Pottawattomie, Kansas, after a pro-slavery militia attacked Lawrence. When he returned to the East in late 1856, Brown's fame for these exploits gained him access to very wealthy and very radical circles of abolitionists in Boston and New York, where he cultivated relationships and raised the money necessary to finance his ultimate plan for slave liberation: an attack on the federal arsenal at **Harper's Ferry**, Virginia.

Brown carefully planned his mission for two years, during which he stockpiled weapons and recruited men to accompany him. Finally, in 1859, he and twenty-two black and white fighters (including three of his sons), seized the arsenal. They hoped that by capturing weaponry they would inspire neighborhood slaves to join them in a generalized uprising. Brown later testified that he hoped to lead the runaway armed slaves to the interior of the Appalachians, where they would set up an independent black nation. The plan fell far short of this goal. Besieged by the local militia, Brown's position was stormed by Marines led by Colonel Robert E. Lee. Several of his men were killed; Brown was wounded and captured.

The event was dramatic enough on its face: white Southerners lived in dread of just such an event and had long emphasized the likelihood that abolitionist rhetoric would foster slave rebellion. But what made John Brown's raid into an event of another political order was the discovery, among Brown's captured effects, of letters between him and his Northern abolitionist benefactors. Most of the so-called "Secret Six"—a group of influential New England abolitionists who raised money for Brown before his raid—had learned of him through their work with Kansas emigrant aid societies. All had distinguished careers as abolitionist activists, and many had advocated civil disobedience to the Fugitive Slave Act of 1850.

Charged with treason against the state of Virginia, Brown was tried, convicted, and hanged, to the great satisfaction of Southerners who found in his actions proof positive that the Republican Party could not control its supporters. Seward, perhaps unsurprisingly, came in for particularly vehement denunciation as the ideological instigator of John Brown's actions. A correspondent to a Richmond, Virginia, newspaper, for instance, noted that he was "one of one hundred" who stood ready "to pay five hundred dollars each ($50,000) for *the head of William H. Seward.*"[97] Many leading Republicans (including Lincoln) distanced themselves from Brown, but some praised his courage and lionized him as a martyr for the cause.

Many white Kentuckians saw John Brown's raid as a harbinger of things to come. John Copeland, a free black who had accompanied Brown, reportedly confessed his knowledge of plans for a similar operation in Kentucky. His story was corroborated by an anonymous letter to Virginia governor Henry A. Wise who warned that two thousand armed abolitionists drilling in Ohio planned to launch an invasion with the aid of Kentucky abolitionists.[98]

The Election of 1860

The dramatic political consequences of the Lecompton crisis, *Dred Scott*, and John Brown's raid were painfully evident in the 1860 presidential campaign. The Democratic Party, heretofore able to withstand sectional pressures, finally gave way under the weight of the polarized political rhetoric fostered by events of the previous two years. The Republicans gained no support in the South but took advantage of the splintering in their opposition and managed to secure the election of the nation's first purely sectional candidate to the presidency.

The Democratic Party Splits. The Democrats held their presidential nominating convention in May 1860. The leadership hoped that holding the event in Charleston, South Carolina, would mollify the Southern rights members of the party. But Southern rights men had been planning their own strategy for years, and by 1859, Fire-Eater William Lowndes Yancey of Alabama had already visited the city to make alliances and plans with Senator Robert Barnwell Rhett and his supporters in the state. Deeply troubled by Stephen Douglas's split with Buchanan over Lecompton, these Southern rights men were determined to block Douglas's nomination at the convention, or at least to ensure that the party's platform reflected their views on slavery in the territories. Unfortunately for them, a platform that included the Douglas interpretation of popular sovereignty was selected at the convention by a decidedly sectional vote of 165 to 138.[99] Southern rights delegates, in keeping with a pact engineered by Yancey, left the hall. With two-thirds of the elected delegates needed to approve presidential nominations, the convention collapsed.

After much confusion and bitterness, the delegates agreed to reconvene in six weeks in Baltimore.[100] But before they could act, Southern rights men unanimously nominated the sitting vice president John C. Breckinridge of Kentucky on a platform explicitly protecting slavery in the territories. Shaken but undeterred, mainline Democrats continued their Baltimore convention and successfully nominated Douglas. Despite their efforts, however, the Democratic Party was broken.[101]

The Republican and Constitutional Union Parties. Meanwhile, the Republican convention in Chicago brought together delegates from all of the free states as well as the border slave states of Delaware, Maryland, Virginia, Kentucky, Missouri, the District of Columbia, and the Kansas and Nebraska territories.[102] The party faced its own internal division, for though there was considerable eastern support for William Seward, his fiery hostility toward the South had alienated many Midwestern and western voters.

Other favorites for the presidency were similarly polarizing. This left Lincoln.[103] His credentials as a former Whig, a Midwesterner, and an ardent Free Soiler were unblemished and long-standing; moreover, in early 1860, he had built up his political reputation in the East by travelling widely to give political speeches, including his famous address at Cooper Union in New York. It took only three ballots for Lincoln to surpass Seward and gain the nomination. The party's platform was forthrightly Free Soil. It condemned efforts to reopen the African slave trade as "a crime against humanity and a burning shame to our country," bemoaned President Buchanan's "measureless subserviency to the exactions of a sectional interest," and rejected "the new dogma that the Constitution, of its own force, carries Slavery into any or all of the Territories" as "a dangerous political heresy."[104]

Only a few days later, on May 19, the Constitutional Union Party met (also in Baltimore) to nominate a candidate for president. The party had been founded in February before the Democratic Party split, and was composed largely of former-Whigs-turned-Know-Nothings-turned-"Opposition"-men. John Crittenden of Kentucky, the political heir to Henry Clay, served as chair of the nominating convention. Delegates from twenty-three states attended and unanimously endorsed a platform of strident moderation. The convention asserted that it was "the part of patriotism and of duty to recognize no political principle other than THE CONSTITUTION OF THE COUNTRY, THE UNION OF THE STATES AND THE ENFORCEMENT OF THE LAWS," and promised to defend those principles "against all enemies, at home and abroad." The platform was most notable for its studied avoidance of slavery; indeed, scuttlebutt at the convention suggested that members had been threatened with expulsion if they raised the topic.[105]

Though the Constitutional Unionist effort is often viewed as having been quixotic, the party was not wrong to consider the possibility that the election would result in such a close vote in the electoral college that the final decision would fall to the House of Representatives, where they believed they had a significant chance of victory as the party of compromise. Crittenden, at seventy-three years old, refused to allow his name to be put into contention, but he did manage to secure the nomination of his favorite, John Bell of Tennessee, a slaveholder who had championed moderate positions on territorial expansion. Like Henry Clay, he had opposed the war with Mexico; he also opposed Kansas-Nebraska and viewed Southern rights agitation over Kansas as purely ideological.[106]

Kentucky and the 1860 Election. Kentucky's leaders became increasingly worried about slavery and its protection in the state. The state legislature repealed all the laws that forbade the importation of slaves into Kentucky, revised the manumission law to require that all emancipated slaves immediately leave the state, and banned the immigration of free blacks into the state,[107] revealing concerns about slavery's stability and the security of whites. Even more significantly, Governor

Magoffin (a Southern rights man elected in 1859) and Simon B. Buckner (also a Southern rights supporter) encouraged the state legislature to expand and strengthen the militia system of the state. The legislature dutifully created the office of inspector general to "direct and superintend the formation and organization" of the volunteer militia and to exercise "active control and command" over it.[108] Magoffin appointed Buckner to the position. (For the text of the Manumission and Militia Acts, see pp. 143–50).

Press coverage of the 1860 election was intense and divided in the state; of Kentucky's seven major newspapers, four endorsed Breckinridge, two supported Bell, and one stood for Douglas.[109] The camps divided most sharply over the question of secession. The official organ of the Breckinridge campaign, the Louisville *Courier*, openly advocated separation from the Union, while the Lexington *Kentucky Statesman* vociferously objected and insisted that Breckinridge was utterly committed to maintaining the Union. Bell and Douglas papers denounced all the Breckinridge defenses as nonsense, and accused the Southern rights party of scheming to bring about Lincoln's election for the explicit purpose of forcing secession upon the South.

Further complicating the situation, although Breckinridge garnered the support of the majority of the state's newspapers and although the governor and much of the state legislature leaned strongly toward states' rights, most Kentuckians remained cool toward sectionalism and what they perceived to be its likely corollary, secession. Numerous "Union" meetings were held throughout the state, with considerable public discussion not only of the presidential candidates, but also of the possible consequences of the election.[110]

In an effort to counteract growing anxiety, many began to warn against overreaction to a Republican win. They noted that the Republicans were unlikely to gain control of either the House or the Senate, and that the Senate would be able to block any of Lincoln's nominees. Their calm stood in sharp contrast to the fiery rhetoric emanating from the Deep South. There, politicians and newspaper editors emphasized that secession would be justified—indeed, required as a matter of honor—by the election of a "Black Republican" to the presidency. In most states of the Deep South, substantial numbers of Secessionists urged their electors and their legislatures to be prepared to secede if Lincoln was victorious, and in South Carolina and Alabama, preemptive arrangements were made such that Lincoln's election would automatically trigger the election of delegates to a state secession convention.[111]

The Results of the 1860 Election. Just as many had feared, the Democratic vote split and Lincoln made a clean sweep of the free states, taking nearly 60 percent of the electoral college, though his popular vote—not quite 40 percent—represented a mere plurality of the total. Douglas came in a healthy second in the popular vote (though he remained well behind in the electoral count). The Constitutional

Unionists held firm in three states—Virginia, Kentucky, and Tennessee—even though they could claim only about 12 percent of the popular vote.

In Kentucky, John Bell far outstripped native son John Breckinridge 66,016 to 52,836 (41 percent to 33 percent), while Douglas made a surprisingly strong showing with 40,372 votes (25 percent). As in the national poll, Kentucky's combined Democratic vote would have carried the day. (Notably, Lincoln was on the ticket in Kentucky, one of only five slave states where men could vote for the Republican, but he garnered only 1,366 votes.[112] Nonetheless, John Breckinridge polled second to Lincoln in electoral votes nationally (with 23.8 percent), and brought home every Deep South state as well as Maryland, Delaware, and North Carolina, though this represented only 18 percent of the popular vote.

More important were the actions of state legislatures throughout the Deep South, where within three weeks of the presidential election secession conventions had been approved and scheduled. South Carolina acted first: before the election, the newly elected and highly partisan legislature had arranged a convention for early January; after the election, the legislators moved the date to December 17, convinced that the momentum for secession was spreading rapidly throughout the region. They were right. Most Deep South states followed suit and scheduled secession conventions for January.

When South Carolina's convention met and passed an Ordinance of Secession on December 20, it acted independently from the other slaveholding states. This was an important threshold for Secessionists; during the 1850s, even the most vigorous defenders of states' rights had insisted on "cooperation" with other slaveholding states. Those concerns still held sway among some Southern leaders. Even as stalwart a defender of the South as James Henry Hammond protested what he considered to be "most impolitic and assuredly abortive" actions.[113] For Hammond, moving recklessly seemed the height of self-destructiveness, but by transforming secession from a theory to a reality, South Carolina had made the unthinkable possible.

During the remainder of 1860, moderates made a concerted effort to shift the tide of sentiment, if not in the Deep South, at least in the border areas. Probably no Kentuckian played a more significant role in this effort than Senator John J. Crittenden. Like his mentor Henry Clay, Crittenden had been a stalwart Whig, and in the aftermath of his party's demise, he remained opposed to the Democrats. The failure of John Bell's Constitutional Unionist candidacy did not dissuade him from urging calm. Crittenden vowed to "search out, if it be possible, some means for the reconciliation of all the different sections and members of this Union, and see if we cannot again restore that harmony, that fraternity, and that union which once existed in this country, and which gave so much of blessing and so much of benefit to all."[114] In an effort to bind the nation's wounds, he proposed six constitutional amendments, each forever unamendable. (For the text of Crittenden's amendments, see pp. 155–59.)

Pulling in the other direction, agents from the Deep South such as Stephen F. Hale began encouraging Kentucky's leaders to quit the Union. Hale encouraged secession on the basis on white supremacy. (For details, see Hale's "Letter to Governor Beriah Magoffin," pp. 159–68.) To consider Kentucky's stance on these matters, Kentucky's governor Beriah Magoffin called the Kentucky state legislature into special session. This special session is where the game begins.

3

PART 3: **THE GAME**

MAJOR ISSUES FOR DEBATE

In reaction to the secession of South Carolina, the governor of Kentucky has called a special session of the legislature. Perhaps the deepening of the crisis will allow Kentucky to serve once again as a moderating influence in national politics, but if nothing else the people of Kentucky look to their legislators to preserve them from the coming storm. In the likely event that sectional reconciliation fails, Kentuckians must reflect on their own definitions of loyalty. Which of their many allegiances will exert the strongest claims?

Every player adheres to certain principles. Some may discover that these provide clear guidance on particular issues, though most will find it difficult to reconcile them with all of their various needs and interests. In these cases, they are particularly open to persuasion.

Some roles possess an extraordinary devotion to various denominations of Protestant Christianity. The principles that they derive from this faith animate their political consciousness. The devout must struggle to answer questions about slavery, such as whether race-based slavery is ordained by God. When contemplating secession, they will reflect on whether injustice should be resisted by force of arms. Many Protestants are also vehemently anti-Catholic and recently joined the Know-Nothing Party to voice their opposition to Catholic immigrants from Ireland and Germany. Players who can make compelling arguments based on the Bible may be able to win particularly devout players over to their way of thinking.

Political liberty is another principle that Kentuckians hold dear. Advocates characterize secession as a defense of property rights (particularly slavery) as part of states' rights, but the crisis may put other civil rights, such as freedom of the press and due process, in peril as well. Some players will react negatively to the abridgement of their rights through censorship, taxation, conscription, or the exercise of extraordinary powers by government officials. These legislators celebrate the declaration of the Kentucky Constitution of 1850: "That absolute, arbitrary power over the lives, liberty, and property of freemen exists nowhere in a Republic, not even in the largest majority." They might also point to Kentucky's constitutional expression of the freedom of the press: "The free communication of thoughts and opinions is one of the invaluable rights of man, and every citizen may freely speak, write, and print on any subject, being responsible for the abuse of that liberty."[1]

At the outset, only a few players will be outspoken about their sectional allegiances. A majority want to preserve the union but also insist on the preservation of Southern rights and privileges—perhaps most notably the right to own slaves. Most white Kentuckians do not see these two desires as mutually exclusive, and most hope that Kentucky can broker peace between the sections. If sectional conflict does arise, however, Kentucky will likely become a battleground, and therefore there are many who would prefer neutrality to siding with either the North or the South.

In addition, many legislators have strong loyalties to the regions within Kentucky. For the purposes of this game, there are four of these regions. Some are adjacent to slave states (such as Tennessee and Virginia), which may tilt toward their secession-minded neighbors in the Deep South; others are closely tied to the economies of the free states that line the north shore of the Ohio River (Illinois, Indiana, and Ohio). Some possess thriving economies; others are stagnant. Some have large populations of slaves; others have very few. (For more details on the regions of Kentucky, see pp. 75–79.)

If there is one principle upon which white Kentuckians unreflectively agree, it is the creed of white supremacy. They see the United States as a white man's nation and resent any attempt to define it otherwise. None appear to consider the idea of racial equality in any meaningful way. These racist ideas are so ingrained that they are not worth mentioning in the deliberations of the legislature, though they may be invoked by using the Racism Argument. (For more details, see p. 57.) However, there are a handful of legislators who would like to make it easier for individual owners to emancipate their slaves. In most cases, this is not because they sympathize with slaves; rather, they think that the rights of property owners should be absolute. At present, legally freeing one's slaves is quite difficult due to Kentucky's recently implemented Manumission Law of 1860 (see p. 143).

RULES AND PROCEDURES

Objectives and Victory Conditions

Most players achieve victory by persuading others to approve legislation that advances one of the goals described above. For example, pro-immigration legislators will attempt to pass a resolution encouraging unrestricted immigration as valuable to Kentucky. Similarly, legislators who oppose Kentucky's manumission law will probably attempt to amend it. In order to achieve these goals, they must persuade others to support them. Fortunately, all players remain undecided about some of the questions raised by the major issues.

In addition to achieving their goals in relation to the major issues for debate (see p. 51), most players are strongly motivated by self-interest—although they would be loath to admit it publicly.

Some players are particularly motivated by a desire to protect their families. As white patriarchs, they consider themselves the social, cultural, legal, and economic heads of their households. Some define family rather narrowly and only strive to provide for the members of their own households, while others have large extended families. Some even speak of their families "black and white," and include the well-being of their slaves in these calculations.

Other players desire personal renown, for which the current tumult offers them unique opportunities. Those with political ambitions may be able to secure the acclaim of their colleagues (perhaps by serving as Speaker). This will act as a springboard to achieve national office. Military service is another route to fame, but it presents special dangers. Men in uniform risk death, injury, and dismemberment. A daily routine of sleeping under canvas, eating moldy hardtack, and using shallow latrines creates an unhealthy environment. It is quite possible that they will succumb to disease even if they never set foot on a battlefield. In the case of a protracted conflict, the chance of dying or contracting an illness increases significantly.

Almost all players seek to defend their property. Wealth takes many forms, but the most common are land, farms, and slaves. Consequently, they are particularly enthusiastic about the clarity of this declaration in the Kentucky Constitution of 1850:

> The right of property is before and higher than any constitutional sanction; and the right of the owner of a slave to such a slave, and its increase, is the same, and as inviolable as the right of the owner to any property whatever.[2]

Although many argue that slavery is on the wane in Kentucky, slave owners all appear very keen to retain their valuable human property, which may be lost in three ways. The first is by legal emancipation, which could result from actions taken by the state of Kentucky. The state constitution of 1850 lays out the conditions for such a step:

> The General Assembly shall have no power to pass laws for the emancipation of slaves, without the consent of their owners, or without paying their owners, previous to such emancipation, a full equivalent in money, for the slaves so emancipated, and providing for their removal from the State.[3]

Despite this safeguard, some fear that emancipation may be enacted if the radically abolitionist wing of the Republican Party becomes dominant or if war breaks out. In either case, emancipation may be imposed by federal law.

Slaves may also escape. Despite the efforts of the slave patrol and white vigilantes, this is a chronic problem for Kentucky slaveholders because of the proximity of free soil across the Ohio River. Fortunately for slave owners, runaways remain in jeopardy due to the federal Fugitive Slave Law. Since the law allows slaveholders and their agents to track down runaways in Northern states, true sanctuary lies only in Canada.

TIP

Even though emancipation happened historically, it may not occur in this game.

Some argue that if the federal Fugitive Slave Law is suspended, as it certainly would be if Kentucky left the Union, escape could become significantly easier for slaves. If this happened, authorities north of the Ohio River would cease cooperating with slave owners and their bounty hunters. Others believe that secession from the Union would reduce the number of escape attempts by allowing Kentucky to exclude Northern abolitionist agents (who many blame for enticing slaves away from their owners). In addition, it is possible that a closed border could be policed more effectively. This point is debatable, but few would argue that war will improve the runaway problem in the short term. If secession results in war, and if Northern armies begin marching through Kentucky, escape attempts are likely to increase significantly.

Other property (such as cash, valuables, shares of stock, livestock, houses, workshops, and other buildings) may be lost due to heavy state taxes, foraging armies, and mob action. The threat of foraging armies is minimized if Kentucky militiamen spring into action in defense of their homes, but even they will begin looting if they remain in the field for an extended period of time.

After the final session of the game, the players take this into account and calculate the degree to which they have achieved their objectives relative to their positions on the major issues for debate as well as their more personal concerns. They then prepare a written explanation of their victory or defeat (see p. 70).

Proceedings of the Legislature

Once the game begins, the classroom becomes the Kentucky state legislature, which requires a certain amount of decorum. While the passions released by the current crisis may cause protocol to fray at the edges, some rules are sacrosanct. They appear below.

The Speaker. The legislature is presided over by the Speaker. The election of the Speaker is the first order of business when the legislature convenes. The Speaker must be approved by a majority vote in the legislature and can be removed by a majority "no confidence" vote at any time. If the Speaker is absent when the legislature convenes for a new session, the legislature must elect a replacement. The Speaker is a member of the legislature and operates under the protection of the Kentucky State Guard. This player has the following responsibilities:

- Ensure that all of the topics listed on the schedule for each session are addressed

- Manage debates

- Ensure that legislators from all four regions have the opportunity to speak in each session

- Remind legislators that all proposals must be written down and distributed

- Manage amendments to acts and resolutions

- Count votes

- Recognize and introduce guest speakers from the Gallery (see below)

In addition to influencing the direction of the debate, the Speaker may cast two votes in the legislature. This reflects the Speaker's ability to manipulate legislative procedure.

If a vote of "no confidence" is held, the sitting Speaker may not vote. That would be unseemly.

Introductions. When speaking for the first time in the legislature, legislators should identify their home regions and describe their past political affiliations, their family and community life, and the many reasons they love Kentucky. Roles do not include proper names, so players may create their own and share them during these introductions.

Respect the Podium. Anyone speaking from the podium has the right to speak. Audience members (including spectators in the Gallery) are welcome to hiss, boo, cheer, or shout "huzzah" as the speech proceeds, but they cannot prevent anyone from speaking. In a similar spirit, there can be no filibustering from the podium. After a speech concludes, anyone may ask questions. The Speaker manages this debate and decides when it should end. The Speaker may choose to ignore questions from the floor, but may not silence someone who has taken the podium.

The Gallery. The Governor, Inspector General, other guests, and any legislators who resign in order to form militias are welcome to attend the deliberations of the legislature. (For more details on militias, see p. 58). They may speak from the podium and ask questions, but they may not vote (except for the Governor, who may do so to break ties). They should sit apart from members of the legislature to ensure that there is no confusion when it comes to voting.

Drafting Legislation. In order to be considered, proposed legislation must be written down and officially introduced by a legislator. Sufficient copies must be provided so that everyone can easily read the text of any proposed law or resolution. There are two types of legislation. **Acts** are laws which require certain actions. If, for example, the legislature passes an act establishing appropriations for the Kentucky State Guard, then money is allocated. **Resolutions** are nonbinding

TIP

If you are proposing legislation, consider submitting it to a newspaper editor for publication. That way you do not need to make copies.

declarations of the will of the legislature. If, for example, the legislature votes on a resolution supporting South Carolina's right to secede, no one is compelled to do anything, but a political point is made.

In an admirable effort to avoid confusion, the Kentucky Constitution of 1850 demands that no law "shall relate to more than one subject, and that shall be expressed in the title."[4] In order to further minimize confusion, proposals must be written succinctly and in contemporary language. They should focus on the essentials of the proposed policy and avoid technical details. If a proposal requires funding, for example, it should simply state that money will be raised through a tax increase. Going into details such as tax rates is unnecessary.

The following sample act and resolution are illustrative of the straightforwardness that legislators should strive for when constructing their proposals.

Military Cargo Seizure Act

All military cargoes bound for Southern states via Kentucky's railroads or Kentucky's ports on the Ohio and Mississippi Rivers shall be confiscated and turned over to the Kentucky State Guard.

Resolution in Support of Slavery in Kentucky

The legislature affirms the centrality of the institution of slavery to the culture, society, and economy of the commonwealth of Kentucky.

Voting in the Legislature. The Speaker conducts each vote. Secret ballots are not allowed.[5]

- The Speaker may cast two votes in the legislature. Using the Racism Argument allows legislators to cast two votes for a single session, provided they play it in conjunction with a prepared speech delivered from the podium.

- Legislators may cast two votes during the session in which they publish newspapers, but they may not use the Racism Argument in the same session.

- The Governor may cast a vote, but only to break a tie.

- Militia commanders and the Inspector General may not vote in the legislature.

- There is no proxy voting. Those absent when a vote is conducted may not vote.

Finally, remember that the Kentucky constitution states that no law may be passed without "free discussion" unless it concerns a particularly urgent matter. In that case, if a super-majority of four-fifths of the legislature calls for an immediate vote on a measure, the Speaker must allow the vote. But while four-fifths is required to *call* the vote, only a majority is required to approve the measure itself.[6]

The Governor's Veto. The Governor possesses the power to veto legislation which has been passed by a majority vote. To use this power, the Governor returns the bill to the legislature with an explanation. The legislature may dismiss these objections and overturn the veto with a mere majority vote.[7] However, if the Governor vetoes a bill while also delivering a prepared speech which includes a use of the Racism Argument (see below), the veto cannot be overturned until the following session.

The Racism Argument. Stephen F. Hales's letter to Kentucky's governor (pp. 159–68) dramatically illustrates the crucial role of inflammatory racist rhetoric in the struggle over secession. Omitting the virulent racism espoused by many politicians of the period would be a serious distortion of the debates over secession, yet requiring players to spout this hateful rhetoric in order to win other players to their political positions would be unreasonable and unconscionable.

Instead, they may use the Racism Argument. This handout represents the influence of racist rhetoric on the white population of Kentucky. If a player obtains a high score on the reading comprehension quiz on Hale's letter and on racist elements of the other required readings, the GM will award that player use of the Racism Argument.

Legislators may use the Racism Argument as part of a *prepared* speech on any topic. During the speech, the legislator holds the handout aloft while proclaiming, "I am using the Racism Argument." This enables the legislator to cast two votes for the rest of the session.

The Governor may use the Racism Argument when vetoing a piece of legislation. Ordinarily, the Governor's veto can be immediately suspended by a majority vote from the legislature, but if used it in combination with the Racism Argument, the legislature must wait until the following session before attempting an override.

Militia Leaders (including the Inspector General) who use the Racism Argument while giving incendiary speeches gain 1 strength point for their militia.

TIP

The Racism Argument cannot be used on the spur of the moment. It can only be used along with a prepared speech.

TIP

There are no "pocket vetoes." If a law is passed by a majority, it becomes law even if the Governor does not sign it.

TIP

If a veto supported by the Racism Argument is issued in the legislative during the last Game Session, the legislature cannot override it.

TIP

The Governor may not use his veto power during a Sovereignty Convention.

After the Racism Argument is used, the handout must be returned to the GM. Each recipient may use it only once per game.

The Racism Argument may not be used to influence a vote on secession, but it may be used to influence a vote calling for a Sovereignty Convention.

Sovereignty Convention. A Sovereignty Convention may be called at any time by a majority vote of the legislature, but only one such vote is allowed in a given session. If the legislature agrees to call a Sovereignty Convention (a thinly veiled euphemism for a secession convention), the business of the legislature immediately ceases, and (after a pause regulated by the GM) the convention begins. Unfinished legislative business remains unfinished.

A Sovereignty Convention is *not* a session of the legislature, so none of the rules of the legislature apply. All players have a single vote, but players who left the state may not vote or participate in the discussion. In order to avoid confusion, voting and nonvoting groups should sit in different parts of the room. Players who have been murdered, are under arrest, or are otherwise incapacitated should also sit apart if they have not yet received new roles. In the Convention, the majority rules—unless the legislature put a supermajority rule into place when it called for a Sovereignty Convention.

The GM will conduct the vote in the Sovereignty Convention. Before taking a vote on the question of secession, players caucus by region. The Governor and the Inspector General caucus in the Bluegrass. Legislators who resigned in order to form militias should caucus with their home regions. When caucusing, players should discuss the pros and cons of secession. In particular, they should recognize that the more unified a region's vote on the question of secession, the less likely that brutal guerrilla warfare will ensue in that region. If all representatives of a particular region attending the Sovereignty Convention *unanimously* oppose whatever decision the convention makes regarding secession, they may opt to secede *from Kentucky*.

After a vote is taken on secession, the game is not over. Regardless of the outcome, if one or more sessions of the game remain, the players reconvene as the Kentucky state legislature. They may pick up where they left off with unfinished business or they may establish a new agenda. They may also vote to hold another Sovereignty Convention.

MILITIAS

At the beginning of the game, there is a single militia: the Kentucky State Guard, which is controlled by Governor Magoffin and overseen by his appointee, Inspector General Simon Bolivar Buckner. Some suspect that Buckner leans Secessionist because he recently disbanded several allegedly Unionist sections of the militia.[8]

Therefore, many legislators are reluctant to appropriate additional resources for the Kentucky State Guard. However, Buckner insists that external and internal threats necessitate a strong and unified militia.

Militia Proliferation

As the situation develops, the Kentucky State Guard may be challenged (or supported) by new militias. These may be created by legislators with military experience. In order to create a new militia, an eligible legislator must submit a letter to the Speaker resigning his position in the legislature. He must then give a speech explaining why he has decided to leave the legislature in order to form a militia (which must have a distinct and appropriately rousing name). After this speech, the GM will give the new militia commander "Militia Mechanics" (**Handout 1.3**), which is filled with information about how to run a militia. The new commander is then free to order his militia to take action.

TIP

Legislators should only contemplate resignation if they see no way to achieve their objectives through voting in the legislature.

The legal status of militia organizations other than the Kentucky State Guard remains hazy. Two potentially contradictory parts of the Kentucky Constitution of 1850 are operative:

> The rights of the citizens to bear arms in defense of themselves and the State shall not be questioned.

and

> No standing army shall, in time of peace, be kept up, without the consent of the General Assembly; and the military shall, in all cases and at all times, be in strict subordination to the civil power.[9]

Assuming Command

If a militia loses its commander due to absence or death, a subordinate officer of that militia may assume command. If there is no subordinate officer, a like-minded legislator with military experience may choose to resign in order to assume command. He must then give a speech explaining why he is a good replacement for the original commander. If, due to absence, death, or dismissal by the Governor, the Kentucky State Guard lacks a commander, a replacement Inspector General must be named by the Governor.

Militia Strength

All militias begin with 1 strength point. Each strength point represents one regiment of troops.

Militias that receive no orders from their commanders during a session lose 1 strength point. This is because the troops will lose interest. Some will return home. The most hotheaded will slip off in the night and head for militia camps in neighboring states. Consequently, commanders should keep their troops active.

Contrariwise, militias that receive orders from their commanders automatically gain 1 strength point each session. Active volunteers are happy volunteers.

Militias with commanders who are absent during a session lose 1 strength point. Troops want to see their leaders; even if the commanders have successfully issued orders in the past, absent leadership weakens a militia.

Each session, militias may improve by a maximum of 3 strength points. Multiple improvements may be accrued simultaneously, but it is important for commanders to remain realistic; transforming enthusiastic, undrilled volunteers into soldiers capable of military maneuvers takes time.

Militia Actions

Orders to militias take several forms, but only strong and well-organized militias may attempt abductions or deploy their forces. Militia commanders may hasten the improvement of their militias by taking a variety of actions. Other actions may influence events throughout Kentucky and in neighboring states. They may also facilitate shifts in the balance of power in the legislature.

STRENGTH POINTS	ACTIONS PER SESSION
1–4	1
5–8	2
9+	3

In order to act, militias require written orders. Commanders of ill-disciplined militias (with 1–4 strength points) may order their troops to take one action per session. More organized militias (with 5–8 strength points) may take two actions. Particularly well-drilled militias (more than 9 strength points) may take three actions. If no orders are issued during a session, militias will defend in place.

The results of all militia actions are determined by the GM outside of regular sessions, so orders should be submitted to the GM at least two hours before the beginning of each session. The GM will announce the results of these actions and any change in militias' strength at the beginning of each session.

Recruitment (No Minimum Strength Requirement). Militia units are initially rather small. Enlisting more troops will help. Militia commanders may make various efforts to call Kentuckians to their banner. These actions are not particularly confrontational or disruptive, and are likely to succeed.

- **Incendiary Speeches:** If the speeches given by militia commanders are of high quality, Kentuckians will join them. The GM will award 0–1 strength points based on the quality of the speech. Militia commanders who opt to use the Racism Argument as part of such a speech automatically add 1 strength point.

- **Recruitment Notices:** Recruitment posters or newspaper advertisements that are produced and distributed by militia commanders may draw more volunteers to their organizations. These increase their strength points by 0–1, as determined by the GM.

- **Additional Leaders:** If a member of the Kentucky legislature with military experience gives a speech supporting the aims and methods of a particular militia and then resigns from the legislature to join that militia, its power will increase by 1 strength point. The legislator becomes a subordinate officer, and assumes command if the militia commander is unable to serve.

TIP

Try the online search term "civil war recruitment posters" to find inspiration for recruitment notices.

The following legislators have military experience:

- Fire-Eater
- Uncomfortable Heir
- Paternalist Planter
- Jacksonian Democrat
- Breckinridge Democrat
- Ambitious Veteran
- Louisville Attorney
- Bold Cavalier

Acquire Equipment (No Minimum Strength Requirement). Militia commanders may improve the quality and quantity of their equipment. These actions are more dramatic than the recruitment efforts described above because they are likely to involve the acquisition of heavy weapons, irreversible decisions, and out-of-state actors.

- **The State Armory:** The State Armory in Frankfort contains fifty-eight pieces of field artillery as well as eight thousand muskets, rifles, and carbines. Receiving these arms would greatly increase the power of any militia. The distribution of these arms can be authorized by the Governor. Alternatively, a militia commander may attempt to seize the armory by force.

- **Receive Smuggled Arms:** Arms may be smuggled into Kentucky from the North or the South. The former seems significantly more likely. If a militia commander writes a compelling letter to a likely source of arms and delivers it to the GM, it may result in a supply of

TIP

If a single militia receives these arms, it increases in power by 3 strength points. If multiple militias receive the arms, the GM will divide the points among them.

TIP

Outside research may be useful to identify potential sources of weapons outside of Kentucky.

weapons, which will increase the power of the recipient militia by 1–2 strength points.

- **Benefit from Appropriations:** The legislature may pass a bill granting funding to any militia, which then gains 1 strength point. Multiple appropriations may be made, but no more than 1 strength point may be added each session to an individual militia using this method.

Combination (No Minimum Strength Requirement). Militias may join together. Commanders of both militias must publicly announce that they have done so and explain the ideological basis for their decision. One must become the commander, while the other becomes second-in-command. The power of the combined militia is equal to the sum of strength points of the two militias that combined. Once merged, militias may not separate. No more than one combination is allowed for each militia in a given session.

Abduction (3 Strength Points Required). Once a militia reaches 3 strength points, its commander may order it to abduct another player. The possibility of a successful abduction (some prefer to call it an "arrest") depends upon the strength of the militia executing the order. If an abduction attempt fails, it may go unnoticed, but if it is truly botched, it may result in a bloody skirmish. Militia commanders should remember that the people of Kentucky do not want their home to become a battleground; abduction attempts will alienate some legislators.

TIP

Inexperienced militias are likely to bungle abduction attempts.

If the abduction attempt is successful, the prisoner's fate is determined by the militia commander who ordered the abduction. Prisoners may be released, deported, placed under house arrest, or murdered. While held, prisoners may not vote or speak in the legislature, but may still publish newspapers or write pieces for publication in other's newspapers. Prisoners may only be held for one session.

TIP

Rival militias may attempt to abduct players under militia protection, but it is likely that such an attempt will result in bloodshed.

Players under the protection of militias are far less likely to be successfully abducted than those who are not. The Kentucky State Guard always protects the Governor, the Inspector General, and the Speaker. Similarly, militia commanders are protected by their troops.

Deployment (3 Strength Points Required). Militia commanders may deploy their troops to particular locations within Kentucky. When doing so, they must keep all of their troops together; militias cannot be split into subgroups, except for when leaving Kentucky (see next page). Leading militias into the field may bring them into contact with hostile forces. Combat may provide green troops with valuable experience, but it is equally likely to shatter them. Consequently, militia commanders should be cautious when putting their troops into harm's way. It is a high-risk proposition.

- **Occupy:** Militia commanders may position their men in strategically important locations in order to defend Kentucky. Railroads, river towns, the state capitol, and the State Armory are likely possibilities. (3 strength points required)

- **Seize (or Protect) Arms Shipments:** Once their troops occupy a location, commanders may issue orders to seize or protect arms shipments travelling from North to South across Kentucky. Successful interceptions provide 1 strength point from captured arms. (3 strength points required)

Assault (5 Strength Points Required). Particularly well-organized militias may attempt to dislodge rival militias from key locations. Given the aggressiveness of such an action, it is likely to be condemned unless it is publicly supported by both the legislature and the Governor. The GM determines the results of assaults. Successful assaults may add strength points to the victor while lessening the strength of the loser, but given the nature of mid-nineteenth-century warfare, the most likely result is a mutual degradation of strength.

Leave Kentucky (6 Strength Points Required). Militia commanders may order some or all of their troops to leave the commonwealth to join military forces in other states. Each strength point that is deployed out of state represents one regiment. Each regiment deployed degrades the overall quality of the militia by 1 strength point.

BASIC OUTLINE OF THE GAME

Some instructors may opt to include additional readings or additional discussion of the readings in the game book. They may also vary the amount of time spent explaining the workings of the game. The number of sessions will therefore vary from game to game.

SETUP SESSION 1

HISTORICAL BACKGROUND

Required Reading

- Game book: Historical Background, pp. 15–49.

This session should familiarize players with the history of sectionalism in the United States. The various ideas that animated these conflicts can be gathered into four interrelated categories. Instructors may decide to use these as guidelines for reading or as prompts for writing assignments.

Federal vs. State Power

- How, in the nineteenth century, did federal and state governments reflect the "will of the people" in different ways?

- How did the Tenth Amendment seek to clarify the balance between federal and state authority?

- How clearly did the Constitution address questions about the expansion of slavery into the territories?

- How did the Virginia and Kentucky Resolutions propose to check federal power?

- What was the struggle over nullification launched by South Carolina? What positions did Calhoun and Jackson take? How was this crisis resolved?

- Why did Secessionists think that Lincoln's election would create a constitutional crisis?

Support for Slavery and Abolitionism

- Why did slavery end in the North?

- What provoked the Missouri crisis in 1820? How was it resolved?

- How did advocates of slavery seek to uphold the righteousness of their position?

- What are the key differences between the different varieties of abolitionism (gradual, immediate, colonization)?

Western Expansion

- How did the Mexican War complicate questions about the expansion of slavery into the West? How did the Compromise of 1850 attempt to resolve this?

- Why did the Kansas-Nebraska Act lead to a bloody mess?

- How did the Supreme Court's *Dred Scott* decision complicate disagreements over the expansion of slavery?

- Why did John Brown's raid on Harper's Ferry terrify white Southerners?

- What was the Republican stance on slavery?

Economics

- Why did slavery grow in economic importance in the early nineteenth century?

- Why did it decline in importance in Kentucky?

SETUP SESSION 2

THE LINCOLN PROBLEM

Required Reading

- Abraham Lincoln, "House Divided," pp. 123–27.

- Abraham Lincoln and Stephen Douglas, "Freeport Debate," pp. 127–34.

- William Henry Seward, "An Irrepressible Conflict," pp. 135–43.

The current crisis was touched off by the election of Republican Abraham Lincoln in November 1860. Many white Southerners are particularly concerned about his stance on slavery. Read and discuss these documents and develop a sophisticated idea of Lincoln's position on this issue.

When exploring these documents, return to the end of the Historical Background section of the game book and consider how the election of Lincoln represents the culmination of conflicts around states' rights and slavery. Reflect on Seward's role as a leader of the Republican Party and an influential advisor to the president.

Consider the following questions:

- What are the clues that indicate Lincoln's position on slavery?

- How might his stances on slavery in the West and slavery in the South differ?

- What does he think about the Fugitive Slave Act of 1850?

- On what issues do Seward and Lincoln differ, if any?

SETUP SESSION 3

INTRODUCTION TO THE GAME

Required Reading

- Stephen F. Hale, "Letter to Governor Beriah Magoffin," pp. 159–68.

- Frederick Douglass, "The Meaning of July Fourth for the Negro," pp. 112–17.

- James Henry Hammond, "Cotton Is King," pp. 117–23.

Class Activities

- Racism Argument Quiz: Racist arguments should not be a substantive element of any speech that is given in this class, but historically they were an important element of these debates. To represent the power of these ideas, everyone will take a short quiz testing comprehension of the required reading. Those who score particularly well may collect a Racism Argument handout from the GM. (See p. 57.)

- Regional Caucuses: Legislators should caucus by region. The Governor and Inspector General may talk to anyone they like. Legislators from some regions will discover a diversity of political views; others will find that their colleagues share their opinions.

- Newspaper Publication Schedule: Legislators must set a publication schedule ensuring that at least two newspapers are published for every Game Session. (The GM should facilitate this process.)

- Speaker of the House: Before the session ends, legislators may nominate a Speaker. Candidates may not self-nominate—that would be unseemly. The Speaker must carry a majority vote. (The GM should facilitate this process. After it is complete, the GM may step back, and the Speaker may begin organizing the class.)

THE FUTURE OF SLAVERY

South Carolina seceded on December 20, 1860.

Oath of Office for Legislators

The Speaker should swear in all of the legislators at the beginning of the special session with the following oath from the Kentucky constitution:

> I do solemnly swear (or affirm, as the case may be), that I will support the Constitution of the United States and the Constitution of this State, and be faithful and true to the Commonwealth of Kentucky so long as I continue a citizen thereof, and that I will faithfully execute, to the best of my abilities, the office of legislator according to law; and I do further solemnly swear (or affirm) that since the adoption of the present Constitution I, being a citizen of this State, have not fought a duel with deadly weapons within this State nor out of it, with a citizen of this State; nor have I sent or accepted a challenge to fight a duel with deadly weapons with a citizen of this State; nor have I acted as second in carrying a challenge, or aided or assisted any person thus offending, so help me God.[10]

Speech Topics

During this session, the legislature shall consider the future of slavery in Kentucky. Lincoln's election has brought this idea into focus. What had been somewhat abstract has become more immediate.

In the debate, everyone should consider the history of the Republican Party and its relationship with abolitionism, the positions that Lincoln developed in the Freeport debate and the "House Divided" speech as well as the ideas expressed by William H. Seward's "Irrepressible Conflict" speech. Everyone is free to mine these and other pre-December 1860 speeches for additional material to answer the burning question: What are Lincoln and the Republicans likely to do about slavery?

Anyone may speak on this matter, but the following players *must* address this topic with prepared speeches. The Speaker should ensure that they have sufficient time to present their speeches and receive questions from the floor and gallery.

- The Governor
- Bookish Lawyer (Cumberland Plateau)

- Uncomfortable Heir (Bluegrass)

- Self-Made Planter (Pennyroyal)

- Presbyterian Planter (Jackson Purchase)

SUBSEQUENT LEGISLATIVE SESSIONS

Events caused by outside forces will drive much of the debate in the Kentucky legislature once the game begins. These events remain in the cloudy future, so at the end of each session, the GM will distribute the readings and agenda for the subsequent session. Some of these will be the texts of speeches by important figures; others will announce political and military developments.

Players should collect this important news as they depart each session.

DEBRIEFING AND POSTMORTEM

After the game ends, the GM will calculate the results of the war (provided one occurs), and conduct a debriefing during which players may explain their actions. This session is also an opportunity to compare the events in the game with those that happened historically. In advance of this session, players should prepare two-to-three-page explanations of the degree to which they have achieved the objectives stated on their role sheets.

ASSIGNMENTS

Speeches

Most players must give at least one speech. The Governor and the Inspector General must give two. Players must deliver their speeches engagingly and enthusiastically, and avoid simply reading from a piece of paper. The fewer notes the better, but some may be necessary and useful. The strongest speeches include properly contextualized quotations from historical documents as well as apt references to speeches and newspapers produced by other players. The vast majority of legislators are undecided about most issues and are therefore likely to be persuaded by inspiring rhetoric.

About half of the players have had the topic and day of their speech assigned to them, almost all during the first two sessions. Players who do not have set topics should therefore plan on giving their speeches during the last two-thirds of the game.

Players should provide the GM with a copy of every speech at the outset of the Game Session in which the speech is delivered. Speeches should be three to five pages in length, though GMs may modify this requirement.

Newspapers

In addition to delivering speeches, every legislator must produce and publish a four-to-eight-page newspaper. Newspapers possess the ability to filter, interpret, and disseminate news of the acts in the legislature, events in Kentucky, and developments across the nation. This gives them a great deal of influence. As events unfold, everyone should look for more information about the situation in the rest of the United States. Newspapers offer rich sources of information, but they are rarely objective due to the partisan loyalties of newspaper editors.

Each newspaper should include all of the following elements (unless your instructor gives you an alternative assignment):

- A **masthead** at the top of the front page that lists the newspaper's title, editor, month of publication, and the region of Kentucky in which it is being published.

- One three-to-five-paragraph **editorial** written by the editor on the *front page*, featuring a headline that makes its position on a particular issue *very clear*.

- A three-to-five-paragraph **news story**, written by the editor, describing current events in Kentucky. Everyone counts on newspapers to keep them up to date with political developments, so these stories might include descriptions of official actions taken by the legislature, Governor, or Inspector General. (Newspapers published for the first session should use this section to describe the Manumussion Act of 1860 [p. 143] and the Militia Act of 1860 [p. 145], which were both recently passed into law).

- Two **excerpts** of stories copied from actual newspapers published during the appropriate month of 1861. Each should be three to five paragraphs in length, and each should be introduced with a paragraph written by the editor.

- One **illustration** from an 1861 publication with an appropriate caption written by the editor.

- One **letter to the editor or illustration** created by another player.

- Two **advertisements** from 1861 publications.

- A **colophon**, which is a statement that contains all citations, the names of the editor and contributors, and any other information that seems pertinent.

Players receive two votes for the entire session when they publish newspapers.

Sources. There are number of good online sources that you can mine for articles and illustrations to be used in newspapers. They include:

- Kentucky Digital Library

- *Harper's Weekly*

- Furman University's "Secession Era Editorials Project"

- George Mason University's "The Editorials on Secession Project"

- *Frank Leslie's Illustrated Newspaper* is an excellent source for period illustrations. There is no comprehensive archive of the newspaper, but many libraries have microform copies of various articles and illustrations and many scanned images are available online.

Many libraries hold microform copies of other mid-nineteenth-century newspapers as well, and many of these newspapers have been digitized. Players may even find libraries that have retained a print collection of these newspapers.

Distribution. Players need to coordinate with one another to make sure that a steady stream of newspapers is published throughout the game.

Editors should distribute their papers as soon as the classroom becomes available so that everyone can look through them before the session officially starts. Alternatively, editors may distribute their papers electronically. The Speaker may choose to set aside the first five minutes of every session for players to glance through the papers.

Provide the GM with a copy of your newspaper. It should be four to eight pages in length, though GMs may modify this requirement.

Postmortem Assessment

Finally, for the debriefing session at the end of the game, players must prepare a two-to-three-page explanation of the degree to which they have fulfilled the objectives listed on their role sheets.

COUNTERFACTUALS

In order to facilitate the smooth operation of the game, we have manipulated some elements of the history of Kentucky during this period.

First, the structure of the government of Kentucky is simplified. The judicial branch has been eliminated, as has the position of lieutenant governor. Furthermore, rather than modeling both halves of the bicameral Kentucky legislature, the game only includes the proceedings of a single house.

Second, the special session, called to decide whether a Sovereignty Convention should be held, begins in the game with a general discussion of the future of slavery in Kentucky. Historically, the legislature did not thoroughly discuss the future of slavery in early January 1861. The ideas in this discussion relate strongly to other questions in the game, however, so the debate helps to set the scene. As an aid to this discussion, the number of outspoken anti-slavery members of the legislature is higher in this game than it was historically.

PART 4: **ROLES AND FACTIONS**

THE GOVERNOR

Governor Magoffin is a terribly conflicted man. He loves the Union, but he fears the Republican Party. He hates the idea of secession, but he is a devoted advocate of states' rights. Many see him as the de facto leader of the Secessionists, but he is reluctant to carry Kentucky out of the Union; he does not want it to become a battleground. Ideally, for the Governor, Kentucky would isolate itself from the fray and serve as an honest broker between North and South. To this end, he hopes to create a neutralist coalition of states.

TIP

The Governor and Inspector General must each write and present two speeches.

The Governor's responsibilities include the preparation and presentation of two speeches. Importantly, the Governor must present the very first speech of the game, which opens the special session of the legislature.[1]

The Governor is the chief executive of the government of the commonwealth of Kentucky. As such, his responsibilities are similar to those of the president of the United States, with several important differences. Under the 1850 state constitution, the powers of the Governor are limited but far from inconsequential.

First, the Governor possesses the power to veto proposed legislation. If he opts to do so, he must return the bill to the legislature with his objections by the end of the session in which it is passed. The legislature may dismiss these objections and overturn the a mere majority vote, but not until the next session of the legislature. The Governor may use the Racism Argument to make a veto stick until the following session. (For details on the Racism Argument, see p. 57.)

The Governor controls the State Arsenal and the Kentucky State Guard except, as the state constitution notes, "when they shall be called into the service of the United States." He may appoint officers to the State Guard. Inspector General Buckner, who serves as the overall commander of the State Guard, is a recent appointment. While the Governor is the commander in chief, the state constitution explains that "he shall not command them personally in the field, unless advised so to do by a resolution of the General Assembly." This is Buckner's job, but he serves at the pleasure of the Governor.[2]

The Governor may vote in the legislature, but only as a tiebreaker.[3]

The Governor's final power is prestige. In some ways, his status as chief executive of Kentucky carries more weight outside of the state than in the commonwealth itself. In the course of the game, anyone may opt to write a letter to someone outside of Kentucky (Abraham Lincoln, Charles Sumner, Jefferson Davis, etc.), but such a letter will carry the greatest weight if the Governor himself signs it. These letters should be delivered to the GM.

TIP

In smaller games, the functions of the Inspector General are performed by the Governor.

THE INSPECTOR GENERAL

In reaction to chronic problems with runaway slaves and John Brown's raid, a new, comprehensive state law reorganized and centralized oversight of the Kentucky State Guard in March 1860. (See p. 145.) This overhaul included clarification of the duties of the Inspector General, who is responsible for overseeing the quality and organization of the disparate local militia units. He now possesses the authority to disband low-quality companies of the militia.[4]

The Inspector General's responsibilities include the preparation and presentation of two speeches. Each *must* be accompanied by orders for the State Guard. Without such a call, the men under arms will grow restless and may return home or leave the state. Especially powerful speeches calling for dramatic action, however, may cause Kentuckians to flock to the banner of the State Guard, which could increase its power and capabilities.

With an estimated four thousand enrolled volunteers, the Kentucky State Guard remains the largest militia in the state. It is not, however, a cohesive organization at the beginning of the game. The allegiance of many militiamen is unknown. They may be swayed by the actions and words of other players, outside events, or what they read in Kentucky's many fine newspapers. Ordinarily, as time passes, the Inspector General will exert greater control and the State Guard will become more cohesive and capable of action.

According to the state constitution, the Governor is the commander in chief while his appointee, the Inspector General, is in charge of overseeing and organizing the militia, but in the current tumult this chain of command may become tenuous. As long as no one objects, the Kentucky State Guard will obey orders from the Inspector General. However, if the state government appears seriously divided and contradictory orders are issued by the legislature and the Governor, the State Guard may become paralyzed.

TIP

The Inspector General serves at the pleasure of the Governor. The Governor may not remove the Inspector General, however, unless a qualified replacement has volunteered to accept his commission. (For details, see the "Assuming Command" section on p. 59.)

MEMBERS OF THE LEGISLATURE

Members of the Kentucky legislature are drawn from throughout the commonwealth. They are popularly elected and represent a range of interests. They are all white, Christian slaveholders, and they are intimately familiar with the documents that appear in the game book.

The Cumberland Plateau

This region includes the hills, valleys, and mountains of eastern Kentucky. Few slaveholders live in this area. Most of the economy is based upon subsistence farming. There are no railways and few reliable roads. Legislators from this region include:

TIP

Each legislator is responsible for preparing and presenting one speech and one newspaper.

The Baptist Farmer. Despite holding a handful of slaves, the Baptist Farmer finds much to criticize about the institution of slavery. Inspired by the writings of James Pendleton, he criticizes the tendency of pro-slavery ideologues to idealize slavery as an abstraction instead of seeing the institution as it actually is. *Voted Bell.*

The Constitutional Unionist. The Constitutional Unionist was inspired to seek political office by the career of Kentucky's favorite son, the Great Compromiser Henry Clay; he seeks a middle road of moderation for Kentucky. He will speak on the indivisibility of the Union during the second session. *Voted Bell.*

The Bookish Lawyer. After traveling the world, the Bookish Lawyer returned to Kentucky to take over his family's assets after his brother died. He is a voracious reader; among the works currently stacked on his desk are Hinton Helper's *Impending Crisis*, Harriet Beecher Stowe's *Uncle Tom's Cabin*, and sheaves of *DeBow's Review*. He won his seat as a Jackson-style champion of the common man, and is known as an advocate of gradual emancipation. He will speak on this issue (and may even propose legislation) during the first session. *Voted Douglas.*

The Genteel Sportsman. A wealthy South Carolina plantation owner, the Genteel Sportsman decided to move to the hills of eastern Kentucky in pursuit of a simpler life and more abundant game and fish. His friends and neighbors prevailed upon him to stand for election in 1860 because of his experience opposing nullification as a member of the South Carolina senate. *Voted Douglas.*

The Bluegrass

Bounded on the north by the Ohio River, this region includes the wheat fields, horse pastures, and hemp plantations of northern and central Kentucky. Many of Kentucky's largest slaveholders live in this region, which also includes numerous pockets of subsistence farmers who are not directly invested in slavery. The Bluegrass is also home to Kentucky's largest cities: Louisville and Lexington, which are connected to one another and the state capital, Frankfort, by rail. The recently completed Louisville and Nashville Railroad—connecting Cincinnati, Ohio, and Nashville, Tennessee—runs through this region as well. The Bluegrass is the most populated of Kentucky's regions and is home to the Governor, the Inspector General, and the following legislators:

The Louisville Attorney. The Louisville Attorney has lived on both sides of the Ohio River. He served as a captain of volunteers in the Mexican War and as a Whig in the Indiana legislature. He later relocated to Louisville to practice law. He is experienced in politics but is new to the Kentucky legislature. *Voted Bell.*

The Homespun Lawyer. After his inheritance was squandered by his legal guardian, the Homespun Lawyer rebuilt his family fortune. He is enamored of the writings of the Fire-Eaters of the Deep South, such as Louis Wigfall, Barnwell Rhett, and William Yancey. Their unapologetic defense of Southern rights, honor, and slavery makes them his political idols. He will speak during the second session. *Voted Breckinridge.*

The Uncomfortable Heir. Despite his anti-slavery sentiments, which began developing during his time at Yale, the Uncomfortable Heir owns several slaves. He insists that he is eager to free them but finds himself stymied by Kentucky's restrictive manumission law (see p. 143). Fearless and indomitable like Kentucky's most belligerent abolitionist, Cassius Clay (they served together in the Mexican War), he will speak during the first session and may propose legislation. *Voted Lincoln.*

The Bold Cavalier. Another veteran of the Mexican War, the Bold Cavalier is heavily invested in hemp manufacturing. He supplements his income by hiring out teams of slaves to riverboat captains. Given his penchant for carousing and apparent disinterest in politics, many wonder why he even stood for office, which he won thanks to the votes of his local militia company, the Lexington Rifles. *Forgot to vote.*

The Hemp Planter. The well-connected Hemp Planter supports his considerable political ambitions with wealth gained by selling his excess slaves to the Deep South. He started his political career as a member of the anti-immigrant American Party, also known as the "Know-Nothings." An advocate of expansionist adventurers like William Walker, who attempted to conquer both the Sonora province of Mexico and the nation of Nicaragua, he supports the expansion of slavery into the Caribbean by force. *Voted Bell.*

The Cautious Banker. From an established Kentucky family, the Cautious Banker is connected to the planter elite through various kin networks. Most of the shareholders in his bank are local slaveholders, but there are also depositors from Ohio and Indiana. He is heavily invested in the Louisville and Nashville Railroad and sees industrialization rather than agriculture as the best source of future prosperity. *Voted Douglas.*

The Arch-Unionist. Unlike most legislators, the Arch-Unionist has a clear position on the question of secession. He opposes it utterly and believes that the legislature should condemn it as treason, unequivocally affirming Kentucky's loyalty to the Union. *Voted Douglas.*

The Striving Manufacturer. The owner of a steam-powered rope and bagging factory, the Striving Manufacturer is at the vanguard of Kentucky's industrialization. He is eager to expand his operations and sees immigrants as the best source of inexpensive labor in the future, though his workforce currently comprises enslaved, free black, and white workers. *Voted Bell.*

The Douglas Democrat. Unlike many of his fellow legislators, the Douglas Democrat was not born into a noted political family. Instead, he worked his way up the ladder as a loyal operative of the Democratic Party in and around the city of Louisville. While members of the Kentucky elite tend to read law at Transylvania University in Lexington, he learned the craft under the tutelage of a wily, self-taught trial attorney. An incredibly handsome man, he will be a powerful force in Frankfort if his cleverness matches his vanity. *Voted Douglas.*

The Rising Star. The Rising Star appears to be something of an opportunist. A Know-Nothing at the start of his political career, he recast himself as a Douglas Democrat. More recently, he pivoted again by dropping the Democrats and advocating for the Constitutional Unionists. In the past month he appears to have changed his colors once again and he now calls himself a Secessionist. *Voted Bell.*

The Pennyroyal

This region west of the Bluegrass includes the tobacco plantations and woodlands of central and southern Kentucky. Plantation settlement came to this area fairly recently, but the region has developed quickly. Large tobacco plantations range along the Tennessee border, while smaller farms dominate elsewhere. The recent completion of the Louisville and Nashville Railroad will facilitate even greater economic development.

The Fire-Eater. Unlike most legislators, the Fire-Eater has a clear position on the question of secession. He supports it with every fiber of his being and believes that the legislature should call a Sovereignty Convention as quickly as possible and then march straight out of the Union. *Voted Breckinridge.*

The Die-Hard Whig. The Die-Hard Whig clings to the memory of the Great Compromiser Henry Clay and his colleague Daniel Webster of Massachusetts. Their stellar careers and steadfast commitment to the nation convinced him to become a proud member of the Whig Party fifteen years ago, and he is not giving up those loyalties now. Throughout his political life he enthusiastically supported Clay's "American System," which echoed the philosophy of the Hamiltonians during the early Republic. He will speak on the ideas of Clay and Webster during the second session. *Voted Bell.*

The Jacksonian Democrat. The Jacksonian Democrat embraces his idol's nationalism and prickly sense of honor. Although he joined the volunteers in the Mexican War as a private, he came home an officer. He plans to speak on Andrew Jackson's concept of nationalism during the second session. *Voted Douglas.*

The Breckinridge Democrat. By rejecting the notion that the federal government possesses any authority over the institution of slavery, the Breckinridge Democrat has managed to weather the past fifteen years of sectional tension. He wants everyone to remain calm. As a result of his military service in the Mexican War, everyone calls him "colonel." He hopes to leverage his record on slavery and his military service into national political office. *Voted Breckinridge.*

The Proud Autodidact. Journeying to the Kentucky frontier as a young man, the Proud Autodidact and a handful of slaves carved a plantation out of heavily wooded bottomlands along the Green River. By relentlessly driving himself and his slaves, he has become the wealthiest man in his county. He recently turned to politics in an attempt to establish a new image for himself as a statesman and man of substance. He will speak in support of slavery during the first session. *Voted Breckinridge.*

The Ambitious Veteran. Born to a wealthy, slaveholding family in North Carolina, the Ambitious Veteran attended the United States Military Academy at West Point and served as an officer in the U.S. Army on the western frontier. During a journey by riverboat down the Missouri River, he met his future father-in-law, a wealthy tobacco planter from Kentucky, who subsequently helped him launch a successful political career. *Voted Bell.*

The True Kentuckian. Determined to keep the commonwealth united, the True Kentuckian is confident that as long as Kentuckians work together, the other sections will come to see reason. *Voted Bell.*

The Jackson Purchase

Bounded to the north by the Ohio River and to the west by the Mississippi River and home to the port of Paducah, this is the most recently settled region of Kentucky. Locked into a network of river transportation, the area will soon become better connected to Memphis, Tennessee, by the completion of the Mobile and Ohio Railroad. If everything goes according to plan, the rail line will be completed in the spring of 1861.

The Presbyterian Planter. The Presbyterian Planter is inspired by one of the most accomplished defenders of slavery in the South, Old School Presbyterian theologian James Henley Thornwell. He will speak on the issue of slavery during the first session. *Voted Breckinridge.*

The Paternalist Planter. A third-generation Kentuckian, the Paternalist Planter was a young man when he sold his ancestral lands in the eastern part of the commonwealth, bought slaves, and moved to new lands in the westernmost portion of the state. Consequently, he sees the opportunity created by new lands in the West as integral to the continued vitality of the institution of slavery. He has lived his ideology by volunteering for service in the Mexican War in which he served with distinction, receiving a commission as a lieutenant. He is particularly enamored of the writings of South Carolina senators John C. Calhoun and John H. Hammond, and will speak on South Carolina's right to secede during the second session. *Voted Breckinridge.*

The Obdurate Planter. After reading George Fitzhugh's 1849 pamphlet *Slavery Justified*, the Obdurate Planter took the pro-slavery position further than any of his fellow legislators. A critic of heartless Northern capitalists, he condemns the Declaration of Independence as a tissue of lies (all men are *not* created equal!) and advocates slavery as the best social institution imaginable. Intellectually combative, he is frequently on edge because his New England wife is known to read abolitionist tracts. *Voted Bell.*

PART 5: **CORE TEXTS**

NOTE ON THE TEXTS

In order to play the game well, one must have a grasp of the documents that follow. Editorial comments by the authors of this game book appear in the margins. The formatting and spelling in the documents have been silently modernized to facilitate comprehension.

DANIEL WEBSTER

"The Second Reply to Hayne," January 1830

On January 26 and 27 of 1830, Webster countered Senator Robert Hayne's claims of South Carolina's right to nullification (or, in Webster's words, annulment) in a speech mainly directed at Vice President John C. Calhoun. The speech was given before the U.S. Senate and is therefore addressed to the president of the Senate.

SOURCE: *Kenneth E. Shewmaker, ed.,* Daniel Webster: The Completest Man *(Hanover, N.H.: University Press of New England, 1990), 113–21, available at www.dartmouth.edu/~dwebster/speeches /hayne-speech.html.*

. . . Sir, let me recur to pleasing recollections; let me indulge in refreshing remembrance of the past; let me remind you that, in early times, no States cherished greater harmony, both of principle and feeling, than Massachusetts and South Carolina. Would to God that harmony might again return! Shoulder to shoulder they went through the Revolution, hand in hand they stood round the administration of Washington, and felt his own great arm lean on them for support. Unkind feeling, if it exist, alienation, and distrust are the growth, unnatural to such soils, of false principles since sown. They are weeds, the seeds of which that same great arm never scattered.

Mr. President, I shall enter on no encomium upon Massachusetts; she needs none. There she is. Behold her, and judge for yourselves. There is her history; the world knows it by heart. The past, at least, is secure. There is Boston, and Concord, and Lexington, and Bunker Hill; and there they will remain for ever. The bones of her sons, falling in the great struggle for Independence, now lie mingled with the soil of every State from New England to Georgia; and there they will lie for ever. And Sir, where American Liberty raised its first voice, and where its youth was nurtured and sustained, there it still lives, in the strength of its manhood, and full of its original spirit. If discord and disunion shall wound it, if party strife and blind ambition shall hawk at and tear it, if folly and madness, if uneasiness under salutary and necessary restraint, shall succeed in separating it from that Union, by which alone its existence is made sure, it will stand, in the end, by the side of that cradle in which its infancy was rocked; over the friends who gather round it; and it will fall at last, if fall it must, amidst the proudest monuments of its own glory, and on the very spot of its origin.

There yet remains to be performed, Mr. President, by far the most grave and important duty, which I feel to be devolved on me by this occasion. It is to state, and to defend, what I conceive to be the true principles of the Constitution under which we are here assembled. I might well have desired that so weighty a task should have fallen into other and abler hands. I could have wished that it should have been executed by those whose character and experience give weight and influence to their opinions, such as cannot possibly belong to mine. But, Sir, I have met the occasion, not sought it; and I shall proceed to state my own sentiments, without challenging for them any particular regard, with studied plainness, and as much precision as possible.

I understand the honorable gentleman from South Carolina to maintain, that it is a right of the State legislatures to interfere, whenever, in their judgment, this government transcends its constitutional limits, and to arrest the operation of its laws.

I understand him to maintain this right, as a right existing *under* the Constitution, not as a right to overthrow it on the ground of extreme necessity, such as would justify violent revolution.

I understand him to maintain an authority, on the part of the States, thus to interfere, for the purpose of correcting the exercise of power by the general government, of checking it, and of compelling it to conform to their opinion of the extent of its powers.

I understand him to maintain that the ultimate power of judging of the constitutional extent of its own authority is not lodged exclusively in the general government, or any branch of it: but that, on the contrary, the States may lawfully decide for themselves, and each State for itself, whether, in a given case, the act of the general government transcends its power.

I understand him to insist, that, if the exigency of the case, in the opinion of any State government, require it, such State government may, by its own sovereign authority, annul an act of the general government which it deems plainly and palpably unconstitutional.

This is the sum of what I understand from him to be the South Carolina doctrine, and the doctrine which he maintains. I propose to consider it, and compare it with the Constitution. Allow me to say, as a preliminary remark, that I call this the South Carolina doctrine only because the gentleman himself has so denominated it. I do not feel at liberty to say that South Carolina, as a State, has ever advanced these sentiments. I hope she has not, and never may. That a great majority of her people are opposed to the tariff laws, is doubtless true. That a majority, somewhat less than that just mentioned, conscientiously believe that these laws are unconstitutional, may probably also be true. But that any majority holds the right of direct State interference at State discretion, the right of nullifying acts of Congress by acts of State legislation, is more than I know, and what I shall be slow to believe.

* * *

This leads us to inquire into the origin of this government and the source of its power. Whose agent is it? Is it the creature of the State legislatures, or the creature of the people? If the government of the United States be the agent of the State governments, then they may control it, provided they can agree in the manner of controlling it; if it be the agent of the people, then the people alone can control it, restrain it, modify, or reform it. It is observable enough, that the doctrine for which the honorable gentleman contends leads him to the necessity of maintaining, not only that this general government is the creature of the States, but that it is the creature of each of the States severally, so that each may assert the power for itself of determining whether it acts within the limits of its authority. It is the servant of four-and-twenty masters, of different will and different purposes and yet bound to obey all. This absurdity (for it seems no less) arises from a misconception as to the origin of this government and its true character. It is, Sir, the people's Constitution, the people's government, made for the people, made by the people, and answerable to the people. The people of the United States have declared that the Constitution shall be the supreme law. We must either admit the proposition, or dispute their authority. The States are, unquestionably, sovereign, so far as their sovereignty is not affected by this supreme law. But the State legislatures, as political bodies, however sovereign, are yet not sovereign over the people. So far as the people have given the power to the general government, so far the grant is unquestionably good, and the government holds of the people, and not of the State governments. We are all agents of the same supreme power, the people. The general government and the State governments derive their authority from the same source. Neither can, in relation to the other, be called primary, though one is definite and restricted, and the other general and residuary. The national government possesses those powers which it will be shown the people have conferred upon it, and no more. All the rest belongs to the State governments, or to the people themselves. So far as the people have restrained State sovereignty, by the expression of their will, in the Constitution of the United States, so far, it must be admitted. State sovereignty is effectually controlled. I do not contend that it is, or ought to be, controlled farther. The sentiment to which I have referred propounds that State sovereignty is only to be controlled by its own "feeling of justice": that is to say, it is not to be controlled at all, for one who is to follow his own feelings is under no legal control. Now, however men may think this ought to be, the fact is, that the people of the United States have chosen to impose control on State sovereignties. There are those, doubtless, who wish they had been left without restraint; but the Constitution has ordered the matter differently. To make war, for instance, is an exercise of sovereignty; but the Constitution declares that no State shall make war. To coin money is another exercise of sovereign power, but no State is at liberty to coin money. Again, the Constitution says that no sovereign State shall be so sovereign as to make a treaty. These prohibitions, it must be confessed, are a control on the State sovereignty of South Carolina, as well as of the other States, which does not arise "from her own feelings of honorable justice." The opinion referred to, therefore, is in defiance of the plainest provisions of the Constitution.

* * *

I must now beg to ask, Sir, Whence is this supposed right of the States derived? Where do they find the power to interfere with the laws of the Union? Sir the opinion which the honorable gentleman maintains is a notion founded in a total misapprehension, in my judgment, of the origin of this government, and of the foundation on which it stands. I hold it to be a popular government, erected by the people; those who administer it, responsible to the people; and itself capable of being amended and modified, just as the people may choose it should be. It is as popular, just as truly emanating from the people, as the State governments. It is created for one purpose; the State governments for another. It has its own powers; they have theirs. There is no more authority with them to arrest the operation of a law of Congress, than with Congress to arrest the operation of their laws. We are here to administer a Constitution emanating immediately from the people, and trusted by them to our administration. It is not the creature of the State governments. It is of no moment to the argument, that certain acts of the State legislatures are necessary to fill our seats in this body. That is not one of their original State powers, a part of the sovereignty of the State. It is a duty which the people, by the Constitution itself, have imposed on the State legislatures; and which they might have left to be performed elsewhere, if they had seen fit. So they have left the choice of President with electors; but all this does not affect the proposition that this whole government, President, Senate, and House of Representatives, is a popular government. It leaves it still all its popular character. The governor of a State (in some of the States) is chosen, not directly by the people, but by those who are chosen by the people, for the purpose of performing, among other duties, that of electing a governor. Is the government of the State, on that account, not a popular government? This government, Sir, is the independent offspring of the popular will. It is not the creature of State legislatures; nay, more, if the whole truth must be told, the people brought it into existence, established it, and have hitherto supported it, for the very purpose, amongst others, of imposing certain salutary restraints on State sovereignties. The States cannot now make war; they cannot contract alliances; they cannot make, each for itself, separate regulations of commerce; they cannot lay imposts; they cannot coin money. If this Constitution, Sir, be the creature of State legislatures, it must be admitted that it has obtained a strange control over the volitions of its creators.

The people, then, Sir, erected this government. They gave it a Constitution, and in that Constitution they have enumerated the powers which they bestow on it. They have made it a limited government. They have defined its authority. They have restrained it to the exercise of such powers as are granted; and all others, they declare, are reserved to the States or the people. But, Sir, they have not stopped here. If they had, they would have accomplished but half their work. No definition can be so clear, as to avoid possibility of doubt; no limitation so precise, as to exclude all uncertainty. Who, then, shall construe this grant of the people? Who shall interpret their will, where it may be supposed they have left it doubtful? With whom do they repose this ultimate right of deciding on the powers of government? Sir, they have settled all this in the fullest manner. They have left it with the government itself, in its appropriate branches. Sir, the very chief end, the main design, for which the whole Constitution was framed and adopted, was to establish a government that should not be obliged to act through State agency, or depend on State opinion and State discretion. The people had had quite enough of that kind of government under the Confederation. Under that system, the legal action, the application of law to individuals, belonged exclusively to the States. Congress could only recommend; their acts were not of binding force, till the States had adopted and sanctioned them. Are we in that condition still? Are we yet at the mercy of State discretion and State construction? Sir, if we are, then vain will be our attempt to maintain the Constitution under which we sit.

But, Sir, the people have wisely provided, in the Constitution itself, a proper, suitable mode and tribunal for settling questions of Constitutional law. There are in the Constitution grants of powers to Congress, and restrictions on these powers. There are, also, prohibitions on the States. Some authority must, therefore, necessarily exist, having the ultimate jurisdiction to fix and ascertain the interpretation of these grants, restrictions, and prohibitions. The Constitution has itself pointed out, ordained, and established that authority. How has it accomplished this great and essential end? By declaring, Sir, that *"the Constitution, and the laws of the United States made in pursuance thereof, shall be the supreme law of the land, any thing in the constitution or laws of any State to the contrary notwithstanding."*

This, Sir, was the first great step. By this the supremacy of the Constitution and laws of the United States is declared. The people so will it. No State law is to be valid which comes in conflict with the Constitution, or any law of the United States passed in pursuance of it. But who shall decide this question of interference? To whom lies the last appeal? This, Sir, the Constitution itself decides also, by declaring, *"That the judicial power shall extend to all cases arising under the Constitution and laws of the United States."* These two provisions cover the whole ground. They are, in truth, the keystone of the arch! With these it is a government; without them it is a confederation. In pursuance of these clear and express provisions, Congress established, at its very first session, in the judicial act, a mode for carrying them into full effect, and for bringing all questions of constitutional power to the final decision of the Supreme Court. It then, Sir, became a government. It then had the means of self-protection; and but for this, it would, in all probability, have been now among things which are past. Having constituted the government, and declared its powers, the people have further said, that, since somebody must decide on the extent of these powers, the government shall itself decide; subject always, like other popular governments, to its responsibility to the people.

* * *

I have not allowed myself, Sir, to look beyond the Union, to see what might lie hidden in the dark recess behind. I have not coolly weighed the chances of preserving liberty when the bonds that unite us together shall be broken asunder. I have not accustomed myself to hang over the precipice of disunion, to see whether, with my short sight, I can fathom the depth of the abyss below; nor could I regard him as a safe counsellor in the affairs of this government, whose thoughts should be mainly bent on considering, not how the Union may be best preserved, but how tolerable might be the condition of the people when it should be broken up and destroyed. While the Union lasts, we have high, exciting, gratifying prospects spread out before us and our children. Beyond that I seek not to penetrate the veil. God grant that in my day, at least, that curtain may not rise! God grant that on my vision never may be opened what lies behind! When my eyes shall be turned to behold for the last time the sun in heaven, may I not see him shining on the broken and dishonored fragments of a once glorious Union; on States dissevered, discordant, belligerent; on a land rent with civil feuds, or drenched, it may be, in fraternal blood! Let their last feeble and lingering glance rather behold the gorgeous ensign of the republic, now known and honored throughout the earth, still full high advanced, its arms and trophies streaming in their original lustre, not a stripe erased or polluted, not a single star obscured, bearing for its motto, no such miserable interrogatory as "What is all this worth?" nor those other words of delusion and folly, "Liberty first and Union afterwards"; but everywhere, spread all over in characters of living light, blazing on all its ample folds, as they float over the sea and over the land, and in every wind under the whole heavens, that other sentiment, dear to every true American heart,—Liberty *and* Union, now and for ever, one and inseparable!

JOHN C. CALHOUN

A Disquisition on Government, 1849

In the course of the Disquisition, *Calhoun argues that the principles of government are as certain and as unquestionable as the laws of gravitation or astronomy. Beginning with the two incontestable facts that man is a social animal and that society cannot exist without government, Calhoun immediately announces a third fact, that man feels what affects him directly more intensely than what affects him indirectly through others. This means that men tend to be selfish. Consequently, government will tend to be abused and corrupted because it must be staffed by people.*

From these three suppositions, Calhoun constructs all of his other arguments and theories, including his doctrine of the concurrent majority, which guarantees every significant interest in the community a concurrent voice in either the enactment or the enforcement of public policy. This concurrent majority serves as a necessary check on the abuse of power by the numerical majority. The presence of such a check, Calhoun argues, distinguishes constitutional governments from tyranny.

SOURCE: *John C. Calhoun,* A Disquisition on Government and a Discourse on the Constitution and Government of the United States, *ed. Richard K. Cralle (Charleston, S.C.: Steam Power-Press of Walker and James, 1851).*

... *P*ower can only be resisted by power—and tendency by tendency. Those who exercise power and those subject to its exercise—the rulers and the ruled—stand in antagonistic relations to each other. The same constitution of our nature which leads rulers to oppress the ruled—regardless of the object for which government is ordained—will, with equal strength, lead the ruled to resist, when possessed of the means of making peaceable and effective resistance. Such an organism, then, as will furnish the means by which resistance may be systematically and peaceably made on the part of the ruled, to oppression and abuse of power on the part of the rulers, is the first and indispensable step towards *forming* a constitutional government. And as this can only be effected by or through the right of suffrage—(the right on the part of the ruled to choose their rulers at proper intervals, and to hold them thereby responsible for their conduct)—the responsibility of the rulers to the ruled, through the right of suffrage, is the indispensable and primary principle in the *foundation* of a constitutional government. When this right is properly guarded, and the people sufficiently enlightened to understand their own rights and the interests of the community, and duly to appreciate the motives and conduct of those appointed to make and execute the laws, it is all-sufficient to give to those who elect, effective control over those they have elected.

* * *

If the whole community had the same interests, so that the interests of each and every portion would be so affected by the action of the government, that the laws which oppressed or impoverished one portion, would necessarily oppress and impoverish all others—or the reverse—then the right of suffrage, of itself, would be all-sufficient to counteract the tendency of the government to oppression and abuse of its powers; and, of course, would form, of itself, a perfect constitutional government. The interest of all being the same, by supposition, as far as the action of the government was concerned, all would have like interests as to what laws should be made, and how they should be executed. All strife and struggle would cease as to who should be elected to make and execute them. The only question would be, who was most fit; who the wisest and most capable of understanding the common interest of the whole. This decided, the election would pass off quietly, and without party discord; as no one portion could advance its own peculiar interest without regard to the rest, by electing a favorite candidate.

But such is not the case. On the contrary, nothing is more difficult than to equalize the action of the government, in reference to the various and diversified interests of the community; and nothing more easy than to pervert its powers into instruments to aggrandize and enrich one or more interests by oppressing and impoverishing the others; and this too, under the operation of laws, couched in general terms—and which, on their face, appear fair and equal. Nor is this the case in some particular communities only. It is so in all; the small and the great—the poor and the rich—irrespective of pursuits, productions, or degrees of civilization—with, however, this difference, that the more extensive and populous the country, the more diversified the condition and pursuits of its population, and the richer, more luxurious, and dissimilar the people, the more difficult is it to equalize the action of the government—and the more easy for one portion of the community to pervert its powers to oppress, and plunder the other.

Such being the case, it necessarily results, that the right of suffrage, by placing the control of the government in the community must, from the same constitution of our nature which makes government necessary to preserve society, lead to conflict among its different interests—each striving to obtain possession of its powers, as the means of protecting itself against the others—or of advancing its respective interests, regardless of the interests of others. For this purpose, a struggle will take place between the various interests to obtain a majority, in order to control the government. If no one interest be strong enough, of itself, to obtain it, a combination will be formed between those whose interests are most alike—each conceding something to the others, until a sufficient number is obtained to make a majority. The process may be slow, and much time may be required before a compact, organized majority can be thus formed; but formed it will be in time, even without preconcert or design, by the sure workings of that principle or constitution of our nature in which government itself originates. When once formed, the community will be divided into two great parties—a major and minor—between which there will be incessant struggles on the one side to retain, and on the other to obtain the majority—and, thereby, the control of the government and the advantages it confers.

* * *

Few, comparatively, as they are, the agents and employees of the government constitute that portion of the community who are the exclusive recipients of the proceeds of the taxes. Whatever amount is taken from the community, in the form of taxes, if not lost, goes to them in the shape of expenditures or disbursements. The two—disbursement and taxation—constitute the fiscal action of the government. They are correlatives. What the one takes from the community, under the name of taxes, is transferred to the portion of the community who are the recipients, under that of disbursements. But, as the recipients constitute only a portion of the community, it follows, taking the two parts of the fiscal process together, that its action must be unequal between the payers of the taxes and the recipients of their proceeds. Nor can it be otherwise, unless what is collected from each individual in the shape of taxes, shall be returned to him, in that of disbursements; which would make the process nugatory and absurd. Taxation may, indeed, be made equal, regarded separately from disbursement. Even this is no easy task; but the two united cannot possibly be made equal.

Such being the case, it must necessarily follow, that some one portion of the community must pay in taxes more than it receives back in disbursements; while another receives in disbursements more than it pays in taxes. It is, then, manifest, taking the whole process together, that taxes must be, in effect, bounties to that portion of the community which receives more in disbursements than it pays in taxes; while, to the other which pays in taxes more than it receives in disbursements, they are taxes in reality—burthens, instead of bounties. This consequence is unavoidable. It results from the nature of the process, be the taxes ever so equally laid, and the disbursements ever so fairly made, in reference to the public service.

* * *

The necessary result, then, of the unequal fiscal action of the government is, to divide the community into two great classes; one consisting of those who, in reality, pay the taxes, and, of course, bear exclusively the burthen of supporting the government; and the other, of those who are the recipients of their proceeds, through disbursements, and who are, in fact, supported by the government; or, in fewer words, to divide it into tax-payers and tax-consumers.

But the effect of this is to place them in antagonistic relations, in reference to the fiscal action of the government, and the entire course of policy therewith connected. For, the greater the taxes and disbursements, the greater the gain of the one and the loss of the other—and *vice versa*; and consequently, the more the policy of the government is calculated to increase taxes and disbursements, the more it will be favored by the one and opposed by the other.

The effect, then, of every increase is, to enrich and strengthen the one, and impoverish and weaken the other. This, indeed, may be carried to such an extent, that one class or portion of the community may be elevated to wealth and power, and the other depressed to abject poverty and dependence, simply by the fiscal action of the government; and this too, through disbursements only—even under a system of equal taxes imposed for revenue only. If such may be the effect of taxes and disbursements, when confined to their legitimate objects—that of raising revenue for the public service—some conception may be formed, how one portion of the community may be crushed, and another elevated on its ruins, by systematically perverting the power of taxation and disbursement, for the purpose of aggrandizing and building up one portion of the community at the expense of the other. That it *will* be so used, unless prevented, is, from the constitution of man, just as certain as that it *can* be so used; and that, if not prevented, it must give rise to two parties, and to violent conflicts and struggles between them, to obtain the control of the government, is, for the same reason, not less certain.

* * *

The only difference in this respect is, that in the government of a majority, the minority may become the majority, and the majority the minority, through the right of suffrage; and thereby change their relative positions, without the intervention of force and revolution. But the duration, or uncertainty of the tenure, by which power is held, cannot, of itself, counteract the tendency inherent in government to oppression and abuse of power. On the contrary, the very uncertainty of the tenure, combined with the violent party warfare which must ever precede a change of parties under such governments, would rather tend to increase than diminish the tendency to oppression.

* * *

Having clearly stated his propositions regarding human nature and government oppression, Calhoun moves on to his proposed solution to the tendency of government to abuse power.

There is but one certain mode in which this result can be secured; and that is, by the adoption of some restriction or limitation, which shall so effectually prevent any one interest, or combination of interests, from obtaining the exclusive control of the government, as to render hopeless all attempts directed to that end.

There is, again, but one mode in which this can be effected; and that is, by taking the sense of each interest or portion of the community, which may be unequally and injuriously affected by the action of the government, separately, through its own majority, or in some other way by which its voice may be fairly expressed; and to require the consent of each interest, either to put or to keep the government in action.

This, too, can be accomplished only in one way—and that is, by such an organism of the government—and, if necessary for the purpose, of the community also—as will, by dividing and distributing the powers of government, give to each division or interest, through its appropriate organ, either a concurrent voice in making and executing the laws, or a veto on their execution. It is only by such an organism, that the assent of each can be made necessary to put the government in motion; or the power made effectual to arrest its action, when put in motion—and it is only by the one or the other that the different interests, orders, classes, or portions, into which the community may be divided, can be protected, and all conflict and struggle between them prevented—by rendering it impossible to put or to keep it in action, without the concurrent consent of all.

* * *

It may be readily inferred, from what has been stated, that the effect of organism is neither to supersede nor diminish the importance of the right of suffrage; but to aid and perfect it. The object of the latter is, to collect the sense of the community. The more fully and perfectly it accomplishes this, the more fully and perfectly it fulfils its end. But the most it can do, of itself, is to collect the sense of the greater number; that is, of the stronger interests, or combination of interests; and to assume this to be the sense of the community. It is only when aided by a proper organism, that it can collect the sense of the entire community—of each and all its interests; of each, through its appropriate organ, and of the whole, through all of them united. This would truly be the sense of the entire community; for whatever diversity each interest might have within itself—as all would have the same interest in reference to the action of the government, the individuals composing each would be fully and truly represented by its own majority or appropriate organ, regarded in reference to the other interests. In brief, every individual of every interest might trust, with confidence, its majority or appropriate organ, against that of every other interest.

Suffrage is a blunt instrument because it only reflects the will of the majority. Calhoun argues that his notion of a concurrent majority is superior because it actually represents everyone.

It results, from what has been said, that there are two different modes in which the sense of the community may be taken; one, simply by the right of suffrage, unaided; the other, by the right through a proper organism. Each collects the sense of the majority. But one regards numbers only, and considers the whole community as a unit, having but one common interest throughout; and collects the sense of the greater number of the whole, as that of the community. The other, on the contrary, regards interests as well as numbers—considering the community as made up of different and conflicting interests, as far as the action of the government is concerned; and takes the sense of each, through its majority or appropriate organ, and the united sense of all, as the sense of the entire community. The former of these I shall call the numerical, or absolute majority; and the latter, the concurrent, or constitutional majority. I call it the constitutional majority, because it is an essential element in every constitutional government—be its form what it may. So great is the difference, politically speaking, between the two majorities, that they cannot be confounded, without leading to great and fatal errors; and yet the distinction between them has been so entirely overlooked, that when the term *majority* is used in political discussions, it is applied exclusively to designate the numerical—as if there were no other. Until this distinction is recognized, and better understood, there will continue to be great liability to error in properly constructing constitutional governments, especially of the popular form, and of preserving them when properly constructed. Until then, the latter will have a strong tendency to slide, first, into the government of the numerical majority, and, finally, into absolute government of some other form.

* * *

The first and leading error which naturally arises from overlooking the distinction referred to, is, to confound the numerical majority with the people; and this so completely as to regard them as identical. This is a consequence that necessarily results from considering the numerical as the only majority. All admit, that a popular government, or democracy, is the government of the people; for the terms imply this. A perfect government of the kind would be one which would embrace the consent of every citizen or member of the community; but as this is impracticable, in the opinion of those who regard the numerical as the only majority, and who can perceive no other way by which the sense of the people can be taken— they are compelled to adopt this as the only true basis of popular government, in contradistinction to governments of the aristocratical or monarchical form.

Being thus constrained, they are, in the next place, forced to regard the numerical majority, as, in effect, the entire people; that is, the greater part as the whole; and the government of the greater part as the government of the whole. It is thus the two come to be confounded, and a part made identical with the whole. And it is thus, also that all the rights, powers, and immunities of the whole people come to be attributed to the numerical majority; and, among others, the supreme, sovereign authority of establishing and abolishing governments at pleasure.

This radical error, the consequence of confounding the two, and of regarding the numerical as the only majority, has contributed more than any other cause, to prevent the formation of popular constitutional governments—and to destroy them even when they have been formed. It leads to the conclusion that, in their formation and establishment nothing more is necessary than the right of suffrage—and the allotment to each division of the community a representation in the government, in proportion to numbers. If the numerical majority were really the people; and if, to take its sense truly, were to take the sense of the people truly, a government so constituted would be a true and perfect model of a popular constitutional government; and every departure from it would detract from its excellence. But, as such is not the case—as the numerical majority, instead of being the people, is only a portion of them—such a government, instead of being a true and perfect model of the people's government, that is, a people self-governed, is but the government of a part, over a part—the major over the minor portion.

* * *

A written constitution certainly has many and considerable advantages; but it is a great mistake to suppose, that the mere insertion of provisions to restrict and limit the powers of the government, without investing those for whose protection they are inserted with the means of enforcing their observance, will be sufficient to prevent the major and dominant party from abusing its powers. Being the party in possession of the government, they will, from the same constitution of man which makes government necessary to protect society, be in favor of the powers granted by the constitution, and opposed to the restrictions intended to limit them. As the major and dominant party, they will have no need of these restrictions for their protection. The ballot box, of itself, would be ample protection to them. Needing no other, they would come, in time, to regard these limitations as unnecessary and improper restraints—and endeavor to elude them, with the view of increasing their power and influence.

Calhoun then takes up the question of written constitutions and develops an argument in stark opposition to Jackson's enthusiastic celebration of the U.S. Constitution in his "Proclamation Regarding Nullification."

The minor, or weaker party, on the contrary, would take the opposite direction—and regard them as essential to their protection against the dominant party. And, hence, they would endeavor to defend and enlarge the restrictions, and to limit and contract the powers. But where there are no means by which they could compel the major party to observe the restrictions, the only resort left them would be, a strict construction of the constitution, that is, a construction which would confine these powers to the narrowest limits which the meaning of the words used in the grant would admit.

To this the major party would oppose a liberal construction—one which would give to the words of the grant the broadest meaning of which they were susceptible. It would then be construction against construction; the one to contract, and the other to enlarge the powers of the government to the utmost. But of what possible avail could the strict construction of the minor party be, against the liberal interpretation of the major, when the one would have all the powers of the government to carry its construction into effect—and the other be deprived of all means of enforcing its construction? In a contest so unequal, the result would not be doubtful. The party in favor of the restrictions would be overpowered. At first, they might command some respect, and do something to stay the march of encroachment; but they would, in the progress of the contest, be regarded as mere abstractionists; and, indeed, deservedly, if they should indulge the folly of supposing that the party in possession of the ballot box and the physical force of the country, could be successfully resisted by an appeal to reason, truth, justice, or the obligations imposed by the constitution. For when these, of themselves, shall exert sufficient influence to stay the hand of power, then government will be no longer necessary to protect society, nor constitutions needed to prevent government from abusing its powers. The end of the contest would be the subversion of the constitution, either by the undermining process of construction—where its meaning would admit of possible doubt—or by substituting in practice what is called party-usage, in place of its provisions—or, finally, when no other contrivance would subserve the purpose, by openly and boldly setting them aside. By the one or the other, the restrictions would ultimately be annulled, and the government be converted into one of unlimited powers.

Having dismissed written constitutions as a bulwark against the tyranny of the majority, Calhoun sketches out a possible solution.

Nor would the division of government into separate, and, as it regards each other, independent departments, prevent this result. Such a division may do much to facilitate its operations, and to secure to its administration greater caution and deliberation; but as each and all the departments—and, of course, the entire government—would be under the control of the numerical majority, it is too clear to require explanation, that a mere distribution of its powers among its agents or representatives, could do little or nothing to counteract its tendency to oppression and abuse of power. To effect this, it would be necessary to go one step further, and make the several departments the organs of the distinct interests or portions of the community; and to clothe each with a negative on the others. But the effect of this would be to change the government from the numerical into the concurrent majority.

* * *

The necessary consequence of taking the sense of the community by the concurrent majority is, as has been explained, to give to each interest or portion of the community a negative on the others. It is this mutual negative among its various conflicting interests, which invests each with the power of protecting itself—and places the rights and safety of each, where only they can be securely placed, under its own guardianship. Without this there can be no systematic, peaceful, or effective resistance to the natural tendency of each to come into conflict with the others: and without this there can be no constitution. It is this negative power—the power of preventing or arresting the action of the government—be it called by what term it may—veto, interposition, nullification, check, or balance of power—which, in fact, forms the constitution. They are all but different names for the negative power. In all its forms, and under all its names, it results from the concurrent majority. Without this there can be no negative; and, without a negative, no constitution. The assertion is true in reference to all constitutional governments, be their forms what they may. It is, indeed, the negative power which makes the constitution—and the positive which makes the government. The one is the power of acting—and the other the power of preventing or arresting action. The two, combined, make constitutional governments.

But, as there can be no constitution without the negative power, and no negative power without the concurrent majority—it follows, necessarily, that where the numerical majority has the sole control of the government, there can be no constitution; as constitution implies limitation or restriction—and, of course, is inconsistent with the idea of sole or exclusive power. And hence, the numerical, unmixed with the concurrent majority, necessarily forms, in all cases, absolute government.

It is, indeed, the single, or *one power*, which excludes the negative, and constitutes absolute government; and not the *number* in whom the power is vested. The numerical majority is as truly a *single power*, and excludes the negative as completely as the absolute government of one, or of the few. The former is as much the absolute government of the democratic, or popular form, as the latter of the monarchical or aristocratical. It has, accordingly, in common with them, the same tendency to oppression and abuse of power.

* * *

[T]he government of the concurrent majority, where the organism is perfect, excludes the possibility of oppression, by giving to each interest, or portion, or order—where there are established classes—the means of protecting itself, by its negative, against all measures calculated to advance the peculiar interests of others at its expense. Its effect, then, is, to cause the different interests, portions, or orders—as the case may be—to desist from attempting to adopt any measure calculated to promote the prosperity of one, or more, by sacrificing that of others; and thus to force them to unite in such measures only as would promote the prosperity of all, as the only means to prevent the suspension of the action of the government—and, thereby, to avoid anarchy, the greatest of all evils. It is by means of such authorized and effectual resistance, that oppression is prevented, and the necessity of resorting to force superseded, in governments of the concurrent majority—and, hence, compromise, instead of force, becomes their conservative principle.

Calhoun now begins describing the virtues of his proposal. First, he explains how the need for a concurrent majority forces government to operate through compromise rather than coercion.

It would, perhaps, be more strictly correct to trace the conservative principle of constitutional governments to the necessity which compels the different interests, or portions, or orders, to compromise—as the only way to promote their respective prosperity, and to avoid anarchy—rather than to the compromise itself. No necessity can be more urgent and imperious, than that of avoiding anarchy. It is the same as that which makes government indispensable to preserve society; and is not less imperative than that which compels obedience to superior force. Traced to this source, the voice of a people—uttered under the necessity of avoiding the greatest of calamities, through the organs of a government so constructed as to suppress the expression of all partial and selfish interests, and to give a full and faithful utterance to the sense of the whole community, in reference to its common welfare—may, without impiety, be called *the voice of God*. To call any other so, would be impious.

* * *

Among the other advantages which governments of the concurrent have over those of the numerical majority—and which strongly illustrates their more popular character, is—that they admit, with safety, a much greater extension of the right of suffrage. It may be safely extended in such governments to universal suffrage: that is—to every male citizen of mature age, with few ordinary exceptions; but it cannot be so far extended in those of the numerical majority, without placing them ultimately under the control of the more ignorant and dependent portions of the community. For, as the community becomes populous, wealthy, refined, and highly civilized, the difference between the rich and the poor will become more strongly marked; and the number of the ignorant and dependent greater in proportion to the rest of the community. With the increase of this difference, the tendency to conflict between them will become stronger; and, as the poor and dependent become more numerous in proportion, there will be, in governments of the numerical majority, no want of leaders among the wealthy and ambitious, to excite and direct them in their efforts to obtain the control.

The case is different in governments of the concurrent majority. There, mere numbers have not the absolute control; and the wealthy and intelligent being identified in interest with the poor and ignorant of their respective portions or interests of the community, become their leaders and protectors. And hence, as the latter would have neither hope nor inducement to rally the former in order to obtain the control, the right of suffrage, under such a government, may be safely enlarged to the extent stated, without incurring the hazard to which such enlargement would expose governments of the numerical majority.

In another particular, governments of the concurrent majority have greatly the advantage. I allude to the difference in their respective tendency, in reference to dividing or uniting the community. That of the concurrent, as has been shown, is to unite the community, let its interests be ever so diversified or opposed; while that of the numerical is to divide it into two conflicting portions, let its interests be, naturally, ever so united and identified.

That the numerical majority will divide the community, let it be ever so homogeneous, into two great parties, which will be engaged in perpetual struggles to obtain the control of the government, has already been established. The great importance of the object at stake, must necessarily form strong party attachments and party antipathies—attachments on the part of the members of each to their respective parties, through whose efforts they hope to accomplish an object dear to all; and antipathies to the opposite party, as presenting the only obstacle to success.

Calhoun does not see political parties as a solution to sectional divisions.

* * *

It is thus, that, in such governments, devotion to party becomes stronger than devotion to country—the promotion of the interests of party more important than the promotion of the common good of the whole, and its triumph and ascendancy, objects of far greater solicitude, than the safety and prosperity of the community. It is thus, also, that the numerical majority, by regarding the community as a unit, and having, as such, the same interests throughout all its parts, must, by its necessary operation, divide it into two hostile parts, waging, under the forms of law, incessant hostilities against each other.

The concurrent majority, on the other hand, tends to unite the most opposite and conflicting interests, and to blend the whole in one common attachment to the country. By giving to each interest, or portion, the power of self-protection, all strife and struggle between them for ascendancy, is prevented; and, thereby, not only every feeling calculated to weaken the attachment to the whole is suppressed, but the individual and the social feelings are made to unite in one common devotion to country. Each sees and feels that it can best promote its own prosperity by conciliating the goodwill, and promoting the prosperity of the others. And hence, there will be diffused throughout the whole community kind feelings between its different portions; and, instead of antipathy, a rivalry amongst them to promote the interests of each other, as far as this can be done consistently with the interest of all. Under the combined influence of these causes, the interests of each would be merged in the common interests of the whole; and thus, the community would become a unit, by becoming the common centre of attachment of all its parts. And hence, instead of faction, strife, and struggle for party ascendancy, there would be patriotism, nationality, harmony, and a struggle only for supremacy in promoting the common good of the whole.

But the difference in their operation, in this respect, would not end here. Its effects would be as great in a moral, as I have attempted to show they would be in a political point of view. Indeed, public and private morals are so nearly allied, that it would be difficult for it to be otherwise. That which corrupts and debases the community, politically, must also corrupt and debase it morally. The same cause, which, in governments of the numerical majority, gives to party attachments and antipathies such force, as to place party triumph and ascendancy above the safety and prosperity of the community, will just as certainly give them sufficient force to overpower all regard for truth, justice, sincerity, and moral obligations of every description. It is, accordingly, found that in the violent strifes between parties for the high and glittering prize of governmental honors and emoluments—falsehood, injustice, fraud, artifice, slander, and breach of faith, are freely resorted to, as legitimate weapons—followed by all their corrupting and debasing influences.

In the government of the concurrent majority, on the contrary, the same cause which prevents such strife, as the means of obtaining power, and which makes it the interest of each portion to conciliate and promote the interests of the others, would exert a powerful influence towards purifying and elevating the character of the government and the people, morally, as well as politically. The means of acquiring power—or, more correctly, influence—in such governments, would be the reverse. Instead of the vices, by which it is acquired in that of the numerical majority, the opposite virtues—truth, justice, integrity, fidelity, and all others, by which respect and confidence are inspired, would be the most certain and effectual means of acquiring it.

Nor would the good effects resulting thence be confined to those who take an active part in political affairs. They would extend to the whole community. For of all the causes which contribute to form the character of a people, those by which power, influence, and standing in the government are most certainly and readily obtained, are, by far, the most powerful. These are the objects most eagerly sought of all others by the talented and aspiring; and the possession of which commands the greatest respect and admiration. But, just in proportion to this respect and admiration will be their appreciation by those, whose energy, intellect, and position in society, are calculated to exert the greatest influence in forming the character of a people. If knowledge, wisdom, patriotism, and virtue, be the most certain means of acquiring them, they will be most highly appreciated and assiduously cultivated; and this would cause them to become prominent traits in the character of the people. But if, on the contrary, cunning, fraud, treachery, and party devotion be the most certain, they will be the most highly prized, and become marked features in their character.

So powerful, indeed, is the operation of the concurrent majority, in this respect, that, if it were possible for a corrupt and degenerate community to establish and maintain a well-organized government of the kind, it would of itself purify and regenerate them; while, on the other hand, a government based wholly on the numerical majority, would just as certainly corrupt and debase the most patriotic and virtuous people. So great is their difference in this respect, that, just as the one or the other element predominates in the construction of any government, in the same proportion will the character of the government and the people rise or sink in the scale of patriotism and virtue. Neither religion nor education can counteract the strong tendency of the numerical majority to corrupt and debase the people.

* * *

To perfect society, it is necessary to develop the faculties, intellectual and moral, with which man is endowed. But the main spring to their development, and, through this, to progress, improvement and civilization, with all their blessings, is the desire of individuals to better their condition. For this purpose, liberty and security are indispensable. Liberty leaves each free to pursue the course he may deem best to promote his interest and happiness, as far as it may be compatible with the primary end for which government is ordained—while security gives assurance to each, that he shall not be deprived of the fruits of his exertions to better his condition. These combined, give to this desire the strongest impulse of which it is susceptible. For, to extend liberty beyond the limits assigned, would be to weaken the government and to render it incompetent to fulfill its primary end—the protection of society against dangers, internal and external. The effect of this would be, insecurity; and, of insecurity—to weaken the impulse of individuals to better their condition, and thereby retard progress and improvement. On the other hand, to extend the powers of the government,

Calhoun switches his focus and returns to the topic of self-interest and its relationship to liberty and security. He describes the balance between them and the relationship of this balance to the idea of progress.

PART 5: CORE TEXTS

so as to contract the sphere assigned to liberty, would have the same effect, by disabling individuals in their efforts to better their condition.

* * *

But some communities require a far greater amount of power than others to protect them against anarchy and external dangers; and, of course, the sphere of liberty in such, must be proportionally contracted. The causes calculated to enlarge the one and contract the other, are numerous and various. Some are physical—such as open and exposed frontiers, surrounded by powerful and hostile neighbors. Others are moral—such as the different degrees of intelligence, patriotism, and virtue among the mass of the community, and their experience and proficiency in the art of self-government. Of these, the moral are, by far, the most influential. A community may possess all the necessary moral qualifications, in so high a degree, as to be capable of self-government under the most adverse circumstances; while, on the other hand, another may be so sunk in ignorance and vice, as to be incapable of forming a conception of liberty, or of living, even when most favored by circumstances, under any other than an absolute and despotic government.

Although it never explicitly addresses slavery, this section of exposition is a defense of slavery more than any other.

The principle, in all communities, according to these numerous and various causes, assigns to power and liberty their proper spheres. To allow to liberty, in any case, a sphere of action more extended than this assigns, would lead to anarchy; and this, probably, in the end, to a contraction instead of an enlargement of its sphere. Liberty, then, when forced on a people unfit for it, would, instead of a blessing, be a curse; as it would, in its reaction, lead directly to anarchy—the greatest of all curses. No people, indeed, can long enjoy more liberty than that to which their situation and advanced intelligence and morals fairly entitle them. If more than this be allowed, they must soon fall into confusion and disorder—to be followed, if not by anarchy and despotism, by a change to a form of government more simple and absolute; and, therefore, better suited to their condition. And hence, although it may be true, that a people may not have as much liberty as they are fairly entitled to, and are capable of enjoying—yet the reverse is questionably true—that no people can long possess more than they are fairly entitled to.

Liberty, indeed, though among the greatest of blessings, is not so great as that of protection; inasmuch, as the end of the former is the progress and improvement of the race—while that of the latter is its preservation and perpetuation. And hence, when the two come into conflict, liberty must, and ever ought, to yield to protection; as the existence of the race is of greater moment than its improvement.

It follows, from what has been stated, that it is a great and dangerous error to suppose that all people are equally entitled to liberty. It is a reward to be earned, not a blessing to be gratuitously lavished on all alike—a reward reserved for the intelligent, the patriotic, the virtuous and deserving—and not a boon to be bestowed on a people too ignorant, degraded and vicious, to be capable either of appreciating or of enjoying it. Nor is it any disparagement to liberty, that such is, and ought to be the case. On the contrary, its greatest praise—its proudest distinction is, that an all-wise Providence has reserved it, as the noblest and highest reward for the development of our faculties, moral and intellectual. A reward more appropriate than liberty could not be conferred on the deserving—nor a punishment inflicted on the undeserving more just, than to be subject to lawless and despotic rule. This dispensation seems to be the result of some fixed law—and every effort to disturb or defeat it, by attempting to elevate a people in the scale of liberty, above the point to which they are entitled to rise, must ever prove abortive, and end in disappointment. The progress of a people rising from a lower to a higher point in the scale of liberty, is necessarily slow—and by attempting to precipitate, we either retard, or permanently defeat it.

There is another error, not less great and dangerous, usually associated with the one which has just been considered. I refer to the opinion, that liberty and equality are so intimately united, that liberty cannot be perfect without perfect equality.

That they are united to a certain extent—and that equality of citizens, in the eyes of the law, is essential to liberty in a popular government, is conceded. But to go further, and make equality of *condition* essential to liberty, would be to destroy both liberty and progress. The reason is, that inequality of condition, while it is a necessary consequence of liberty, is, at the same time, indispensable to progress. In order to understand why this is so, it is necessary to bear in mind, that the main spring to progress is, the desire of individuals to better their condition; and that the strongest impulse which can be given to it is, to leave individuals free to exert themselves in the manner they may deem best for that purpose, as far at least as it can be done consistently with the ends for which government is ordained—and to secure to all the fruits of their exertions.

Now, as individuals differ greatly from each other, in intelligence, sagacity, energy, perseverance, skill, habit of industry and economy, physical power, position and opportunity—the necessary effect of leaving all free to exert themselves to better their condition, must be a corresponding inequality between those who may possess these qualities and advantages in a high degree, and those who may be deficient in them.

The only means by which this result can be prevented are, either to impose such restrictions on the exertions of those who may possess them in a high degree, as will place them on a level with those who do not; or to deprive them of the fruits of their exertions. But to impose such restrictions on them would be destructive of liberty—while, to deprive them of the fruits of their exertions, would be to destroy the desire of bettering their condition. It is, indeed, this inequality of condition between the front and rear ranks, in the march of progress, which gives so strong an impulse to the former to maintain their position, and to the latter to press forward into their files. This gives to progress its greatest impulse. To force the front rank back to the rear, or attempt to push forward the rear into line with the front, by the interposition of the government, would put an end to the impulse, and effectually arrest the march of progress.

These great and dangerous errors have their origin in the prevalent opinion that all men are born free and equal—than which nothing can be more unfounded and false. It rests upon the assumption of a fact, which is contrary to universal observation, in whatever light it may be regarded. It is, indeed, difficult to explain how an opinion so destitute of all sound reason, ever could have been so extensively entertained, unless we regard it as being confounded with another, which has some semblance of truth—but which, when properly understood, is not less false and dangerous. I refer to the assertion, that all men are equal in the state of nature; meaning, by a state of nature, a state of individuality, supposed to have existed prior to the social and political state; and in which men lived apart and independent of each other. If such a state ever did exist, all men would have been, indeed, free and equal in it; that is, free to do as they pleased, and exempt from the authority or control of others—as, by supposition, it existed anterior to society and government. But such a state is purely hypothetical. It never did, nor can exist; as it is inconsistent with the preservation and perpetuation of the race. It is, therefore, a great misnomer to call it *the state of nature*. Instead of being the natural state of man, it is, of all conceivable states, the most opposed to his nature—most repugnant to his feelings, and most incompatible with his wants. His natural state is, the social and political—the one for which his Creator made him, and the only one in which he can preserve and perfect his race. As, then, there never was such a state as the, so called, state of nature, and never can be, it follows, that men, instead of being born in it, are born in the social and political state; and of course, instead of being born free and equal, are born subject, not only to parental authority, but to the laws and institutions of the country where born, and under whose protection they draw their first breath.

DANIEL WEBSTER

"Seventh of March Speech," March 7, 1850

Webster began this speech with his support for the Fugitive Slave Law. Although his constitutional argument is logical and compelling, this position was a controversial one which cost Webster any hope he might have had of winning the presidency. The rest of this address is a passionate call for unity at a time when "peaceable secession" was being offered by Southern states as an alternative to the Union's problems. The speech was given before the U.S. Senate and is therefore addressed to the president of the Senate.

SOURCE: *Kenneth E. Shewmaker, ed.,* Daniel Webster: The Completest Man *(Hanover, N.H.: University Press of New England, 1990), 121–30, available at www.dartmouth.edu/~dwebster/speeches/ seventh-march.html.*

Mr. President, I wish to speak to-day, not as a Massachusetts man, nor as a Northern man, but as an American, and a member of the Senate of the United States. It is fortunate that there is a Senate of the United States; a body not yet moved from its propriety, not lost to a just sense of its own dignity and its own high responsibilities, and a body to which the country looks, with confidence, for wise, moderate, patriotic, and healing counsels. It is not to be denied that we live in the midst of strong agitations, and are surrounded by very considerable dangers to our institutions and our government. The imprisoned winds are let loose. The East, the North, and the stormy South combine to throw the whole sea into commotion, to toss its billows to the skies, and disclose its profoundest depths. I do not affect to regard myself, Mr. President, as holding, or as fit to hold, the helm in this combat with the political elements; but I have a duty to perform, and I mean to perform it with fidelity, not without a sense of existing dangers, but not without hope. I have a part to act, not for my own security or safety, for I am looking out for no fragment upon which to float away from the wreck, if wreck there must be, but for the good of the whole, and the preservation of all; and there is that which will keep me to my duty during this struggle, whether the sun and the stars shall appear, or shall not appear for many days. I speak to-day for the preservation of the Union. "Hear me for my cause." I speak to-day, out of a solicitous and anxious heart for the restoration to the country of that quiet and harmonious harmony which make the blessings of this Union so rich, and so dear to us all. These are the topics I propose to myself to discuss; these are the motives, and the sole motives, that influence me in the wish to communicate my opinions to the Senate and the country; and if I can do any thing, however little, for the promotion of these ends, I shall have accomplished all that I expect.

* * *

Now, Sir, upon the general nature and influence of slavery there exists a wide difference of opinion between the northern portion of this country and the southern. It is said on the one side, that, although not the subject of any injunction or direct prohibition in the New Testament, slavery is a wrong; that it is founded merely in the right of the strongest; and that is an oppression, like unjust wars, like all those conflicts by which a powerful nation subjects a weaker to its will; and that, in its nature, whatever may be said of it in the modifications which have taken place, it is not according to the meek spirit of the Gospel. It is not "kindly affectioned";

it does not "seek another's, and not its own"; it does not "let the oppressed go free." These are the sentiments that are cherished, and of late with greatly augmented force, among the people of the Northern States. They have taken hold of the religious sentiment of that part of the country, as they have, more or less, taken hold of the religious feeling of a considerable portion of mankind. The South, upon the other side, having been accustomed to this relation between two races all their lives, from their birth, having been taught, in general, to treat the subjects of this bondage with care and kindness, and I believe, in general, feeling great kindness for them, have not taken the view of the subject which I have mentioned. There are thousands of religious men, with consciences as tender as any of their brethren at the North, who do not see the unlawfulness of slavery; and there are more thousands, perhaps, that whatsoever they may think of it in its origin, and as a matter depending upon natural right, yet take things as they are, and, finding slavery to be an established relation of the society in which they live, can see no way in which, let their opinions on the abstract question be what they may, it is in the power of the present generation to relieve themselves from this relation. And candor obliges me to say, that I believe they are just as conscientious, many of them, and the religious people, all of them, as they are at the North who hold different opinions.

The honorable Senator from South Carolina [John C. Calhoun] the other day alluded to the separation of that great religious community, the Methodist Episcopal Church. That separation was brought about by differences of opinion upon this particular subject of slavery. I felt great concern, as that dispute went on, about the result. I was in hopes that the difference of opinion might be adjusted, because I looked upon that religious denomination as one of the great props of religion and morals throughout the whole country, from Maine to Georgia, and westward to our utmost boundary. The result was against my wishes and against my hopes. I have read all their proceedings and all their arguments; but I have never yet been able to come to the conclusion that there was any real ground for that separation; in other words, that any good could be produced by that separation. I must say I think there was some want of candor or charity. Sir, when a question of this kind seizes on the religious sentiments of mankind, and comes to be discussed in religious assemblies of the clergy and laity, there is always to be expected, or always to be feared, a great degree of excitement. It is in the nature of man, manifested in his whole history, that religious disputes are apt to become warm in proportion to the strength of the convictions which men entertain of the magnitude of the questions at issue. In all such disputes, there will sometimes be found men with whom every thing is absolute; absolutely wrong, or absolutely right. They see the right clearly; they think others ought so to see it, and they are disposed to establish a broad line of distinction between what is right and what is wrong. They are not seldom willing to establish that line upon their own convictions of truth or justice; and are ready to mark and guard it by placing along it a series of dogmas, as lines of boundary on the earth's surface are marked by posts and stones. There are men who, with clear perception, as they think, of their own duty, do not see how too eager a pursuit of one duty may involve them in the violation of others, or how too warm an embracement of one truth may lead to a disregard of other truths equally important. As I heard it stated strongly, not many days ago, these persons are disposed to mount upon some particular duty, as upon a war-horse, and to drive furiously on and upon and over all other duties that may stand in the way. There are men who, in reference to disputes of that sort, are of the opinion that human duties may be ascertained with the exactness of mathematics. They deal with morals as with mathematics; and they think what is right may be distinguished from what is wrong with the precision of an algebraic equation. They have, therefore, none too much charity towards others who differ from them. They are apt, too, to think that nothing is good but what is perfect, and that there are no compromises or modifications to be made in consideration of difference of opinion or in deference to other men's judgment. If their perspicacious vision enables them to detect a spot on the face of the sun, they think that a good reason why the sun should be struck down from heaven. They prefer the chance of running into utter darkness to living in heavenly light, if that heavenly light be not absolutely without any imperfection. There are impatient men; too impatient always to give heed to the admonition of St. Paul, that we are not to "do evil that good may come"; too impatient to wait for the slow progress of moral causes in the improvement of mankind.

* * *

Mr. President, in the excited times in which we live, there is found to exist a state of crimination and recrimination between the North and South. There are lists of grievances produced by each; and those grievances, real or supposed, alienate the minds of one portion of the country from the other, exasperate the feelings, and subdue the sense of fraternal affection, patriotic love, and mutual regard. I shall bestow a little attention, Sir, upon these various grievances existing on the one side and on the other. I begin with complaints of the South. I will not answer, further than I have, the general statements of the honorable Senator from South Carolina [Calhoun], that the North has prospered at the expense of the South in consequence of the manner of administering this government, in the collecting of its revenues, and so forth. These are disputed topics, and I have no inclination to enter into them. But I will allude to the other complaints of the South, and especially to one which has in my opinion just foundation; and that is, that there has been found at the North, among individuals and among legislators, a disinclination to perform fully their constitutional duties in regard to the return of persons bound to service who have escaped into the free States. In that respect, the South, in my judgment, is right, and the North is wrong. Every member of every Northern legislature is bound by oath, like every other officer in the country, to support the Constitution of the United States; and the article of the Constitution which says to these States that they shall deliver up fugitives from service is as binding in honor and conscience as any other article. No man fulfills his duty in any legislature who sets himself to find excuses, evasions, escapes from this constitutional obligation. I have always thought that the Constitution addressed itself to the legislatures of the States or to the States themselves. It says that those persons escaping to other States "shall be delivered up," and I confess I have always been of the opinion that it was an injunction upon the States themselves. When it is said that a person escaping into another State, and coming therefore within the jurisdiction of that State, shall be delivered up, it seems to me the import of the clause is, that the State itself, in obedience to the Constitution, shall cause him to be delivered up. That is my judgment. I have always entertained that opinion, and I entertain it now. But when the subject, some years ago, was before the Supreme Court of the United States, the majority of the judges held that the power to cause fugitives from service to be delivered up was a power to be exercised under the authority of this government. I do not know, on the whole, that it may not have been a fortunate decision. My habit is to respect the result of judicial deliberations and the solemnity of judicial decisions. As it now stands, the business of seeing that these fugitives are delivered up resides in the power of Congress and the national judicature, and my friend at the head of the Judiciary Committee has a bill on the subject now before the Senate, which, with some amendments to it, I propose to support, with all its provisions, to the fullest extent. And I desire to call the attention of all sober-minded men at the North, of all conscientious men, of all men who are not carried away by some fanatical idea or some false impression, to their constitutional obligations. I put it to all the sober and sound minds at the North as a question of morals and a question of conscience. What right have they, in their legislative capacity or any other capacity, to endeavor to get round this Constitution, or to embarrass the free exercise of the rights secured by the Constitution to the persons whose slaves escape from them? None at all; none at all. Neither in the forum of conscience, nor before the face of the Constitution, are they, in my opinion, justified in such an attempt. Of course it is a matter for their consideration. They probably, in the excitement of the times, have not stopped to consider of this. They have followed what seemed to be the current of thought and of motives, as the occasion arose, and they have neglected to investigate fully the real question, and to consider their constitutional obligations; which, I am sure, if they did consider, they would fulfill with alacrity. I repeat, therefore, Sir, that here is a well-founded ground of complaint against the North, which ought to be removed, which it is now in the power of the different departments of this government to remove; which calls for the enactment of proper laws authorizing the judicature of this government, in the several States, to do all that is necessary for the recapture of fugitive slaves and for their restoration to those who claim them. Wherever I go, and whenever I speak on the subject, and when I speak here I desire to speak to the whole North, I say that the South has been injured in this respect, and has a right to complain; and the North has been too careless of what I think the Constitution peremptorily and emphatically enjoins upon her as a duty.

* * *

Then, Sir, there are the Abolition societies, of which I am unwilling to speak, but in regard to which I have very clear notions and opinions. I do not think them useful. I think their operations for the last twenty years have produced nothing good or valuable. At the same time, I believe thousands of their members to be honest and good men, perfectly well-meaning men. They have excited feelings; they think they must do something for the cause of liberty; and, in their sphere of action, they do not see what else they can do than to contribute to an Abolition press, or an Abolition society, or to pay an Abolition lecturer. I do not mean to impute gross motives even to the leaders of these societies, but I am not blind to the consequences of their proceedings. I cannot but see what mischiefs their interference with the South has produced. And is it not plain to every man? Let any gentleman who entertains doubts on this point recur to the debates in the Virginia House of Delegates in 1832, and he will see with what freedom a proposition made by Mr. [Thomas] Jefferson Randolph for the gradual abolition of slavery was discussed in that body. Every one spoke of slavery as he thought; very ignominious and disparaging names and epithets were applied to it. The debates in the House of Delegates on that occasion, I believe, were all published. They were read by every colored man who could read, and to those who could not read, those debates were read by others. At that time Virginia was not unwilling or unafraid to discuss this question, and to let that part of her population know as much of discussion as they could learn. That was in 1832. As has been said by the honorable member from South Carolina [Calhoun], these Abolition societies commenced their course of action in 1835. It is said, I do not know how true it may be, that they sent incendiary publications into the slave States; at any rate, they attempted to arouse, and did arouse, a very strong feeling; in other words, they created great agitation in the North against Southern slavery. Well, what was the result? The bonds of the slave were bound more firmly than before, their rivets were more strongly fastened. Public opinion, which in Virginia had begun to be exhibited against slavery, and was opening out for the discussion of the question, drew back and shut itself up in its castle. I wish to know whether any body in Virginia can now talk openly as Mr. Randolph, Governor [James] McDowell, and others talked in 1832 and sent their remarks to the press? We all know the fact, and we all know the cause; and every thing that these agitating people have done has been, not to enlarge, but to restrain, not to set free, but to bind faster the slave population of the South.

* * *

Mr. President, I should much prefer to have heard from every member on this floor declarations of opinion that this Union could never be dissolved, than the declaration of opinion by any body, that, in any case, under the pressure of any circumstances, such a dissolution was possible. I hear with distress and anguish the word "secession," especially when it falls from the lips of those who are patriotic, and known to the country, and known all over the world, for their political services. Secession! Peaceable secession! Sir, your eyes and mine are never destined to see that miracle. The dismemberment of this vast country without convulsion! The breaking up of the fountains of the great deep without ruffing the surface! Who is so foolish, I beg every body's pardon, as to expect to see any such thing? Sir, he who sees these States, now revolving in harmony around a common centre, and expects to see them quit their places and fly off without convulsion, may look the next hour to see heavenly bodies rush from their spheres, and jostle against each other in the realms of space, without causing the wreck of the universe. There can be no such thing as peaceable secession. Peaceable secession is an utter impossibility. Is the great Constitution under which we live, covering this whole country, is it to be thawed and melted away by secession, as the snows on the mountain melt under the influence of a vernal sun, disappear almost unobserved, and run off? No, Sir! No, Sir! I will not state what might produce the disruption of the Union; but, Sir, I see as plainly as I see the sun in heaven what that disruption itself must produce; I see that it must produce war, and such a war as I will not describe, *in its twofold character*.

Peaceable secession! Peaceable secession! The concurrent agreement of all the members of this great republic to separate! A voluntary separation, with alimony on one side and on the other. Why, what would be the result? Where is the line to be drawn? What States are to secede? What is to remain American? What am I to be? An American no longer? Am I to become a sectional man, a local man, a separatist, with no country in common with the gentlemen who sit around me here, or who fill the other house of Congress? Heaven forbid! Where is the flag of the republic to remain? Where is the eagle still to tower? or is he to cower, and shrink, and fall to the ground? Why, Sir, our ancestors, our fathers and our grandfathers, those of them that are yet living amongst us with prolonged lives, would rebuke and reproach us; and our children and our grandchildren would cry out shame upon us, if we of this generation should dishonor these ensigns of the power of the government and the harmony of that Union which is every day felt among us with so much joy and gratitude. What is to become of the army? What is to become of the navy? What is to become of the public lands? How is each of the thirty States to defend itself? I know, although the idea has not been stated distinctly, there is to be, or it is supposed possible that there will be, a Southern Confederacy. I do not mean, when I allude to this statement, that any one seriously contemplates such a state of things. I do not mean to say that it is true, but I have heard it suggested elsewhere, that the idea has been entertained, that, after the dissolution of this Union, a Southern Confederacy might be formed. I am sorry, Sir, that it has ever been thought of, talked of, or dreamed of, in the wildest flights of human imagination. But the idea, so far as it exists, must be of a separation, assigning the slave States to one side and the free States to the other. Sir, I may express myself too strongly, perhaps, but there are impossibilities in the natural as well as in the physical world, and I hold the idea of a separation of these States, those that are free to form one government, and those that are slave-holding to form another, as such an impossibility. We could not separate the States by any such line, if we were to draw it. We could not sit down here to-day and draw a line of separation that would satisfy any five men in the country. There are natural causes that would keep and tie us together, and there are social and domestic relations which we could not break if we would, and which we should not if we could.

Sir, nobody can look over the face of this country at the present moment, nobody can see where its population is the most dense and growing, without being ready to admit, and compelled to admit, that ere long the strength of America will be in the Valley of the Mississippi. Well, now, Sir, I beg to inquire what the wildest enthusiast has to say about the possibility of cutting that river in two, and leaving free States at its source and on its branches, and slave States down near its mouth, each forming a separate government? Pray, Sir, let me say to the people of this country, that these things are worthy of their pondering and of their consideration. Here, Sir, are five millions of freemen in the free States north of the river of Ohio. Can any body suppose that this population can be severed, by a line that divides them from the territory of a foreign and alien government, down somewhere, the Lord knows where, upon the lower banks of the Mississippi? What would become of Missouri? Will she join the *arrondissement* of the slave States? Shall the man from the Yellow Stone and the Platte be connected, in the new republic, with the man who lives on the southern extremity of the Cape of Florida? Sir, I am ashamed to pursue this line of remark. I dislike it, I have an utter disgust for it. I would rather hear of natural blasts and mildews, war, pestilence, and famine, than to hear gentlemen talk of secession. To break up this great government! to dismember this glorious country! to astonish Europe with an act of folly such as Europe for two centuries has never beheld in any government or any people! No, Sir! no, Sir! There will be no secession! Gentlemen are not serious when they talk of secession.

* * *

And now, Mr. President, I draw these observations to a close. I have spoken freely, and I meant to do so. I have sought to make no display. I have sought to enliven the occasion by no animated discussion, nor have I attempted any train of elaborate argument. I have wished only to speak my sentiments, fully and at length, being desirous, once and for all, to let the Senate know, and to let the country know, the opinions and sentiments which I entertain on all these subjects. These opinions are not likely to be suddenly changed. If there be any future service that I can render to the country, consistently with these sentiments and opinions, I shall cheerfully render it. If there be not, I shall still be glad to have had an opportunity to disburden myself from the bottom of my heart, and to make known every political sentiment that therein exists.

And now, Mr. President, instead of speaking of the possibility or utility of secession, instead of dwelling in those caverns of darkness, instead of groping with those ideas so full of all that is horrid and horrible, let us come out into the light of day; let us enjoy the fresh air of Liberty and Union; let us cherish those hopes which belong to us; let us devote ourselves to those great objects that are fit for our consideration and action; let us raise our conceptions to the magnitude and the importance of the duties that devolve upon us; let our comprehension be as broad as the country for which we act, our aspirations as high as its certain destiny; let us not be pigmies in a case that calls for men. Never did there devolve on any generation of men higher trusts than now devolve upon us, for the preservation of this Constitution and the harmony and peace of all who are destined to live under it. Let us make our generation one of the strongest and brightest links in that golden chain which is destined, I fondly believe, to grapple the people of all the States to this Constitution for ages to come. We have a great, popular, constitutional government, guarded by law and by judicature, and defended by the affections of the whole people. No monarchical throne presses these States together, no iron chain of military power encircles them; they live and stand under a government popular in its form, representative in its character, founded upon principles of equality, and so constructed, we hope, as to last for ever. In all its history it has been beneficent; it has trodden down no man's liberty; it has crushed no State. Its daily respiration is liberty and patriotism; its yet youthful veins are full of enterprise, courage, and honorable love of glory and renown. Large before, the country has now, by recent events, become vastly larger. This republic now extends, with a vast breadth, across the whole continent. The two great seas of the world wash the one and the other shore. We realize, on a mighty scale, the beautiful description of the ornamental border of the buckler of Achilles:—

> Now, the broad shield completed, the artist crowned
> With his last hand, and poured the ocean round;
> In living silver seemed the waves to roll,
> And beat the bucklers verge, and bound the whole.[1]

---

1. From Alexander Pope's translation of the Iliad, Book 18.

HENRY CLAY

"On the Compromise Bills," July 22, 1850

Clay gave a lengthy speech on July 22, 1850, in support of the Compromise of 1850, a package of laws that he and Democratic senator Stephen Douglas cobbled together in an attempt to forestall disunion over the question of slavery's place in the territories after the War with Mexico. This excerpt focuses on Clay's belief in the necessity of compromise to the United States' system of government and reveals his bleak vision for the country should his proposals fail to pass in Congress. The speech was given before the U.S. Senate and is therefore addressed to the president of the Senate.

SOURCE: *"A General Review of the Debate on the Compromise Bills, In Senate, July 22, 1850,"* in The Works of Henry Clay: Comprising His Life, Correspondence, and Speeches, in Ten Volumes, *vol. 9, ed. Calvin Colton (New York and London: G. P. Putnam and Sons, 1904), 529–67.*

It has been objected against this measure that it is a compromise. It has been said that it is a compromise of principle, or of a principle. Mr. President, what is a compromise? It is a work of mutual concession—an agreement in which there are reciprocal stipulations—a work in which, for the sake of peace and concord, one party abates his extreme demands in consideration of an abatement of extreme demands by the other party: it is a measure of mutual concession—a measure of mutual sacrifice. Undoubtedly, Mr. President, in all such measures of compromise, one party would be very glad to get what he wants, and reject what he does not desire but which the other party wants. But when he comes to reflect that, from the nature of the government and its operations, and from those with whom he is dealing, it is necessary upon his part, in order to secure what he wants, to grant something to the other side, he should be reconciled to the concession which he has made in consequence of the concession which he is to receive, if there is no great principle involved, such as a violation of the Constitution of the United States. I admit that such a compromise as that ought never to be sanctioned or adopted. But I now call upon any senator in his place to point out from the beginning to the end, from California to New Mexico, a solitary provision in this bill which is violative of the Constitution of the United States.

* * *

The responsibility of this great measure passes from the hands of the committee, and from my hands. They know, and I know, that it is an awful and tremendous responsibility. I hope that you will meet it with a just conception and a true appreciation of its magnitude, and the magnitude of the consequences that may ensue from your decision one way or the other. The alternatives, I fear, which the measure presents, are concord and increased discord; a servile civil war, originating in its causes, on the lower Rio Grande, and terminating, possibly, in its consequences, on the upper Rio Grande in the Santa Fe country—or the restoration of harmony and fraternal kindness.

I believe from the bottom of my soul that the measure is the reunion of this Union. I believe it is the dove of peace, which, taking its aerial flight from the dome of the Capitol, carries the glad tidings of assured peace and restored harmony to all the remotest extremities of this distracted land. I believe that it will be attended with all these beneficent effects. And now let us discard all resentment, all passions, all petty jealousies, all personal desires, all love of place, all hankerings after the gilded crumbs which fall from the table of power. Let us forget popular fears, from whatever quarter they may spring. Let us go to the limpid fountain of unadulterated patriotism, and, performing a solemn lustration, return divested of all selfish, sinister, and sordid impurities, and think alone of our God, our country, our consciences, and our glorious Union—that Union without which we shall be torn into hostile fragments, and sooner or later become the victims of military despotism or foreign domination.

* * *

Let us look at our country and our cause, elevate ourselves to the dignity of pure and disinterested patriots, and save our country from all impending dangers. What if, in the march of this nation to greatness and power, we should be buried beneath the wheels that propel it onward.

* * *

I call upon all the South. Sir, we have heard hard words—bitter words, bitter thoughts, unpleasant feelings toward each other in the progress of this great measure. Let us forget them. Let us sacrifice these feelings. Let us go to the altar of our country and swear, as the oath was taken of old, that we will stand by her; that we will support her; that we will uphold her Constitution; that we will preserve her Union; and that we will pass this great, comprehensive, and healing system of measures, which will hush all the jarring elements and bring peace and tranquility to our homes.

Let me, Mr. President, in conclusion, say that the most disastrous consequences would occur, in my opinion, were we to go home, doing nothing to satisfy and tranquillize the country upon these great questions. What will be the judgment of mankind, what the judgment of that portion of mankind who are looking upon the progress of this scheme of self-government as being that which holds the highest hopes and expectations of ameliorating the condition of mankind—what will their judgment be? Will not all the monarchs of the Old World pronounce our glorious republic a disgraceful failure? What will be the judgment of our constituents, when we return to them and they ask us, How have you left your country? Is all quiet—all happy—are all the seeds of distraction or division crushed and dissipated?... Will you go home and leave all in disorder and confusion, all unsettled, all open? The contentions and agitations of the past will be increased and augmented by the agitations resulting from our neglect to decide them. Sir, we shall stand condemned by all human judgment below, and of that above it is not for me to speak. We shall stand condemned in our own consciences, by our own constituents, and by our own country. The measure may be defeated. I have been aware that its passage for many days was not absolutely certain.... But, if defeated, it will be a triumph of ultraism and impracticability—a triumph of a most extraordinary conjunction of extremes; a victory won by abolitionism; a victory achieved by free-soilism; a victory of discord and agitation over peace and tranquility; and I pray to Almighty God that it may not, in consequence of the inauspicious result, lead to the most unhappy and disastrous consequences to our beloved country.

FREDERICK DOUGLASS

"The Meaning of July Fourth for the Negro," July 5, 1852

An escaped slave from the border state of Maryland, Frederick Douglass travelled throughout the North giving speeches in support of the abolitionist cause. He settled in Rochester, New York, where he began publishing the influential abolitionist newspaper The North Star *in 1847. On July 5, 1852, Douglass gave the following speech in Rochester. In it, he stridently condemns hypocritical Northern complicity in the perpetuation of slavery in the South. He closes with a poem by radical abolitionist William Lloyd Garrison.*

SOURCE: Philip S. Foner, ed., *Pre-Civil War Decade 1850–1860, vol. 2 of* The Life and Writings of Frederick Douglass *(New York: International Publishers Co., 1950).*

Fellow Citizens, I am not wanting in respect for the fathers of this republic. The signers of the Declaration of Independence were brave men. They were great men, too—great enough to give frame to a great age. It does not often happen to a nation to raise, at one time, such a number of truly great men. The point from which I am compelled to view them is not, certainly, the most favorable; and yet I cannot contemplate their great deeds with less than admiration. They were statesmen, patriots and heroes, and for the good they did, and the principles they contended for, I will unite with you to honor their memory.

* * *

Fellow-citizens, pardon me, allow me to ask, why am I called upon to speak here to-day? What have I, or those I represent, to do with your national independence? Are the great principles of political freedom and of natural justice, embodied in that Declaration of Independence, extended to us? and am I, therefore, called upon to bring our humble offering to the national altar, and to confess the benefits and express devout gratitude for the blessings resulting from your independence to us?

Would to God, both for your sakes and ours, that an affirmative answer could be truthfully returned to these questions! Then would my task be light, and my burden easy and delightful. For who is there so cold, that a nation's sympathy could not warm him? Who so obdurate and dead to the claims of gratitude, that would not thankfully acknowledge such priceless benefits? Who so stolid and selfish, that would not give his voice to swell the hallelujahs of a nation's jubilee, when the chains of servitude had been torn from his limbs? I am not that man. In a case like that, the dumb might eloquently speak, and the "lame man leap as an hart."

But such is not the state of the case. I say it with a sad sense of the disparity between us. I am not included within the pale of glorious anniversary! Your high independence only reveals the immeasurable distance between us. The blessings in which you, this day, rejoice, are not enjoyed in common. The rich inheritance of justice, liberty, prosperity and independence, bequeathed by your fathers, is shared by you, not by me. The sunlight that brought light and healing to you, has brought stripes and death to me. This Fourth July is yours, not mine. You may rejoice, I must mourn. To drag a man in fetters into the grand illuminated temple of liberty, and call upon him to join you in joyous anthems, were inhuman mockery and sacrilegious irony. Do you mean, citizens, to mock me, by asking me to speak to-day? If so, there is a parallel to your conduct. And let me warn you that it is dangerous to copy the example of a nation whose crimes, towering up to heaven, were thrown down by the breath of the Almighty, burying that nation in irrevocable ruin! I can to-day take up the plaintive lament of a peeled and woe-smitten people!

By the rivers of Babylon, there we sat down. Yea! we wept when we remembered Zion. We hanged our harps upon the willows in the midst thereof. For there, they that carried us away captive, required of us a song; and they who wasted us required of us mirth, saying, Sing us one of the songs of Zion. How can we sing the Lord's song in a strange land? If I forget thee, O Jerusalem, let my right hand forget her cunning. If I do not remember thee, let my tongue cleave to the roof of my mouth.

Fellow-citizens, above your national, tumultuous joy, I hear the mournful wail of millions! whose chains, heavy and grievous yesterday, are, to-day, rendered more intolerable by the jubilee shouts that reach them. If I do forget, if I do not faithfully remember those bleeding children of sorrow this day, "may my right hand forget her cunning, and may my tongue cleave to the roof of my mouth!" To forget them, to pass lightly over their wrongs, and to chime in with the popular theme, would be treason most scandalous and shocking, and would make me a reproach before God and the world. My subject, then, fellow-citizens, is American slavery. I shall see this day and its popular characteristics from the slave's point of view. Standing there identified with the American bondman, making his wrongs mine, I do not hesitate to declare, with all my soul, that the character and conduct of this nation never looked blacker to me than on this 4th of July! Whether we turn to the declarations of the past, or to the professions of the present, the conduct of the nation seems equally hideous and revolting. America is false to the past, false to the present, and solemnly binds herself to be false to the future. Standing with God and the crushed and bleeding slave on this occasion, I will, in the name of humanity which is outraged, in the name of liberty which is fettered, in the name of the constitution and the Bible which are disregarded and trampled upon, dare to call in question and to denounce, with all the emphasis I can command, everything that serves to perpetuate slavery—the great sin and shame of America! "I will not equivocate; I will not excuse"; I will use the severest language I can command; and yet not one word shall escape me that any man, whose judgment is not blinded by prejudice, or who is not at heart a slaveholder, shall not confess to be right and just.

But I fancy I hear some one of my audience say, "It is just in this circumstance that you and your brother abolitionists fail to make a favorable impression on the public mind. Would you argue more, and denounce less; would you persuade more, and rebuke less; your cause would be much more likely to succeed." But, I submit, where all is plain there is nothing to be argued. What point in the anti-slavery creed would you have me argue? On what branch of the subject do the people of this country need light? Must I undertake to prove that the slave is a man? That point is conceded already. Nobody doubts it. The slaveholders themselves acknowledge it in the enactment of laws for their government. They acknowledge it when they punish disobedience on the part of the slave. There are seventy-two crimes in the State of Virginia which, if committed by a black man (no matter how ignorant he be), subject him to the punishment of death; while only two of the same crimes will subject a white man to the like punishment. What is this but the acknowledgment that the slave is a moral, intellectual, and responsible being? The manhood of the slave is conceded. It is admitted in the fact that Southern statute books are covered with enactments forbidding, under severe fines and penalties, the teaching of the slave to read or to write. When you can point to any such laws in reference to the beasts of the field, then I may consent to argue the manhood of the slave. When the dogs in your streets, when the fowls of the air, when the cattle on your hills, when the fish of the sea, and the reptiles that crawl, shall be unable to distinguish the slave from a brute, then will I argue with you that the slave is a man!

For the present, it is enough to affirm the equal manhood of the Negro race. Is it not astonishing that, while we are ploughing, planting, and reaping, using all kinds of mechanical tools, erecting houses, constructing bridges, building ships, working in metals of brass, iron, copper, silver and gold; that, while we are reading, writing and ciphering, acting as clerks, merchants and secretaries, having among us lawyers, doctors, ministers, poets, authors, editors, orators and teachers; that, while we are engaged in all manner of enterprises common to other men, digging gold in California, capturing the whale in the Pacific, feeding sheep and cattle on the hill-side, living, moving, acting, thinking, planning, living in families as husbands, wives and children, and, above all, confessing and worshipping the

Christian's God, and looking hopefully for life and immortality beyond the grave, we are called upon to prove that we are men!

Would you have me argue that man is entitled to liberty? that he is the rightful owner of his own body? You have already declared it. Must I argue the wrongfulness of slavery? Is that a question for Republicans? Is it to be settled by the rules of logic and argumentation, as a matter beset with great difficulty, involving a doubtful application of the principle of justice, hard to be understood? How should I look to-day, in the presence of Americans, dividing, and subdividing a discourse, to show that men have a natural right to freedom? speaking of it relatively and positively, negatively and affirmatively. To do so, would be to make myself ridiculous, and to offer an insult to your understanding. There is not a man beneath the canopy of heaven that does not know that slavery is wrong for him.

What, am I to argue that it is wrong to make men brutes, to rob them of their liberty, to work them without wages, to keep them ignorant of their relations to their fellow men, to beat them with sticks, to flay their flesh with the lash, to load their limbs with irons, to hunt them with dogs, to sell them at auction, to sunder their families, to knock out their teeth, to burn their flesh, to starve them into obedience and submission to their masters? Must I argue that a system thus marked with blood, and stained with pollution, is wrong? No! I will not. I have better employment for my time and strength than such arguments would imply.

What, then, remains to be argued? Is it that slavery is not divine; that God did not establish it; that our doctors of divinity are mistaken? There is blasphemy in the thought. That which is inhuman, cannot be divine! Who can reason on such a proposition? They that can, may; I cannot. The time for such argument is passed.

At a time like this, scorching irony, not convincing argument, is needed. O! had I the ability, and could reach the nation's ear, I would, to-day, pour out a fiery stream of biting ridicule, blasting reproach, withering sarcasm, and stern rebuke. For it is not light that is needed, but fire; it is not the gentle shower, but thunder. We need the storm, the whirlwind, and the earthquake. The feeling of the nation must be quickened; the conscience of the nation must be roused; the propriety of the nation must be startled; the hypocrisy of the nation must be exposed; and its crimes against God and man must be proclaimed and denounced.

What, to the American slave, is your 4th of July? I answer; a day that reveals to him, more than all other days in the year, the gross injustice and cruelty to which he is the constant victim. To him, your celebration is a sham; your boasted liberty, an unholy license; your national greatness, swelling vanity; your sounds of rejoicing are empty and heartless; your denunciation of tyrants, brass fronted impudence; your shouts of liberty and equality, hollow mockery; your prayers and hymns, your sermons and thanksgivings, with all your religious parade and solemnity, are, to Him, mere bombast, fraud, deception, impiety, and hypocrisy—a thin veil to cover up crimes which would disgrace a nation of savages. There is not a nation on the earth guilty of practices more shocking and bloody than are the people of the United States, at this very hour.

Go where you may, search where you will, roam through all the monarchies and despotisms of the Old World, travel through South America, search out every abuse, and when you have found the last, lay your facts by the side of the everyday practices of this nation, and you will say with me, that, for revolting barbarity and shameless hypocrisy, America reigns without a rival.

* * *

Allow me to say, in conclusion, notwithstanding the dark picture I have this day presented, of the state of the nation, I do not despair of this country. There are forces in operation which must inevitably work the downfall of slavery. "The arm of the Lord is not shortened," and the doom of slavery is certain. I, therefore, leave off where I began, with hope. While drawing encouragement from "the Declaration of Independence," the great principles it contains, and the genius of American Institutions, my spirit is also cheered by the obvious tendencies of the age. Nations do not now stand in the same relation to each other that they did ages ago. No nation can now shut itself up from the surrounding world and trot round in the same old path of its fathers without interference. The time was when such could be done. Long established customs of hurtful character could formerly fence themselves in, and do their evil work with social impunity. Knowledge was then confined and enjoyed by the privileged few, and the multitude walked on in mental darkness. But a change has now come over the affairs of mankind. Walled cities and empires have become unfashionable. The arm of commerce has borne away the gates of the strong city. Intelligence is penetrating the darkest corners of the globe. It makes its pathway over and under the sea, as well as on the earth. Wind, steam, and lightning are its chartered agents. Oceans no longer divide, but link nations together. From Boston to London is now a holiday excursion. Space is comparatively annihilated.—Thoughts expressed on one side of the Atlantic are distinctly heard on the other.

The far off and almost fabulous Pacific rolls in grandeur at our feet. The Celestial Empire, the mystery of ages, is being solved. The fiat of the Almighty, "Let there be Light," has not yet spent its force. No abuse, no outrage whether in taste, sport or avarice, can now hide itself from the all-pervading light. The iron shoe, and crippled foot of China must be seen in contrast with nature. Africa must rise and put on her yet unwoven garment. "Ethiopia, shall, stretch out her hand unto God." In the fervent aspirations of William Lloyd Garrison, I say, and let every heart join in saying it:

> God speed the year of jubilee The wide world o'er!
> When from their galling chains set free,
> Th' oppress'd shall vilely bend the knee,
> And wear the yoke of tyranny
> Like brutes no more.

That year will come, and freedom's reign,
To man his plundered rights again
Restore.

God speed the day when human blood
Shall cease to flow!
In every clime be understood,
The claims of human brotherhood,
And each return for evil, good,
Not blow for blow;
That day will come all feuds to end,
And change into a faithful friend
Each foe.

God speed the hour, the glorious hour,
When none on earth
Shall exercise a lordly power,
Nor in a tyrant's presence cower;
But to all manhood's stature tower,
By equal birth!
That hour will come, to each, to all,
And from his Prison-house, to thrall
Go forth.

Until that year, day, hour, arrive,
With head, and heart, and hand I'll strive,
To break the rod, and rend the gyve,
The spoiler of his prey deprive—
So witness Heaven!
And never from my chosen post,
Whate'er the peril or the cost,
Be driven.

JAMES HENRY HAMMOND

"Cotton Is King," March 4, 1858

In this response to a speech by New York senator Charles Sumner on the matter of the Lecompton constitution, South Carolina senator James Henry Hammond presents an utterly unapologetic assertion of slavery's status as the premier social

system. In addition, he claims that the economic and military power of the South is
so great that none dare make war upon it.

SOURCE: *Reprinted in* Selections from the Letters and Speeches of the Hon. James H. Hammond, of South Carolina *(New York: John F. Trow & Co., 1866), 311–22.*

... *I*f we never acquire another foot of territory for the South, look at her. Eight hundred and fifty thousand square miles. As large as Great Britain, France, Austria, Prussia and Spain. Is not that territory enough to make an empire that shall rule the world? With the finest soil, the most delightful climate, whose staple productions none of those great countries can grow, we have three thousand miles of continental sea-shore line so indented with bays and crowded with islands, that, when their shore lines are added, we have twelve thousand miles. Through the heart of our country runs the great Mississippi, the father of waters, into whose bosom are poured thirty-six thousand miles of tributary rivers; and beyond we have the desert prairie wastes to protect us in our rear. Can you hem in such a territory as that? You talk of putting up a wall of fire around eight hundred and fifty thousand square miles so situated! How absurd.

But, in this territory lies the great valley of the Mississippi, now the real, and soon to be the acknowledged seat of the empire of the world. The sway of that valley will be as great as ever the Nile knew in the earlier ages of mankind. We own the most of it. The most valuable part of it belongs to us now; and although those who have settled above us are now opposed to us, another generation will tell a different tale. They are ours by all the laws of nature; slave-labor will go over every foot of this great valley where it will be found profitable to use it, and some of those who may not use it are soon to be united with us by such ties as will make us one and inseparable. The iron horse will soon be clattering over the sunny plains of the South to bear the products of its upper tributaries of the valley to our Atlantic ports, as it now does through the ice-bound North. And there is the great Mississippi, a bond of union made by Nature herself. She will maintain it forever.

On this fine territory we have a population four times as large as that with which these colonies separated from the mother country, and a hundred, I might say a thousand fold stronger. Our population is now sixty per cent. greater than that of the whole United States when we entered into the second war of independence [the War of 1812]. It is as large as the whole population of the United States was ten years after the conclusion of that war, and our own exports are three times as great as those of the whole United States then. Upon our muster-rolls we have a million of men. In a defensive war, upon an emergency, every one of them would be available. At any time, the South can raise, equip, and maintain in the field, a larger army than any Power of the earth can send against her, and an army of soldiers—men brought up on horseback, with guns in their hands.

If we take the North, even when the two large States of Kansas and Minnesota shall be admitted, her territory will be one hundred thousand square miles less than ours. I do not speak of California and Oregon; there is no antagonism between the South and those countries, and never will be. The population of the North is fifty per cent. greater than ours. I have nothing to say in disparagement either of the soil of the North, or the people of the North, who are a brave and energetic race, full of intellect. But they produce no great staple that the South does not produce; while we produce two or three, and these the very greatest, that she can never produce. As to her men, I may be allowed to say, they have never proved themselves to be superior to those of the South, either in the field or in the Senate.

But the strength of a nation depends in a great measure upon its wealth, and the wealth of a nation, like that of a man, is to be estimated by its surplus production. You may go to your trashy census books, full of falsehoods and nonsense—they tell you, for example, that in the State of Tennessee, the whole number of house-servants is not equal to that of those in my own house, and such things as that. You may estimate what is made throughout the country from these census books, but it is no matter how much is made if it is all consumed. If a man possess millions of dollars and consumes his income, is he rich? Is he competent to embark in any new enterprises? Can he long build ships or railroads? And could a people in that condition build ships and roads or go to war without a fatal strain on capital? All the enterprises of peace and war depend upon the surplus productions of a people. They may be happy, they may be comfortable, they may enjoy themselves in consuming what they make; but they are not rich, they are not strong. It appears, by going to the reports of the Secretary of the Treasury, which are authentic, that last year the United States exported in round numbers $279,000,000 worth of domestic produce, excluding gold and foreign merchandise re-exported. Of this amount $158,000,000 worth is the clear produce of the South; articles that are not and cannot be made at the North. There are then $80,000,000 worth of exports of products of the forest, provisions and breadstuffs. If we assume that the South made but one third of these, and I think that is a low calculation, our exports were $185,000,000, leaving to the North less than $95,000,000.

In addition to this, we sent to the North $30,000,000 worth of cotton, which is not counted in the exports. We sent to her $7 or $8,000,000 worth of tobacco, which is not counted in the exports. We sent naval stores, lumber, rice, and many other minor articles. There is no doubt that we sent to the North $40,000,000 in addition; but suppose the amount to be $35,000,000, it will give us a surplus production of $220,000,000. But the recorded exports of the South now are greater than the whole exports of the United States in any year before 1856. They are greater than the whole average exports of the United States for the last twelve years, including the two extraordinary years of 1856 and 1857. They are nearly double the amount of the average exports of the twelve preceding years. If I am right in my calculations as to $220,000,000 of surplus produce, there is not a nation on the face of the earth, with any numerous population, that can compete with us in produce per capita. It amounts to $16.66 per head, supposing that we have twelve millions of people. England with all her accumulated wealth, with her concentrated and educated energy, makes but sixteen and a half dollars of surplus production per head. I have not made a calculation as to the North, with her $95,000,000 surplus; admitting that she exports as much as we do, with her eighteen millions of population it would be but little over twelve dollars a head. But she cannot export to us and abroad exceeding ten dollars a head against our sixteen dollars. I know well enough that the North sends to the South a vast amount of the productions of her industry. I take it for granted that she, at least, pays us in that way for the thirty or forty million dollars worth of cotton and other articles we send her. I am willing to admit that she sends us considerably more; but to bring her up to our amount of surplus production—to bring her up to $220,000,000 a year, the South must take from her $125,000,000; and this, in addition to our share of the consumption of the $330,000,000 worth introduced into the country from abroad, and paid for chiefly by our own exports. The thing is absurd; it is impossible; it can never appear anywhere but in a book of statistics, or a Congress speech.

With an export of $220,000,000 under the present tariff, the South organized separately would have $40,000,000 of revenue. With one-fourth the present tariff, she would have a revenue with the present tariff adequate to all her wants, for the South would never go to war; she would never need an army or a navy, beyond a few garrisons on the frontiers and a few revenue cutters. It is commerce that breeds war. It is manufactures that require to be hawked about the world, and that give rise to navies and commerce. But we have nothing to do but to take off restrictions on foreign merchandise and open our ports, and the whole world will come to us to trade. They will be too glad to bring and carry us, and we never shall dream of a war. Why the South has never yet had a just cause of war except with the North. Every time she has drawn her sword it has been on the point of honor, and that point of honor has been mainly loyalty to her sister colonies and sister States, who have ever since plundered and calumniated her.

But if there were no other reason why we should never have war, would any sane nation make war on cotton? Without firing a gun, without drawing a sword, should they make war on us we could bring the whole world to our feet. The South is perfectly competent to go on, one, two, or three years without planting a seed of cotton. I believe that if she was to plant but half her cotton, for three years to come, it would be an immense advantage to her. I am not so sure but that after three years' entire abstinence she would come out stronger than ever she was before, and better prepared to enter afresh upon her great career of enterprise. What would happen if no cotton was furnished for three years? I will not stop to depict what every one can imagine, but this is certain: England would topple headlong and carry the whole civilized world with her, save the South. No, you dare not make war on cotton. No power on earth dares to make war upon it. Cotton is king. Until lately the Bank of

England was king; but she tried to put her screws as usual, the fall before last, upon the cotton crop, and was utterly vanquished. The last power has been conquered. Who can doubt, that has looked at recent events, that cotton is supreme? When the abuse of credit had destroyed credit and annihilated confidence; when thousands of the strongest commercial houses in the world were coming down, and hundreds of millions of dollars of supposed property evaporating in thin air; when you came to a dead lock, and revolutions were threatened, what brought you up? Fortunately for you it was the commencement of the cotton season, and we have poured in upon you one million six hundred thousand bales of cotton just at the crisis to save you from destruction. That cotton, but for the bursting of your speculative bubbles in the North, which produced the whole of this convulsion, would have brought us $100,000,000. We have sold it for $65,000,000 and saved you. Thirty-five million dollars we, the slaveholders of the South, have put into the charity box for your magnificent financiers, your "cotton lords," your "merchant princes."

But, sir, the greatest strength of the South arises from the harmony of her political and social institutions. This harmony gives her a frame of society, the best in the world, and an extent of political freedom, combined with entire security, such as no other people ever enjoyed upon the face of the earth. Society precedes government; creates it, and ought to control it; but as far as we can look back in historic times we find the case different; for government is no sooner created than it becomes too strong for society, and shapes and moulds, as well as controls it. In later centuries the progress of civilization and of intelligence has made the divergence so great as to produce civil wars and revolutions; and it is nothing now but the want of harmony between governments and societies which occasions all the uneasiness and trouble and terror that we see abroad. It was this that brought on the American Revolution. We threw off a Government not adapted to our social system, and made one for ourselves. The question is, how far have we succeeded? The South, so far as that is concerned, is satisfied, harmonious, and prosperous, but demands to be let alone.

In all social systems there must be a class to do the menial duties, to perform the drudgery of life. That is, a class requiring but a low order of intellect and but little skill. Its requisites are vigor, docility, fidelity. Such a class you must have, or you would not have that other class which leads progress, civilization, and refinement. It constitutes the very mud-sill of society and of political government; and you might as well attempt to build a house in the air, as to build either the one or the other, except on this mud-sill. Fortunately for the South, she found a race adapted to that purpose to her hand. A race inferior to her own, but eminently qualified in temper, in vigor, in docility, in capacity to stand the climate, to answer all her purposes. We use them for our purpose, and call them slaves. We found them slaves by the common "consent of mankind," which, according to Cicero, "lex naturae est."[1] The highest proof of what is Nature's law. We are

---

1. *"This is the law of nature."*

old-fashioned at the South yet; slave is a word discarded now by "ears polite;" I will not characterize that class at the North by that term; but you have it; it is there; it is everywhere; it is eternal.

The Senator from New York [William Seward] said yesterday that the whole world had abolished slavery. Aye, the name, but not the thing; all the powers of the earth cannot abolish that. God only can do it when he repeals the fiat, "the poor ye always have with you;" for the man who lives by daily labor, and scarcely lives at that, and who has to put out his labor in the market, and take the best he can get for it; in short, your whole hireling class of manual laborers and "operatives," as you call them, are essentially slaves. The difference between us is, that our slaves are hired for life and well compensated; there is no starvation, no begging, no want of employment among our people, and not too much employment either. Yours are hired by the day, not cared for, and scantily compensated, which may be proved in the most painful manner, at any hour in any street of your large towns. Why, you meet more beggars in one day, in any single street of the city of New York, than you would meet in a lifetime in the whole South. We do not think that whites should be slaves either by law or necessity. Our slaves are black, of another and inferior race. The status in which we have placed them is an elevation. They are elevated from the condition in which God first created them, by being made our slaves. None of that race on the whole face of the globe can be compared with the slaves of the South. They are happy, content, unaspiring, and utterly incapable, from intellectual weakness, ever to give us any trouble by their aspirations. Yours are white, of your own race; you are brothers of one blood. They are your equals in natural endowment of intellect, and they feel galled by their degradation. Our slaves do not vote. We give them no political power. Yours do vote, and, being the majority, they are the depositaries [sic] of all your political power. If they knew the tremendous secret, that the ballot-box is stronger than "an army with banners," and could combine, where would you be? Your society would be reconstructed, your government overthrown, your property divided, not as they have mistakenly attempted to initiate such proceedings by meeting in parks, with arms in their hands, but by the quiet process of the ballot-box. You have been making war upon us to our very hearthstones. How would you like for us to send lecturers and agitators North, to teach these people this, to aid in combining, and to lead them?

* * *

Transient and temporary causes have thus far been your preservation. The great West has been open to your surplus population, and your hordes of semi-barbarian immigrants, who are crowding in year by year. They make a great movement, and you call it progress. Whither? It is progress; but it is progress toward Vigilance Committees. The South have sustained you in great measure. You are our factors. You fetch and carry for us. One hundred and fifty million dollars of our money passes annually through your hands. Much of it sticks; all of it assists to keep your machinery together and in motion. Suppose we were to discharge you; suppose we were to take our business out of your hands;—we should consign you to anarchy and poverty. You complain of the rule of the South; that has been another cause that has preserved you. We have kept the Government conservative to the great purposes of the Constitution. We have placed it, and kept it, upon the Constitution; and that has been the cause of your peace and prosperity. The Senator from New York says that that is about to be at an end; that you intend to take the Government from us; that it will pass from our hands into yours. Perhaps what he says is true; it may be; but do not forget—it can never be forgotten—it is written on the brightest page of human history—that we, the slaveholders of the South, took our country in her infancy, and, after ruling her for sixty out of the seventy years of her existence, we surrendered her to you without a stain upon her honor, boundless in prosperity, incalculable in her strength, the wonder and admiration of the world. Time will show what you will make of her; but no time can diminish our glory or your responsibility.

ABRAHAM LINCOLN

"A House Divided," June 16, 1858

At the Illinois Republican convention in Springfield, Lincoln kicked off his campaign for incumbent Stephen Douglas's Senate seat in this speech, which sketches out the idea of a "Slave Power conspiracy" to extend slavery into the West. The first act of this conspiracy, according to Lincoln, was Douglas's Kansas-Nebraska Act, which relied upon popular or "squatter" sovereignty to organize these territories into states. Lincoln chides Douglas for blithely entrusting the settlers to decide the question of slavery for themselves, an act which paved the way for Kansas to devolve into bloody struggle. The next act of the Slave Power conspiracy was the Supreme Court decision in Dred Scott v. Sandford, *which opened the western territories and potentially the entire nation to slavery.*

In the conclusion of his speech, Lincoln insists that Douglas, President Franklin Pierce (who was in office when Kansas-Nebraska passed), Justice Roger Taney (author of the Dred Scott *majority decision), and James Buchanan (the sitting president) "all understood one another from the beginning, and all worked upon a common plan or draft drawn up before the first blow [of the conspiracy] was struck."*

SOURCE: The Annals of America: 1858–1865, A House Dividing *(Chicago: Encyclopædia Britannica, 1968), 1–4.*

*I*f we could first know where we are and whither we are tending, we could better judge what to do and how to do it. We are now far into the fifth year since a policy was initiated with the avowed object and confident promise of putting an end to slavery agitation. Under the operation of that policy, that agitation has not only not ceased but has constantly augmented. In my opinion, it will not cease until a crisis shall have been reached and passed. "A house divided against itself cannot stand." I believe this government cannot endure, permanently, half slave and half free. I do not expect the Union to be dissolved; I do not expect the house to fall; but I do expect it will cease to be divided. It will become all one thing, or all the other. Either the opponents of slavery will arrest the further spread of it and place it where the public mind shall rest in the belief that it is in the course of ultimate extinction, or its advocates will push it forward till it shall become alike lawful in all the states, old as well as new, North as well as South.

Have we no tendency to the latter condition?

Let anyone who doubts carefully contemplate that now almost complete legal combination—piece of machinery, so to speak—compounded of the Nebraska doctrine and the Dred Scott decision. Let him consider, not only what work the machinery is adapted to do, and how well adapted, but also let him study the history of its construction and trace, if he can, or rather fail, if he can, to trace the evidences of design and concert of action among its chief architects, from the beginning.

The new year of 1854 found slavery excluded from more than half the states by state constitutions and from most of the national territory by congressional prohibition. Four days later commenced the struggle which ended in repealing that congressional prohibition. This opened all the national territory to slavery and was the first point gained.

But, so far, Congress *only* had acted; and an endorsement by the people, real or apparent, was indispensable to save the point already gained and give chance for more.

This necessity had not been overlooked, but had been provided for, as well as might be, in the notable argument of "squatter sovereignty," other-wise called "sacred right of self-government," which latter phrase, though expressive of the only rightful basis of any government, was so perverted in this attempted use of it as to amount to just this: That if any *one* man choose to enslave *another*, no *third* man shall be allowed to object. That argument was incorporated into the Nebraska Bill itself, in the language which follows:

> It being the true intent and meaning of this act not to legislate slavery into any territory or state, nor to exclude it therefrom, but to leave the people there-of perfectly free to form and regulate their domestic institutions in their own way, subject only to the Constitution of the United States.

Then opened the roar of loose declamation in favor of "squatter sovereignty" and "sacred right of self-government." "But," said opposition members, "let us amend the bill so as to expressly declare that the people of the territory may exclude slavery." "Not we," said the friends of the measure; and down they voted the amendment.

While the Nebraska Bill was passing through Congress, a law case, involving the question of a Negro's freedom, by reason of his owner having voluntarily taken him first into a free state and then into a territory covered by the congressional prohibition, and held him as a slave for a long time in each, was passing through the United States Circuit Court for the district of Missouri; and both Nebraska Bill and lawsuit were brought to a decision in the same month of May 1854. The Negro's name was Dred Scott, which name now designates the decision finally made in the case. Before the then next presidential election, the law case came to, and was argued in, the Supreme Court of the United States; but the decision of it was deferred until after the election. Still, before the election, Senator Trumbull, on the floor of the Senate, requested the leading advocate of the Nebraska Bill to state his opinion whether the people of a territory can constitutionally exclude slavery from their limits; and the latter answers: "That is a question for the Supreme Court."

The election came. Mr. Buchanan was elected, and the endorsement, such as it was, secured. That was the second point gained. The endorsement, however, fell short of a clear popular majority by nearly 400,000 votes, and so, perhaps, was not overwhelmingly reliable and satisfactory. The outgoing President, in his last annual message, as impressively as possible echoed back upon the people the weight and authority of the endorsement. The Supreme Court met again, did not announce their decision, but ordered a reargument.

The presidential inauguration came, and still no decision of the Court; but the incoming President, in his inaugural address, fervently exhorted the people to abide by the forthcoming decision, whatever it might be. Then, in a few days, came the decision.

The reputed author of the Nebraska Bill [Sen. Stephen Douglas] finds an early occasion to make a speech at this capital endorsing the Dred Scott decision, and vehemently denouncing all opposition to it. The new President, too, seizes the early occasion of the Silliman letter to endorse and strongly construe that decision, and to express his astonishment that any different view had ever been entertained!

At length a squabble springs up between the President and the author of the Nebraska Bill, on the mere question of *fact*, whether the Lecompton constitution was or was not in any just sense made by the people of Kansas; and in that quarrel the latter declares that all he wants is a fair vote for the people, and that he cares not whether slavery be voted *down* or voted *up*. I do not understand his declaration, that he cares not whether slavery be voted down or voted up, to be intended by him other than as an apt definition of the policy he would impress upon the public mind—the principle for which he declares he has suffered so much and is ready to suffer to the end. And well may he cling to that principle! If he has any parental feeling, well may he cling to it. That principle is the only shred left of his original Nebraska doctrine.

Under the Dred Scott decision, "squatter sovereignty" squatted out of existence, tumbled down like temporary scaffolding; like the mold at the foundry, served through one blast and fell back into loose sand; helped to carry an election and then was kicked to the winds. His late joint struggle with the Republicans against the Lecompton constitution involves nothing of the original Nebraska doctrine. That struggle was made on a point—the right of a people to make their own constitution—upon which he and the Republicans have never differed.

The several points of the Dred Scott decision, in connection with Senator Douglas' "care not" policy, constitute the piece of machinery in its present state of advancement. This was the third point gained. The working points of that machinery are:

First, that no Negro slave, imported as such from Africa, and no descendant of such slave can ever be a citizen of any state in the sense of that term as used in the Constitution of the United States. This point is made in order to deprive the Negro, in every possible event, of the benefit of that provision of the United States Constitution which declares that "the citizens of each state shall be entitled to all the privileges and immunities of citizens in the several states."

Second, that, "subject to the Constitution of the United States," neither Congress nor a territorial legislature can exclude slavery from any United States territory. This point is made in order that individual men may fill up the territories with slaves, without danger of losing them as property, and thus enhance the chances of permanency to the institution through all the future.

Third, that whether the holding a Negro in actual slavery in a free state makes him free, as against the holder, the United States courts will not decide, but will leave to be decided by the courts of any slave state the Negro may be forced into by the master. This point is made, not to be pressed immediately but, if acquiesced in for awhile, and apparently endorsed by the people at an election, then to sustain the logical conclusion that what Dred Scott's master might lawfully do with Dred Scott in the free state of Illinois, every other master may lawfully do with any other one, or 1,000 slaves, in Illinois or in any other free state.

Auxiliary to all this, and working hand in hand with it, the Nebraska doctrine, or what is left of it, is to educate and mold public opinion, at least Northern public opinion, not to care whether slavery is voted down or voted up. This shows exactly where we now are; and partially, also, whither we are tending.

It will throw additional light on the latter to go back and run the mind over the string of historical facts already stated. Several things will now appear less dark and mysterious than they did when they were transpiring. The people were to be left "perfectly free," "subject only to the Constitution." What the Constitution had to do with it, outsiders could not then see. Plainly enough, now, it was an exactly fitted niche for the Dred Scott decision to afterward come in and declare the perfect freedom of the people to be just no freedom at all.

Why was the amendment expressly declaring the right of the people voted down? Plainly enough, now, the adoption of it would have spoiled the niche for the

Dred Scott decision. Why was the Court decision held up? Why even a senator's individual opinion withheld till after the presidential election? Plainly enough, now, the speaking out then would have damaged the "perfectly free" argument upon which the election was to be carried. Why the outgoing President's felicitation on the endorsement? Why the delay of a reargument? Why the incoming President's advance exhortation in favor of the decision? These things look like the cautious patting and petting of a spirited horse preparatory to mounting him when it is dreaded that he may give the rider a fall. And why the hasty after-endorsement of the decision by the President and others?

We cannot absolutely know that all these exact adaptations are the result of preconcert. But when we see a lot of framed timbers, different portions of which we know have been gotten out at different times and places and by different workmen—Stephen, Franklin, Roger, and James, for instance—and when we see these timbers joined together and see they exactly make the frame of a house or a mill, all the tenons and mortises exactly fitting, and all the lengths and proportions of the different pieces exactly adapted to their respective places, and not a piece too many or too few, not omitting even scaffolding, or, if a single piece be lacking, we see the place in the frame exactly fitted and prepared yet to bring such piece in—in such a case, we find it impossible not to believe that Stephen and Franklin and Roger and James all understood one another from the beginning, and all worked upon a common plan or draft drawn up before the first blow was struck.

ABRAHAM LINCOLN AND STEPHEN DOUGLAS

"Freeport Debate," August 27, 1858

This debate resulted in the clarification of the positions of Abraham Lincoln and Stephen Douglas on the pressing questions of westward expansion and slavery. First, Lincoln answers the questions (or interrogatories) posed by Douglas at the previous debate in Ottawa, Illinois. He repeats the questions Douglas asked for clarity. After answering the questions very briefly, he proceeds to expand on some of his answers. Afterwards, he poses some questions of his own to Douglas, who, in turn, answers in some detail.

Comments from the crowd are shown in brackets.

SOURCE: *Abraham Lincoln and Stephen Douglas, "Second Debate at Freeport, Illinois, August 27, 1858,"* The Complete Works of Abraham Lincoln, *vol. 3, eds. John G. Nicolay and John Hay (New York: Francis D. Tandy Co., 1894).*

LINCOLN'S OPENING

Question 1. "I desire to know whether Lincoln to-day stands as he did in 1854, in favor of the unconditional repeal of the fugitive-slave law?"

Answer. I do not now, nor ever did, stand in favor of the unconditional repeal of the fugitive-slave law.

Question 2. "I desire him to answer whether he stands pledged to-day as he did in 1854, against the admission of any more slave States into the Union, even if the people want them?"

Answer. I do not now, nor ever did, stand pledged against the admission of any more slave States into the Union.

Q. 3. "I want to know whether he stands pledged against the admission of a new State into the Union with such a constitution as the people of that State may see fit to make?"

A. I do not stand pledged against the admission of a new State into the Union with such a constitution as the people of that State may see fit to make.

Q. 4. "I want to know whether he stands to-day pledged to the abolition of slavery in the District of Columbia?"

A. I do not stand to-day pledged to the abolition of slavery in the District of Columbia.

Q. 5. "I desire him to answer whether he stands pledged to the prohibition of the slave trade between the different States?"

A. I do not stand pledged to the prohibition of the slave-trade between the different States.

Q. 6. "I desire to know whether he stands pledged to prohibit slavery in all the Territories of the United States, North as well as South of the Missouri Compromise line?"

A. I am impliedly, if not expressly, pledged to a belief in the right and duty of Congress to prohibit slavery in all the United States Territories.

Q. 7. "I desire him to answer whether he is opposed to the acquisition of any new territory unless slavery is first prohibited therein?"

A. I am not generally opposed to honest acquisition of territory; and, in any given case, I would or would not oppose such acquisition, accordingly as I might think such acquisition would or would not aggravate the slavery question among ourselves.

Now, my friends, it will be perceived upon an examination of these questions and answers, that so far I have only answered that I was not pledged to this, that, or the other. The judge has not framed his interrogatories to ask me anything more than this, and I have answered in strict accordance with the interrogatories, and have answered truly that I am not pledged at all upon any of the points to which I have answered. But I am not disposed to hang upon exact form of his interrogatory. I am then really disposed to take up at least some of these questions, and state what I really think upon them.

As to the first one, in regard to the fugitive slave law, I have never hesitated to say, and I do not now hesitate to say, that I think, under the Constitution of the United States, the people of the Southern States are entitled to a congressional fugitive-slave law. Having said that, I have had nothing to say in regard to the existing fugitive-slave law, further than that I think it should have been framed so as to be free from some of the objections that pertain to it, without lessening its efficiency. And in as much as we are not now in an agitation in regard to an alteration or modification of that law, I would not be the man to introduce it as a new subject of agitation upon the general question of slavery.

In regard to the other question, of whether I am pledged to the admission of any more slave states into the Union, I state to you very frankly that I would be exceedingly sorry ever to be put in a position of having to pass upon that question. I should be exceedingly glad to know that there would never be another slave State admitted into the Union; but I must add that if slavery shall be kept out of the Territories during the territorial existence of any given Territory, and then the people shall, having a fair chance and a clear field, when they come to adopt the Constitution, do such an extraordinary thing as to adopt a slave constitution, uninfluenced by the actual presence of the institution among them, I see no alternative if we own the country, but to admit them into the Union.

The third interrogatory is answered by the answer to the second, it being, as I conceive, the same as the second.

The fourth one is in regard to the abolition of slavery in the District of Columbia. In relation to that, I have my mind very distinctly made up. I should be exceedingly glad to see slavery abolished in the District of Columbia. I believe that Congress possesses the constitutional power to abolish it. Yet as a member of Congress, I should not with my present views be in favor of endeavoring to abolish slavery in the District of Columbia unless it would be upon these conditions: First, that the abolition should be gradual; second, that it should be on a vote of the majority of qualified voters in the District; and third, that compensation should be made to unwilling owners. With these three conditions, I confess I would be exceedingly glad to see Congress abolish slavery in the District of Columbia, and, in the language of Henry Clay, "sweep from our capital that foul blot upon our nation."

In regard to the fifth interrogatory, I must say here that as to the question of the abolition of the slave-trade between the different States, I can truly answer, as I have, that I am pledged to nothing about it. It is a subject to which I have not given that mature consideration that would make me feel authorized to state a position so as to hold myself entirely bound by it. In other words, that question has never been prominently enough before me to induce me to investigate whether we really have the constitutional power to do it. I could investigate it if I had sufficient time to bring myself to a conclusion upon that subject, but I have not done so, and I say so frankly to you here and to Judge Douglas. I must say, however, that if I should be of opinion that Congress does possess the constitutional power to abolish the slave-trade among the different States, I should still not be in favor of the exercise of that power unless upon some conservative principle as I conceive it, akin to what I have said in relation to the abolition of slavery in the District of Columbia.

My answer as to whether I desire that slavery should be prohibited in all the Territories of the United States is full and explicit within itself, and cannot be made clearer by any comments of mine.

So I suppose in regard to the question whether I am opposed to the acquisition of any more territory unless slavery is first prohibited therein, my answer is such that I could add nothing by way of illustration, or making myself better understood, than the answer which I have placed in writing.

Now in all this the judge has me, and he has me on the record. I suppose he had flattered himself that I was really entertaining one set of opinions for one place and another set for another place that I was afraid to say at one place what I uttered at another. What I am saying here I suppose I say to a vast audience as strongly tending to Abolitionism as any audience in the State of Illinois, and I believe I am saying that which, if it would be offensive to any persons and render them enemies to myself, would be offensive to persons in this audience.

I now proceed to propound to the judge the interrogatories so far as I have framed them. I will bring forward a new installment when I get them ready. I will bring them forward now, only reaching to number four.

The first one is:

Question 1. If the people of Kansas shall, by means entirely unobjectionable in all other respects, adopt a State constitution, and ask admission into the Union under it, before they have the requisite number of inhabitants according to the English bill,—some ninety-three thousand,—will you vote to admit them?

Q. 2. Can the people of a United States Territory, in any lawful way, against the wish of any citizen of the United States, exclude slavery from its limits prior to the formation of a State constitution?

Q. 3. If the Supreme Court of the United States shall decide that States cannot exclude slavery from their limits, are you in favor of acquiescing in, adopting, and following such decision as a rule of political action?

Q. 4. Are you in favor of acquiring additional territory, in disregard of how such acquisition may affect the nation on the slavery question?

DOUGLAS REPLIES

Ladies and Gentlemen: The silence with which you have listened to Mr. Lincoln during his hour is creditable to this vast audience, composed of men of various political parties. Nothing is more honorable to any large mass of people assembled for the purpose of a fair discussion, than that kind and respectful attention that is yielded not only to your political friends, but to those who are opposed to you in politics.

I am glad that at last I have brought Mr. Lincoln to the conclusion that he had better define his position on certain political questions to which I called his attention at Ottawa. He there showed no disposition, no inclination, to answer them. I did not present idle questions for him to answer merely for my gratification. I laid the foundation for those interrogatories by showing that they constituted the platform of the party whose nominee he is for the Senate. I did not presume that I had the right to catechize him as I saw proper, unless I showed that his party, or a majority of it, stood upon the platform, and were in favor of the propositions upon which my questions were based. I desired simply to know, inasmuch as he had been nominated as the first, last, and only choice of his party, whether he concurred in the platform which that party had adopted for its government. In a few moments I will proceed to review the answers which he has given to these interrogatories, but in order to relieve his anxiety I will first respond to these which he has presented to me.

* * *

First, he desires to know if the people of Kansas shall form a constitution by means entirely proper and unobjectionable and ask admission into the Union as a State, before they have the requisite population for a member of Congress, whether I will vote for that admission. Well, now, I regret exceedingly that he did not answer that interrogatory himself before he put it to me, in order that we might understand, and not be left to infer, on which side he is.… But I will answer his question. In reference to Kansas, it is my opinion that as she has population enough to constitute a slave State, she has people enough for a Free State. I will not make Kansas an exceptional case to the other States of the Union. I hold it to be a sound rule of universal application to require a Territory to contain the requisite population for a member of Congress, before it is admitted as a State into the Union. I made that proposition in the Senate in 1856, and I renewed it during the last session, in a bill providing that no Territory of the United States should form a constitution and apply for admission until it had the requisite population. On another occasion I proposed that neither Kansas, nor any other Territory, should be admitted until it had the requisite population. Congress did not adopt any of my propositions containing this general rule, but did make an exception of Kansas. I will stand by that exception. Either Kansas must come in as a Free State, with whatever population she may have, or the rule must be applied to all the other Territories alike. I therefore answer at once that, it having been decided that Kansas has people enough for a slave State, I hold that she has enough for a Free State.

I hope Mr. Lincoln is satisfied with my answer; and now I would like to get his answer to his own interrogatory—whether or not he will vote to admit Kansas before she has the requisite population. I want to know whether he will vote to admit Oregon before that Territory has the requisite population.... I would like Mr. Lincoln to answer this question. I would like him to take his own medicine.... [L]et him answer his argument against the admission of Oregon, instead of poking questions at me.

The next question propounded to me by Mr. Lincoln is: Can the people of a Territory in any lawful way, against the wishes of any citizen of the United States, exclude slavery from their limits prior to the formation of a State constitution? I answer emphatically, as Mr. Lincoln has heard me answer a hundred times from every stump in Illinois, that in my opinion the people of a Territory can, by lawful means, exclude slavery from their limits prior to the formation of a State constitution. Mr. Lincoln knew that I had answered that question over and over again. He heard me argue the Nebraska bill on that principle all over the State in 1854, in 1855, and in 1856, and he has no excuse for pretending to be in doubt as to my position on that question. It matters not what way the Supreme Court may hereafter decide as to the abstract question whether slavery may or may not go into a Territory under the Constitution[;] the people have the lawful means to introduce it or exclude it as they please, for the reason that slavery cannot exist a day or an hour anywhere unless it is supported by the local police regulations. Those police regulations can only be established by the local legislature, and if the people are opposed to slavery they will elect representatives to that body who will by unfriendly legislation effectually prevent the introduction of it into their midst. If, on the contrary, they are for it, their legislation will favor its extension. Hence, no matter what the decision of the Supreme Court may be on that abstract question, still the right of the people to make a slave Territory or a free Territory is perfect and complete under the Nebraska bill. I hope Mr. Lincoln deems my answer satisfactory on that point.

* * *

The third question which Mr. Lincoln presented is, if the Supreme Court of the United States shall decide that a State of this Union cannot exclude slavery from its own limits, will I submit to it? I am amazed that Lincoln should ask such a question.

["A school-boy knows better."]

Yes, a school-boy does know better. Mr. Lincoln's object is to cast an imputation upon the Supreme Court. He knows that there never was but one man in America claiming any degree of intelligence or decency, who ever for a moment pretended such a thing. It is true that the Washington "Union," in an article published on the 17th of last December, did put forth that doctrine, and I denounced the article on the floor of the Senate, in a speech which Mr. Lincoln now pretends was against the President. The "Union" had claimed that slavery had a right to go into the free States, and that any provision in the constitution or laws of the free States to the contrary was null and void. I denounced it in the Senate, as I said before, and I was the first man who did. Lincoln's friends, Trumbull, and Seward, and Hale, and Wilson, and the whole Black Republican side of the Senate were silent. They left it to me to denounce it. And what was the reply made to me on that occasion? Mr. Toombs, of Georgia, got up and undertook to lecture me on the ground that I ought not to have deemed the article worthy of notice, and ought not to have replied to it; that there was not one man, woman, or child south of the Potomac, in any slave State, who did not repudiate any such pretensions. Mr. Lincoln knows that that reply was made on the spot, and yet now he asks this question. He might as well ask me, suppose Mr. Lincoln should steal a horse, Would I sanction it? and it would be as genteel in me to ask him, in the event he stole a horse, what ought to be done with him. He casts an imputation upon the Supreme Court of the United States by supposing that they would violate the Constitution of the United States. I tell him that such a thing is not possible. It would be an act of moral treason that no man on the bench could ever descend to. Mr. Lincoln himself would never in his partisan feelings so far forget what was right as to be guilty of such an act.

The fourth question of Mr. Lincoln is: Are you in favor of acquiring additional territory, in disregard as to how such acquisition may affect the Union on the slavery question? This question is very ingeniously and cunningly put.

The Black Republican creed lays it down expressly, that under no circumstances shall we acquire any more territory unless slavery is first prohibited in the country. I ask Mr. Lincoln whether he is in favor of that proposition. Are you [addressing Mr. Lincoln] opposed to the acquisition of any more territory, under any circumstances, unless slavery is prohibited in it? That he does not like to answer. When I ask him whether he stands up to that article in the platform of his party, he turns, Yankee-fashion, and, without answering it, asks me whether I am in favor of acquiring territory without regard to how it may affect the Union on the slavery question. I answer that whenever it becomes necessary, in our growth and progress, to acquire more territory, that I am in favor of it, without reference to the question of slavery, and when we have acquired it, I will leave the people free to do as they please, either to make it slave or free territory, as they prefer. It is idle to tell me or you that we have territory enough. Our fathers supposed that we had enough when our territory extended to the Mississippi River, but a few years' growth and expansion satisfied them that we needed more, and the Louisiana territory, from the west branch of the Mississippi to the British possessions, was acquired. Then we acquired Oregon, then California and New Mexico. We have enough now for the present, but this is a young and a growing nation. It swarms as often as a hive of bees, and as new swarms are turned out each year, there must be hives in which they can gather and make their honey. In less than fifteen years, if the same progress that has distinguished this country for the last fifteen years continues, every foot of vacant land between this and the Pacific Ocean owned by the United States, will be occupied. Will you not continue to increase at the end of fifteen years as well as now? I tell you, increase, and multiply, and expand, is the law of this nation's existence. You cannot limit this great republic by mere boundary lines, saying, "Thus far shalt thou go, and no further." Any one of you gentlemen might as well say to a son twelve years old that he is big enough, and must not grow any larger, and in order to prevent his growth put a hoop around him to keep him to his present size. What would be the result? Either the hoop must burst and be rent asunder, or the child must die. So it would be with this great nation. With our natural increase, growing with a rapidity unknown in any other part of the globe, with the tide of emigration that is fleeing from despotism in the Old World to seek refuge in our own, there is a constant torrent pouring into this country that requires more land, more territory upon which to settle, and just as fast as our interests and our destiny require additional territory in the North, in the South, or on the islands of the ocean, I am for it, and when we acquire it, will leave the people, according to the Nebraska bill, free to do as they please on the subject of slavery and every other question.

I trust now that Mr. Lincoln will deem himself answered on his four points. He racked his brain so much in devising these four questions that he exhausted himself, and had not strength enough to invent the others. As soon as he is able to hold a council with his advisers, Lovejoy, Farnsworth, and Fred Douglass, he will frame and propound others.

["Good, good."]

You Black Republicans who say good, I have no doubt[,] think that they are all good men. I have reason to recollect that some people in this country think that Fred Douglass is a very good man. The last time I came here to make a speech, while talking from the stand to you, people of Freeport, as I am doing today, I saw a carriage, and a magnificent one it was, drive up and take a position on the outside of the crowd; a beautiful young lady was sitting on the box-seat, whilst Fred Douglass and her mother reclined inside, and the owner of the carriage acted as driver. I saw this in your own town.

["What of it?"]

All I have to say of it is this, that if you Black Republicans think that the negro ought to be on a social equality with your wives and daughters, and ride in a carriage with your wife, whilst you drive the team, you have perfect right to do so. I am told that one of Fred Douglass's kinsmen, another rich black negro, is now traveling in this part of the State making speeches for his friend Lincoln as the champion of black men.

["What have you to say against it?"]

All I have to say on that subject is, that those of you who believe that the negro is your equal and ought to be on an equality with you socially, politically, and legally, have a right to entertain those opinions, and of course will vote for Mr. Lincoln.

WILLIAM HENRY SEWARD

"An Irrepressible Conflict," October 25, 1858

New York senator William H. Seward began his political career as a Whig. An outspoken opponent of the expansion of slavery, he fought the Compromise of 1850 by appealing to a "higher law than the Constitution." In this speech, given in Rochester, New York, Seward unleashes abuse on the Democratic Party as the instrument of a Slave Power conspiracy.

One of the architects of the Republican Party, Seward was widely regarded as the leading contender for the Republican presidential nomination in 1860. Due in part to the radicalism of speeches like this, however, he was supplanted by Lincoln. Despite losing the nomination, he spent most of the autumn of 1860 campaigning for Lincoln.

He begins with a fierce denunciation of slavery and a celebration of free labor, which he connects to political liberty.

SOURCE: *William Henry Seward, "Speech of William H. Seward, delivered at Rochester, Monday, October 27, 1858" (Washington, D.C.: Buell & Blanchard, 1858).*

... Our country is a theatre, which exhibits, in full operation, two radically different political systems; the one resting on the basis of servile or slave labor, the other on voluntary labor of freemen. The laborers who are enslaved are all negroes, or persons more or less purely of African derivation. But this is only accidental. The principle of the system is, that labor in every society, by whomsoever performed, is necessarily unintellectual, groveling, and base; and that the laborer, equally for his own good and for the welfare of the State, ought to be enslaved. The white laboring man, whether native or foreigner, is not enslaved, only because he cannot, as yet, be reduced to bondage.

You need not be told now that the slave system is the older of the two, and that once it was universal. The emancipation of our own ancestors, Caucasians and Europeans as they were, hardly dates beyond a period of five hundred years. The great melioration of human society which modern times exhibits is mainly due to the incomplete substitution of the system of voluntary labor for the one of servile labor, which has already taken place. This African slave system is one which, in its origin and in its growth, has been altogether foreign from the habits of the races which colonized these States, and established civilization here. It was introduced on this continent as an engine of conquest, and for the establishment of monarchical power, by the Portuguese and the Spaniards, and was rapidly extended by them all over South America, Central America, Louisiana, and Mexico. Its legitimate fruits are seen in the poverty, imbecility, and anarchy which now pervade all Portuguese and Spanish America. The free-labor system is of German extraction, and it was established in our country by emigrants from Sweden, Holland, Germany, Great Britain, and Ireland. We justly ascribe to its influences the strength, wealth, greatness, intelligence, and freedom, which the whole American people now enjoy. One of the chief elements of the value of human life is freedom in the pursuit of happiness. The slave system is not only intolerable, unjust, and inhuman, toward the laborer, whom, only because he is a laborer, it loads down with chains and converts into merchandise, but is scarcely less severe upon the freeman, to whom, only because he is a laborer from necessity, it denies facilities for employment, and whom it expels from the community because it cannot enslave and convert into merchandise also. It is necessarily improvident and ruinous, because, as a general truth, communities prosper and flourish, or droop and decline, in just the degree that they practice or neglect to practice the primary duties of justice and humanity. The free-labor system conforms to the divine law of equality, which is written in the hearts and consciences of man, and therefore is always and everywhere beneficent.

The slave system is one of constant danger, distrust, suspicion, and watchfulness. It debases those whose toil alone can produce wealth and resources for defense, to the lowest degree of which human nature is capable, to guard against mutiny and insurrection, and thus wastes energies which otherwise might be employed in national development and aggrandizement. The free-labor system educates all alike, and by opening all the fields of industrial employment and all the departments of authority, to the unchecked and equal rivalry of all classes of men, at once secures universal contentment, and brings into the highest possible activity all the physical, moral, and social energies of the whole state. In states where the slave system prevails, the masters, directly or indirectly, secure all political power, and constitute a ruling aristocracy. In states where the free-labor system prevails, universal suffrage necessarily obtains, and the state inevitably becomes, sooner or later, a republic or democracy.

Seward develops the idea that free and slave labor systems must ultimately come into conflict. He begins by describing the situation in Europe and quickly returns to the situation in the United States.

Russia yet maintains slavery, and is a despotism. Most of the other European states have abolished slavery, and adopted the system of free labor. It was the antagonistic political tendencies of the two systems which the first Napoleon was contemplating when he predicted that Europe would ultimately be either all Cossack or all republican. Never did human sagacity utter a more pregnant truth. The two systems are at once perceived to be incongruous. But they are more than incongruous—they are incompatible. They never have permanently existed together in one country, and they never can. It would be easy to demonstrate this impossibility, from the irreconcilable contrast between their great principles and characteristics. But the experience of mankind has conclusively established it. Slavery, as I have intimated, existed in every state in Europe. Free labor has supplanted it everywhere except in Russia and developed in modern times are now Turkey. State necessities developed in modern times are now obliging even those two nations to encourage and employ free labor; and already, despotic as they are, we find them engaged in abolishing slavery. In the United States, slavery came into collision with free labor at the close of the last century, and fell before it in New England, New York, New Jersey, and Pennsylvania, but triumphed over it effectually, and excluded it for a period yet undetermined, from Virginia, the Carolinas, and Georgia. Indeed, so incompatible are the two systems, that every new State which is organized within our ever-extending domain makes its first political act a choice of the one and the exclusion of the other, even at the cost of civil war, if necessary. The slave States, without law, at the last national election, successfully forbade, within their own limits, even the casting of votes for a candidate for President of the United States supposed to be favorable to the establishment of the free-labor system in new States.

Hitherto, the two systems have existed in different States, but side by side within the American Union. This has happened because the Union is a confederation of States. But in another aspect the United States constitute only one nation. Increase of population, which is filling the States out to their very borders, together with a new and extended network of railroads and other avenues, and an internal commerce which daily becomes more intimate, is rapidly bringing the States into a higher and more perfect social unity or consolidation. Thus, these antagonistic systems are continually coming into closer contact, and collision results.

Shall I tell you what this collision means? They who think that it is accidental, unnecessary, the work of interested or fanatical agitators, and therefore ephemeral, mistake the case altogether. It is an irrepressible conflict between opposing and enduring forces, and it means that the United States must and will, sooner or later, become either entirely a slaveholding nation, or entirely a free-labor nation. Either the cotton and rice fields of South Carolina and the sugar plantations of Louisiana will ultimately be tilled by free labor, and Charleston and New Orleans become marts of legitimate merchandise alone, or else the rye-fields and wheat-fields of Massachusetts and New York must again be surrendered by their farmers to slave culture and to the production of slaves, and Boston and New York become once more markets for trade in the bodies and souls of men. It is the failure to apprehend this great truth that induces so many unsuccessful attempts at final compromises between the slave and free States, and it is the existence of this great fact that renders all such pretended compromises, when made, vain and ephemeral. Startling as this saying may appear to you, fellow-citizens, it is by no means an original or even a modern one. Our forefathers knew it to be true, and unanimously acted upon it when they framed the constitution of the United States. They regarded the existence of the servile system in so many of the States with sorrow and shame, which they openly confessed, and they looked upon the collision between them, which was then just revealing itself, and which we are now accustomed to deplore, with favor and hope. They knew that one or the other system must exclusively prevail.

Unlike too many of those who in modern time invoke their authority, they had a choice between the two. They preferred the system of free labor, and they determined to organize the government, and so direct its activity, that that system should surely and certainly prevail. For this purpose, and no other, they based the whole structure of the government broadly on the principle that all men are created equal, and therefore free—little dreaming that, within the short period of one hundred years, their descendants would bear to be told by any orator, however popular, that the utterance of that principle was merely a rhetorical rhapsody; or by any judge, however venerated, that it was attended by mental reservation, which rendered it hypocritical and false. By the ordinance of 1787 they dedicated all of the national domain not yet polluted by slavery to free labor immediately, thenceforth and forever; while by the new constitution and laws they invited foreign free labor from all lands under the sun, and interdicted the importation of African slave labor, at all times, in all places, and under all circumstances whatsoever. It is true that they necessarily and wisely modified this policy of freedom by leaving it to the several States, affected as they were by different circumstances, to abolish slavery in their own way and at their own pleasure, instead of confiding that duty to Congress; and that they secured to the slave States, while yet retaining the system of slavery, a three-fifths representation of slaves in the federal government, until they should find themselves able to relinquish it with safety. But the very nature of these modifications fortifies my position, that the fathers knew that the two systems could not endure within the Union, and expected within a short period slavery would disappear forever. Moreover, in order that these modifications might not altogether defeat their grand design of a republic maintaining universal equality, they provided that two thirds of the States might amend the constitution.

Seward continues invoking the authority of the founding generation in favor of free labor.

It remains to say on this point only one word, to guard against misapprehension. If these States are to again become universally slaveholding, I do not pretend to say with what violations of the constitution that end shall be accomplished. On the other hand, while I do confidently believe and hope that my country will yet become a land of universal freedom, I do not expect that it will be made so otherwise than through the action of the several States co-operating with the federal government, and all acting in strict conformity with their respective constitutions.

The strife and contentions concerning slavery, which gently disposed persons so habitually deprecate, are nothing more than the ripening of the conflict which the fathers themselves not only thus regarded with favor, but which they may be said to have instituted.

It is not to be denied, however, that thus far the course of that contest has not been according to their humane anticipations and wishes. In the field of federal politics, slavery, deriving unlooked-for advantages from commercial changes, and energies unforeseen from the facilities of combination between members of the slaveholding class and between that class and other property classes, early rallied, and has at length made a stand, not merely to retain its original defensive position, but to extend its sway throughout the whole Union. It is certain that the slaveholding class of American citizens indulge this high ambition, and that they derive encouragement for it from the rapid and effective political successes which they have already obtained. The plan of operation is this: By continued appliances of patronage and threats of disunion, they will keep a majority favorable to these designs in the Senate, where each State has an equal representation. Through that majority they will defeat, as they best can, the admission of free States and secure the admission of slave States. Under the protection of the judiciary, they will, on the principle of the Dred Scott case, carry slavery into all the territories of the United States now existing and hereafter to be organized. By the action of the President and Senate, using the treaty-making power, they will annex foreign slaveholding States. In a favorable conjuncture they will induce Congress to repeal the act of 1808 which prohibits the foreign slave trade, and so they will import from Africa, at a cost of only twenty dollars a head, slaves enough to fill up the interior of the continent. Thus relatively increasing the number of slave States, they will allow no amendment to the constitution prejudicial to their interest; and so, having permanently established their power, they expect the federal judiciary to nullify all State laws which shall interfere with internal or foreign commerce in slaves. When the free States shall be sufficiently demoralized to tolerate these designs, they reasonably conclude that slavery will be accepted by those States themselves. I shall not stop to show how speedy or how complete would be the ruin which the accomplishment of these slaveholding schemes would bring upon the country. For one, I should not remain in the country to test the sad experiment. Having spent my manhood, though not my whole life, in a free State, no aristocracy of any kind, much less an aristocracy of slaveholders, shall ever make the laws of the land in which I shall be content to live. Having seen the society around me universally engaged in agriculture, manufactures, and trade, which were innocent and beneficent, I shall never be a denizen of a State where men and women are reared as cattle, and bought and sold as merchandise. When that evil day shall come, and all further effort at resistance shall be impossible, then, if there shall be no better hope for redemption than I can now foresee, I shall say with Franklin, while looking abroad over the whole earth for a new and more congenial home, "Where liberty dwells, there is my country." You will tell me that these fears are extravagant and chimerical. I answer, they are so; but they are so only because the designs of the slaveholders must and can be defeated. But it is only the possibility of defeat that renders them so. They cannot be defeated by inactivity. There is no escape from them compatible

Seward briefly sketches the history of the Slave Power conspiracy, and ultimately names the Democratic Party as the conspirators' chosen instrument.

with non-resistance. How, then, and in what way, shall the necessary resistance be made? There is only one way. The Democratic party must be permanently dislodged from the government. The reason is, that the Democratic party is inextricably committed to the designs of the slaveholders, which I have described. Let me be well understood. I do not charge that the Democratic candidates for public office now before the people are pledged to—much less that the Democratic masses who support them really adopt—those atrocious and dangerous designs. Candidates may, and generally do, mean to act justly, wisely, and patriotically, when they shall be elected; but they become the ministers and servants, not the dictators, of the power which elects them. The policy which a party shall pursue at a future period is only gradually developed, depending on the occurrence of events never fully foreknown. The motives of men, whether acting as electors or in any other capacity, are generally pure. Nevertheless, it is not more true that "hell is paved with good intentions," than it is that earth is covered with wrecks resulting from innocent and amiable motives.

The very constitution of the Democratic party commits it to execute all the designs of the slaveholders, whatever they may be. It is not a party of the whole Union, of all the free States and of all the slave States; nor yet is it a party of the free States in the North and in the Northwest; but it is a sectional and local party, having practically its seat within the slave States, and counting its constituency chiefly and almost exclusively there. Of all its representatives in Congress and in the electoral colleges, two-thirds uniformly come from these States. Its great element of strength lies in the vote of the slaveholders, augmented by the representation of three-fifths of the slaves. Deprive the Democratic party of this strength, and it would be a helpless and hopeless minority, incapable of continued organization. The Democratic party, being thus local and sectional, acquires new strength from the admission of every new slave State, and loses relatively by the admission of every new free State into the Union.

A party is, in one sense, a joint stock association, in which those who contribute most direct the action and management of the concern. The slaveholders contributing in an overwhelming proportion to the capital strength of the Democratic party, they necessarily dictate and prescribe its policy. The inevitable caucus system enables them to do so with a show of fairness and justice. If it were possible to conceive for a moment that the Democratic party should disobey the behests of the slaveholders, we should then see a withdrawal of the slaveholders, which would leave the party to perish. The portion of the party which is found in the free States is a mere appendage, convenient to modify its sectional character, without impairing its sectional constitution, and is less effective in regulating its movements than the nebulous tail of the corset is in determining the appointed, though apparently eccentric, course of the fiery sphere from which it emanates.

To expect the Democratic party to resist slavery and favor freedom is as unreasonable as to look for Protestant missionaries to the Catholic propaganda of Rome.

The history of the Democratic party commits it to the policy of slavery. It has been the Democratic party, and no other agency, which has carried that policy up to its present alarming culmination. Without stopping to ascertain, critically, the origin of the present Democratic party, we may concede its claim to date from the era of good feeling which occurred under the administration of President Monroe. At that time, in this State, and about that time in many others of the free States, the Democratic party deliberately disfranchised the free colored or African citizen, and it has pertinaciously continued this disfranchisement ever since. This was an effective aid to slavery; for, while the slaveholder votes for his slaves against freedom, the freed slave in the free States is prohibited from voting against slavery. In 1824 the democracy resisted the election of John Quincy Adams—himself before that time an acceptable Democrat—and in 1828 it expelled him from the presidency and put a slaveholder in his place, although the office had been filled by slaveholders thirty-two out of forty years.

In 1836, Martin Van Buren—the first non-slaveholding citizen of a free State to whose election the Democratic party ever consented—signalized his inauguration into the presidency by a gratuitous announcement that under no circumstances would he ever approve a bill for the abolition of slavery in the District of Columbia. From 1838 to 1844 the subject of abolishing slavery in the District of Columbia and in the national dockyards and arsenals, was brought before Congress by repeated popular appeals. The Democratic party thereupon promptly denied the right of petition, and effectually suppressed the freedom of speech in Congress, so far as the institution of slavery was concerned.

From 1840 to 1843 good and wise men counseled that Texas should remain outside the Union until she should consent to relinquish her self-instituted slavery; but the Democratic party precipitated her admission into the Union, not only without that condition, but even with a covenant that the State might be divided and reorganized so as to constitute four slave States instead of one.

In 1846, when the United States became involved in a war with Mexico, and it was apparent that the struggle would end in the dismemberment of that republic, which was a non-slaveholding power, the Democratic party rejected a declaration that slavery should not be established within the territory to be acquired. When, in 1850, governments were to be instituted in the territories of California and New Mexico, the fruits of that war, the Democratic party refused to admit New Mexico as a free State, and only consented to admit California as a free State on the condition, as it has since explained the transaction, of leaving all of New Mexico and Utah open to slavery, to which was also added the concession of perpetual slavery in the District of Columbia, and the passage of an unconstitutional, cruel, and humiliating law, for the recapture of fugitive slaves, with a further stipulation that the subject of slavery should never again be agitated in either chamber of Congress. When, in 1854, the slaveholders were contentedly reposing on these great advantages, then so recently won, the Democratic party unnecessarily, officiously,

After a swipe at Catholicism, Seward continues his account of the history of Democratic duplicity.

and with super-serviceable liberality, awakened them from their slumber, to offer and force on their acceptance the abrogation of the law which declared that neither slavery nor involuntary servitude should ever exist within that part of the ancient territory of Louisiana which lay outside of the State of Missouri, and north of the parallel of 36° 30′ of north latitudes law which, with the exception of one other, was the only statute of freedom then remaining in the federal code.

In 1856, when the people of Kansas had organized a new State within the region thus abandoned to slavery, and applied to be admitted as a free State into the Union, the Democratic party contemptuously rejected their petition, and drove them with menaces and intimidations from the halls of Congress, and armed the President with military power to enforce their submission to a slave code, established over them by fraud and usurpation. At every subsequent stage of a long contest which has since raged in Kansas, the Democratic party has lent its sympathies, its aid, and all the powers of the government which it controlled, to enforce slavery upon that unwilling and injured people. And now, even at this day, while it mocks us with the assurance that Kansas is free, the Democratic party keeps the State excluded from her just and proper place in the Union, under the hope that she may be dragooned into the acceptance of slavery.

The Democratic party, finally, has procured from a supreme judiciary, fixed in its interest, a decree that slavery exists by force of the constitution in every territory of the United States, paramount to all legislative authority, either within the territory or residing in Congress.

Such is the Democratic party. It has no policy, state or federal, for finance, or trade, or manufacture, or commerce, or education, or internal improvements, or for the protection or even the security of civil or religious liberty. It is positive and uncompromising in the interest of slavery—negative, compromising, and vacillating, in regard to everything else. It boasts its love of equality, and wastes its strength, and even its life, in fortifying the only aristocracy known in the land. It professes fraternity, and, so often as slavery requires, allies itself with proscription. It magnifies itself for conquests in foreign lands, but it sends the national eagle forth always with chains, and not the olive branch, in his fangs.

This dark record shows you, fellow-citizens, what I was unwilling to announce at an earlier stage of this argument, that of the whole nefarious schedule of slaveholding designs which I have submitted to you, the Democratic party has left only one yet to be consummated—the abrogation of the law which forbids the African slave-trade.

I know—few, I think, know better than I—the resources and energies of the Democratic party, which is identical with the slave power. I do ample justice to its traditional popularity. I know further—few, I think, know better than I—the difficulties and disadvantages of organizing a new political force, like the Republican party, and the obstacles it must encounter in laboring without prestige and without patronage. But, understanding all this, I know that the Democratic party must go down, and that the Republican

At last, Seward argues, the Republicans arise.

party must rise into its place. The Democratic party derived its strength, originally, from its adoption of the principles of equal and exact justice to all men. So long as it practiced this principle faithfully it was invulnerable. It became vulnerable when it renounced the principle, and since that time it has maintained itself, not by virtue of its own strength, or even of its traditional merits, but because there as yet had appeared in the political field no other party that had the conscience and the courage to take up, and avow, and practice the life-inspiring principle which the Democratic party had surrendered. At last, the Republican party has appeared. It avows, now, as the Republican party of 1800 did, in one word, its faith and its works, "Equal and exact justice to all men." Even when it first entered the field, only half organized, it struck a blow which only just failed to secure complete and triumphant victory. In this, its second campaign, it has already won advantages which render that triumph now both easy and certain.

The secret of its assured success lies in that very characteristic which, in the mouth of scoffers, constitutes its great and lasting imbecility and reproach. It lies in the fact that it is a party of one idea; but that is a noble one—an idea that fills and expands all generous souls; the idea of equality—the equality of all men before human tribunals and human laws, as they all are equal before the divine tribunal and divine laws.

I know, and you know, that a revolution has begun. I know, and all the world knows, that revolutions never go backward. Twenty senators and a hundred representatives proclaim boldly in Congress to-day sentiments and opinions and principles of freedom which hardly so many men, even in this free State, dared to utter in their own homes twenty years ago. While the government of the United States, under the conduct of the Democratic party, has been all that time surrendering one plain and castle after another to slavery, the people of the United States have been no less steadily and perseveringly gathering together the forces with which to recover back again all the fields and all the castles which have been lost, and to confound and overthrow, by one decisive blow, the betrayers of the constitution and freedom forever.

Manumission Act of 1860, March 3, 1860

SOURCE: Acts of the General Assembly of the Commonwealth of Kentucky, *vol. 1 (Frankfort: J. B. Major, 1860), 128–31.*

*A*n act concerning free negroes, mulattoes, and emancipation.

Be it enacted by the General Assembly of the Commonwealth of Kentucky:

§ 1. That hereafter no slave shall be deemed to be emancipated by the laws of this State, until the person emancipating such slave, or some person for him, as principal, with good and sufficient resident security, before the county court of the county of his residence, shall give a covenant to the Commonwealth, covenanting that such person shall remove such slave (naming him or her, and giving the age, color, height, and weight) beyond the limits of this State within ninety days after the approval of such covenant by said county court; nor until such slave shall subscribe a written statement, to be indorsed on such covenant, that he or she does then forever abandon his or her residence in, and will, within the time named, remove from this State, which subscription shall be attested by the clerk of such court; upon the breach of such covenant, it shall be the duty of the attorney for the Commonwealth of the district, and the attorney for such county, or either of them, to institute suit upon the same for the recovery of such damages as may be found to be due: *Provided,* That the amount of damages shall not be less than the value of such slave at the time of his or her emancipation, which damages shall be paid into the county treasury, after deducting therefrom twenty per cent. as a compensation for the attorney or attorneys by whom the suit is prosecuted, and also ten dollars to be paid to the person or persons who may have given information of the breach of the covenant.

§ 2. That hereafter, should any free negro or mulatto come into this State with the intention of remaining therein, he or she shall be deemed guilty of felony, and upon conviction thereof, shall be confined in the penitentiary for a period of not less than six years.

§ 3. That hereafter any free negro or mulatto, not a resident of Kentucky, who shall come to this State for any purpose or upon any pretense whatever, unless in obedience to the process of a court, shall likewise be deemed guilty of a felony, and, upon conviction thereof, shall be confined in the penitentiary for a period of not less than one, nor more than five years.

§ 4. That when any free negro or mulatto who may be convicted under either of the two preceding sections of this act, shall have served out one fourth of the time for which he or she was sentenced, any person, as principal, shall have the right to execute a bond to the Commonwealth, with at least one good resident security, to be approved by the Governor, conditioned that such convict will, within ten days, leave this State and never return; and thereupon it shall be the duty of the Governor to deposit such bond in the office of the Secretary of State, and cause the keeper of the penitentiary to be notified that the same has been executed; immediately upon the receipt of such notice, it shall be the duty of the keeper of the penitentiary to discharge such convict, as though the time for which he or she was sentenced had expired.

* * *

§ 11. That any person who shall be convicted of purchasing a free negro or mulatto, for the benefit of such free negro or mulatto, and not with the *bona fide* intention of making him or her a slave, such person shall be fined in any sum not exceeding five hundred dollars.

* * *

§ 14. That this act shall take effect from and after the first day of January, 1861.

Militia Act of 1860, March 5, 1860

The first two articles of this act describe the "Militia of the Reserve" and the "Enrolled Militia," which together include all white male persons older than 18 and younger than 45 years of age and can be called into the service of the State in times of war or public danger.

SOURCE: Acts of the General Assembly of the Commonwealth of Kentucky, *vol. 1 (Frankfort: J. B. Major, 1860), 120–71.*

ARTICLE III. OF THE ACTIVE OR VOLUNTEER MILITIA—OF THE INSPECTOR GENERAL

§ 1. In addition to the staff officers at present authorized by law, the Governor and commander-in-chief shall appoint an inspector general, with the rank of major general.

1. The inspector general shall direct and superintend the formation and organization, and shall exercise, under the commander-in-chief, the active control and command of the Volunteer Militia.

2. He shall cause all existing volunteer companies, and all volunteer companies raised under the authority of this act, to be mustered into the service of the State; and shall thereafter organize them successively into battalions, regiments, brigades, divisions, and army corps, as their strength and the necessities of the service may require.

3. He shall have authority to issue orders for the election, on reasonable notice, of all officers; and when the good of the service requires it, he may delegate any portion of his authority to his assistants or to subordinate commanders.

4. He shall have authority to require from all officers, at any time, such reports and returns as may be necessary to inform himself of the military condition of any portion of the force under his command; and to examine also the books, accounts, and papers of officers charged with the disbursement of military funds, and to demand from such officers a strict and detailed account of all public disbursements. He shall also supervise the action of councils of administration, and restrain their appropriations within the limits prescribed by law.

5. He shall have authority to examine into the condition of the armories, arsenals, or other places of deposit or safekeeping of the public arms; and in case of defective arrangements by any of the counties, for the preservation of the arms held by any portion of the Active Militia therein, he may require the county judge to make better provision for their safe-keeping; or he may require that they shall be surrendered to the State.

6. It shall be his duty to report to the commander-in-chief, in order that the information may reach the Auditor of Public Accounts, any loss or unnecessary damage to the public arms or property of which he may have information; and it shall thereupon

be the duty of the Auditor to direct a levy of the sum which may be found due from any county for the loss or damage to the arms or other public property which may have been charged to said county.

7. He shall have authority at any time, by issuing his orders to that effect, to disband any portion of the military force under his command which may evince a mutinous or disorderly spirit, and to deprive them of their arms; a copy of which order shall be transmitted to the clerk of the county court of the county in which said force was raised, after which it shall be considered a misdemeanor in any person so discharged to appear with State arms in his possession, or as any portion of the volunteer force, until again regularly mustered into service, under the penalty of not less than ten dollars for each offense; and such person shall be proceeded against before any justice of the peace, by the attorney for the county where such person may happen to be, on information given by the inspector general, or any officer of the Volunteer Militia, or by any citizen of the county; and all fines collected from such person, shall be paid over to the county clerk, who shall pay it into the State treasury as part of the military fund.

8. It shall be his duty, when practicable, to drill and inspect in person, at least once in each year, every part of the Volunteer Militia; and he may order such inspections at any time.

9. He shall make annually, prior to the first day of December, a return to the commander-in-chief of the strength and organization of the Volunteer Militia, and of the state of their arms and equipments, accompanied by a report showing the condition of the whole force as to instruction, discipline, and efficiency.

10. He shall have authority, from time to time, to make requisitions on the Auditor of Public Accounts for such stationery and books of record as may be necessary for the business of his department; and it shall be the duty of the Auditor to furnish the same when the requisition has been approved by the commander-in-chief.

11. He shall have authority to publish, for distribution amongst the Volunteer Militia, such general orders and regulations as may be necessary for their use and instruction; the cost of which may be rendered in his account of expenses to the Auditor, and reimbursed when approved by the commander-in-chief.

12. He shall have authority, with the approval of the commander-in-chief, to publish, for like distribution, such blank forms and general regulations as may be necessary for the Volunteer Militia; and the Public Printer is hereby directed to furnish the same.

13. He may convene courts of inquiry to investigate and examine into any matter connected with the discipline or military condition of any part of the volunteer force; and may also convene general courts martial for the trial of any offender against any of the military laws. And it shall be his duty to order the prosecution of all officers against whom he may entertain charges of incapacity, neglect of duty, embezzlement, or misapplication of public money or property, ungentlemanly or

unofficerlike conduct, or any conduct to the prejudice of good order and military discipline.

* * *

15. Under the authority of the commander-in-chief he shall cause to be assembled for purposes of encampment and military instruction, at suitable points, such portions of the Volunteer Militia as can be conveniently and economically brought together; and when thus assembled, it shall be his duty to assume command of said force, and to direct its instruction, both theoretically and practically, according to the systems of tactics and other military instruction prescribed; but no such encampment for purposes only of instruction, in time of peace, shall be required to continue a longer period than six days for the same troops.

* * *

ARTICLE V. OF THE QUARTERMASTER GENERAL

§ 1. The quartermaster general, and the subordinates of his department, shall perform also the duties of the commissariat, or all the duties which especially relate to the subsistence of the troops.

§ 2. The quartermaster general shall be especially charged with the preservation and safe-keeping of the State arms, equipments, and munitions of war, of every kind and description, and shall issue the same only in pursuance of law, on a written order from the Governor.

§ 3. Whenever the State forces shall be called into the service of the State, for any purpose, the officers of the quartermaster's department—subject, however, to the orders of the commanding officer—shall have charge of all wagon trains and transportation of every kind, as well as of all arms, equipments, ordnance, and ordnance stores and subsistence, and shall be responsible for the safe-keeping of the same until properly issued.

The Act then describes other high administrative offices: the adjutant general, the inspector general, and the quartermaster general. The first two offices are combined in this game into the Inspector General. The quartermaster general oversees all of the arms owned by the state, including those in the State Armory in Frankfort.

* * *

§ 7. The quartermaster general shall have authority to pay for the transportation of all arms and public stores issued to troops and received into the State arsenal from other parts of the State. His accounts for the amount of such transportation, when approved by the Governor, shall be paid on the warrant of the Auditor.

ARTICLE VI. OF THE ORGANIZATION OF THE ACTIVE OR VOLUNTEER MILITIA

§ 1. The Volunteer or Active Militia shall be styled the Kentucky State Guard. It shall be composed of all citizens or residents of the State over eighteen years of age who may voluntarily become active, *bona fide* members of the State Guard, and who shall sign the following agreement, or an agreement to that effect:

I solemnly promise and agree that I will honestly and faithfully serve the State of Kentucky against all her enemies or opposers, and that I will do my utmost to support the constitution and laws of the United States, and of the State of Kentucky, against all violence of whatsoever kind or description; and I further declare that I will well and truly execute and obey the legal orders of all officers legally placed over me, when on duty.

Of Supplying Arms and Equipments to Companies of the State Guard

§ 12. The commanding officer of every company of the State Guard shall make a requisition on the quartermaster general for such supply of arms and equipments as may be necessary for his company, on which requisition shall be indorsed the certificate of the county judge that it is made with his consent. This requisition, accompanied by the commanding officer's receipt to the quartermaster general, shall be forwarded to the adjutant general. Should the commander-in-chief approve, he shall give an order on the back of the requisition, directing the quartermaster general to make the issue. The arms having been issued, the quartermaster general will file the receipts and requisition as vouchers to accompany his annual return to the Auditor.

* * *

§ 16. The commander-in-chief shall have authority at any time to demand from the counties, or from any portion of the military force, all arms and military stores and equipments belonging to the State, and which may be in the possession of such counties or military force.

* * *

Of Existing Volunteer Companies

§ 25. Within ninety days after the passage of this act every existing military company which has been furnished with State arms shall conform to the requirements of this act which relate to mustering new companies into the State Guard; but it shall not be an absolute requisite that such companies shall have the full strength required for new companies, or that the members of such companies shall be eighteen years of age. The commanding officer under the present organization of such companies shall make out a statement of all arms, equipments, and public property in possession of the company and of its members, and submit the same to the county judge, who, if he deem it expedient, shall indorse on said statement that it is with his sanction that said arms and equipments are held by said company; after which indorsement the arms and equipments so described shall be charged against such county in like manner as if they had been issued as provided in cases of new companies mustered into the service under this act. The statement of arms, thus indorsed, together with the commander's report of the strength of the company, shall be transmitted to the inspector general, who shall cause the company to be mustered into the State Guard, and the election of officers to take place in the same manner as is provided for a new company.

§ 26. Should any existing company fail, within the required time, to comply with the above prescribed conditions, it shall be considered as disbanded; and it shall be the duty of the county attorney, or the Commonwealth's attorney for the district in which such disbanded company existed, on the representation of any officer of the Active Militia, to take the necessary legal steps to obtain the restitution of the State arms and other property which had been issued for the use of such company.

§ 27. After the expiration of ninety days from the passage of this act, no person who is not a member of the Active Militia, shall retain or have in his possession, at any time, arms or military equipments belonging to the State, unless they have been properly issued to such person in pursuance of law, and he shall be permitted by proper authority to retain the same in the discharge of a public duty; and no person, whether of the Active Militia or not, shall use any public arms or equipments for his private use; under the penalty, in either of the above cases, of not less than five dollars for each offense, to be recovered before a justice of the peace, on information by the county attorney; or in the case of a member of the Active Militia, it may be recovered by sentence of a court martial.

§ 28. No public arms or equipments of any kind shall hereafter be issued to any person not members of the Active Militia, except in time of war, insurrection, or public danger so imminent that the commander-in-chief shall consider that the public safety requires him to make the issue.

* * *

Of Troops in the State Service

§ 35. Whenever any portion of the Active Militia shall be ordered to assemble, for purposes of military instruction, under the authority of the commander-in-chief; or whenever any part of the State forces shall be ordered to assemble under his authority in time of war, invasion, insurrection, or public danger, the rules and articles of war, and the general regulations for the government of the army of the United States, so far as they are applicable, and with such modifications as the commander-in-chief may prescribe, shall be considered in force and regarded as part of this act, during the continuance of such instruction, and to the close of such state of war, invasion, insurrection, or public danger; but no punishment under such rules and articles, which shall extend to the taking of life, shall in any case be inflicted, except in time of actual war, invasion, or insurrection declared by proclamation of the Governor to exist.

* * *

ARTICLE VII. OF TROOPS CALLED OUT BY CIVIL AUTHORITIES

§ 1. Whenever there shall be in any city, town, or county, any tumult, riot, mob, or any body of men acting together by force with intent to commit any felony, or misdemeanor, or to offer violence to persons or property, or by force and violence to break and resist the laws of the Commonwealth, or any such tumult, riot, or mob shall be threatened, and the fact be made to appear to the commander-in-chief, or to the mayor of any city, or to any court of record sitting in said city, or county, or to any judge thereof, or to any judge of the Court of Appeals, or to the sheriff of said county, the commander-in-chief may issue his order, or such mayor, court, judge, or sheriff may, in writing, direct the senior or other military officers convenient to the scene of disturbance to turn out such portion of his or their command as may be necessary to quell, suppress, or prevent such tumult or threatened tumult; and any officer or member of the military who shall fail promptly to obey such orders and directions of said civil officers, shall be subjected to such fines as a court martial shall inflict, and if an officer, shall be cashiered.

§ 2. Whenever it becomes necessary, in order to sustain the supremacy of the law, that the troops should fire upon a mob, the civil officer calling out such troops (in the exercise of a sound discretion) shall give the order to fire to the superior officer present, whenever it can be done, who will at once proceed to carry out the order, and shall direct the firing to cease only when ordered to do so by the proper civil authority.

§ 3. No officer who has been called out to sustain the civil authorities shall, under any pretence, or in compliance with any order, fire blank cartridges on a mob, under penalty of being cashiered by sentence of a court martial.

WILLIAM LOWNDES YANCEY

"Speech of Protest in the Charleston Convention," April 28, 1860

Born in 1814, Yancey was an active figure in South Carolina's nullification movement. He moved to Alabama in 1836, and he became prominent as an Anti-Whig orator in the presidential campaign of 1840. Elected to Congress in 1844, he vigorously opposed the Clay Compromise of 1850 and endorsed the Nashville Convention. As a vociferous Southern nationalist, he led the advocates of secession at the Charleston Democratic Convention in 1860, where he gave this speech.

SOURCE: *William Jennings Bryan, ed.,* America: II (1818–1865), *vol. IX of* The World's Famous Orations *(New York: Bartleby.com, 2003), available at www.bartleby.com/268/9/19.html/.*

It has been charged, in order to demoralize whatever influence we might be entitled to, either from our personal or political characteristics or as representatives of the State of Alabama, that we are disruptionists, disunionists *per se;* that we desire to break up the party in the State of Alabama, to break up the party in the Union, and to dissolve the Union itself. Each and all of these allegations, come from what quarter they may, I pronounce to be false. There is no disunionist, that I know of, in the delegation from the State of Alabama. There is no disruptionist that I know of, and if there are factionists in our delegation they could not have got in there with the knowledge upon the part of our State Convention that they were of so unenviable a character.

We have come here, with the twofold purpose of saving the country and of saving the Democracy; and if the Democracy will not lend itself to that high, holy and elevated purpose; if it can not elevate itself above the mere question of how perfect shall be its mere personal organization and how widespread shall be its mere voting success, then we say to you, gentlemen, mournfully and regretfully, that, in the opinion of the State of Alabama, and I believe, of the whole South, you have failed in your mission, and it will be our duty to go forth and make an appeal to the loyalty of the country to stand by that Constitution which party organizations have deliberately rejected.

The South is in a minority, we have been tauntingly told to-day. In the progress of events and the march of civilization and emigration, the Northwest has grown up, from a mere infant in swaddling clothes, at the formation of the Constitution, into the form and proportions of a giant people; and owing to its institutions and demand for white labor, and the peculiar nature of our institutions, though advancing side by side with us in parallel lines, but never necessarily in conflict, it has surpassed us greatly in numbers. We are, therefore, in a numerical minority. But we do not murmur at this; we cheerfully accept the result; but we as firmly claim the right of the minority—and what is that? We claim the benefit of the Constitution that was made for the protection of minorities.

In the march of events, feeling conscious of your numerical power, you have aggressed upon us. We hold up between us and your advancing columns of numbers that written instrument which your and our fathers made, and by the compact of which, you with your power were to respect as to us and our rights. Our and your fathers made it that they and their children should for ever observe it; that, upon all questions affecting the rights of the minority, the majority should not rely upon their voting numbers, but should look, in restraint upon passion, avarice and lust for power, to the written compact, to see in what the minority was to be respected, and how it was to be protected, and to yield an implicit obedience to that compact. Constitutions are made solely for the protection of the minorities in government, and for the guidance of majorities.

Ours are now the institutions which are at stake; ours is the peace that is to be destroyed; ours is the property that is to be destroyed; ours is the honor at stake—the honor of children, the honor of families, the lives, perhaps, of all of us. It all rests upon what your course may ultimately make out of a great heaving volcano of passion. Bear with us then, while we stand sternly upon what is yet a dormant volcano, and say that we can yield no position until we are convinced that we are wrong. We are in a position to ask you to yield. What right of yours, gentlemen of the North, have we of the South ever invaded? What institution of yours have we ever assailed, directly or indirectly? What laws have we ever passed that have invaded, or induced others to invade, the sanctity of your homes, or to put your lives in jeopardy, or that were likely to destroy the fundamental institutions of your States? The wisest, the most learned and the best among you remain silent, because you can not say that we have done this thing.

If your view is right and ours is not one strictly supported by the compact, still the consequence, in a remote degree, of your proposition, may bring a dreaded result upon us all. If you have no domestic, no municipal peace at stake, and no property at stake, and no fundamental institutions of your liberties at stake, are we asking any too much of you to-day when we ask you to yield to us in this matter as brothers, in order to quiet our doubts? For in yielding you lose nothing that is essentially right. Do I state that proposition, gentlemen, any stronger than your own intellects and your own judgment will thoroughly endorse? If I do, I am unconscious of it.

Turn the pages of the recent past as regards the possessions acquired in the Mexican War, in which, gentlemen, it is but modestly stating the fact when I say that Southern chivalry was equal to Northern chivalry—that Southern blood was poured out in equal quantities with Northern blood—and Southern genius shone as bright upon the battle-field as Northern genius; and yet. when the battle was done, and the glittering spoil was brought forward, a vast and disproportionate quantity was given to the North, while the South was made to take the portion of an almost portionless son.

In the Northern States the Democratic party was once overwhelmingly in the ascendant. Why are they not so now? And why is the South more unitedly Democratic? The answer is ready. Antislavery sentiment is dominant in the North—slavery sentiment is dominant in the South. And, gentlemen, let me tell you, if it is not presumption in me to tell you, why you have grown weaker and weaker. It is my belief, from some observation and reflection upon this subject, that you are not now in the ascendant in the North, because you have tampered with the antislavery feeling of that section. I do not mean that you have tampered with it, or yielded to it, as a matter of choice. I do not mean that you are willful traitors to your convictions of duty; but this is what I do mean: Finding an overwhelming preponderance of power in that antislavery sentiment, believing it to be the common will of your people, you hesitated before it; you trembled at its march. You did not triumph over the young Hercules in his cradle, because you made no direct effort to do so.

There is a conviction in our minds that we can not be safe in the Union, unless we obtain your unequivocal pledge to an administration of this government upon plainly avowed constitutional, congressional, as well as executive and judicial, protection of our rights. You have objected that this is a new feature in Democracy. But I say you have taken jurisdiction of this question in years past. In 1844 you took jurisdiction of the slavery question, to protect it from assaults. In 1848 you again took jurisdiction of the slavery question, though to a limited extent. In 1852 you did the same; and in 1856 when the Territorial issues were forced upon the country by the Freesoilers, you demanded that the Democratic party should take one step farther in advance, in order to be up with the progress of the times, and with the march of aggression. You then added to these former platforms another plank, which it was then deemed would be sufficient to meet the issues urged.

And what was that plank? It was that Congress should not intervene to establish or abolish slavery in State or Territory. What is the fair and just meaning of this proposition? Lawyers and statesmen who are in the habit of construing laws and constitutions by the light of experience and by the rules which the great jurists of all ages have laid down for their construction, know that in order to decide what a law of doubtful import means, you must look at the subject matter, at the cause of its enactment; you must look at the evils it was designed to correct, and the remedy it was designed to give.

Gentlemen of the Convention, that venerable, that able, that revered jurist, the honorable chief justice of the United States, trembling upon the very verge of the grave, for years kept merely alive by the pure spirit of patriotic duty that burns within his breast—a spirit that will not permit him to succumb to the gnawings of disease and to the weaknesses of mortality—which hold him, as it were, suspended between two worlds, with his spotless ermine around him, standing upon the very altar of justice, has given to us the utterance of the Supreme Court of the United States upon this very question.

Let the murmur of the hustings be stilled—let the voices of individual citizens, no matter how great and respected in their appropriate spheres, be hushed, while the law, as expounded by the constituted authority of the country, emotionless, passionless and just, rolls in its silvery cadence over the entire realm, from the Atlantic to the Pacific, and from the ice-bound regions of the North to the glittering waters of the Gulf. What says that decision? That decision tells you, gentlemen, that the Territorial Legislature has no power to interfere with the rights of the slave-owner in the Territory while in a Territorial condition. That decision tells you that this government is a union of sovereign States; which States are coequal, and in trust for which coequal States the government holds the Territories. It tells you that the people of those coequal States have a right to go into these Territories, thus held in trust, with every species of property which is recognized as property by the States in which they live, or by the Constitution of the United States.

But, we are met right here with this assertion: we are told by the distinguished advocate of this doctrine of popular sovereignty that this opinion is not a decision of the Supreme Court, but merely the opinion of citizen Taney. He does not tell you, my countrymen, that it is not the opinion of the great majority of the Supreme Court bench. Oh, no! but he tells you that it is a matter that is *obiter dicta*, outside the jurisdiction of the Court; in other words, extra-judicial—that it is simply the opinion of Chief Justice Taney, as an individual, and not the decision of the Court because it was not the subject-matter before the Court.

Now, Mr. Douglas and all others who make that assertion and undertake to get rid of the moral, the constitutional, the intellectual power of the argument, put themselves directly in conflict with the venerable chief justice of the Supreme Court of the United States, and with the recorded decision of the Court itself; because Chief Justice Taney, after disposing of the demurrer in that case, undertook to go on and to decide the question upon the facts and the merits of the case; and, said he, in doing that we are met with the objection, "That anything we may say upon that part of the case will be extrajudicial and mere *obiter dicta*. This is a manifest mistake," etc.; and the Court—not Chief Justice Taney, but the whole Court, with but two dissenting voices—decided that it was not *obiter dicta;* that it was exactly in point, within the jurisdiction of the Court, and that it was the duty of the Court to decide it.

Now then, who shall the Democracy recognize as authority on this point—a statesman, no matter how brilliant and able and powerful in intellect, in the very meridian of life, animated by an ardent and consuming ambition, struggling as no other man has ever done for the high and brilliant position of candidate for the presidency of the United States, at the hand of this great party; or that old and venerable jurist, who, having filled his years with honor, leaves you his last great decision before stepping from the high place of earthly power into the grave, to appear before his Maker, in whose presence deception is impossible, and earthly position is as dust in the balance?

We simply claim that we, being coequal with you in the Territories, we having property which is as sacred to us as yours is to you, that is recognized as such by the Constitution of our common country—shall enjoy, unmolested, the rights to go into the Territories, and to remain there, and enjoy those rights as citizens of the United States, as long as our common government holds those Territories in trust for the States of which we are citizens. That is all.

We shall go to the wall upon this issue if events shall demand it, and accept defeat upon it. Let the threatened thunders roll and the lightning flash through the sky, and let the dark cloud now resting on the Southern horizon be pointed out by you. Let the world know that our people are in earnest. In accepting defeat upon that issue, my countrymen, we are bound to rise, if there is virtue in the Constitution. But if we accept your policy, where shall we be? We shall then have assented to the great fact involved in adopting your platform, that the government is a failure so far as the protection of the South in the Territories is concerned. We should be estopped for ever from asserting our principle simply by your pointing to the record that we had assented to the fact that the government could not be administered on a clear assertion of our rights. Is it true, gentlemen of the Northwest? Is it true, gentlemen of the whole country, that our government is a failure so far as the plain and unequivocal rights of the South are concerned? If it be a failure, we are not patriots unless we go to work at the very foundation stone of this error and reconstruct this party on a proper basis.

To my countrymen of the South I have a few words here to say. Be true to your constitutional duties and rights. Be true to your own sense of right. Accept of defeat here, if defeat is to attend the assertion of the right, in order that you may secure a permanent victory in whatever contest you carry a constitutional banner. Yield nothing of principle for mere party success—else you will die by the hands of your associates as surely as by the hand of your avowed enemy.

A party, in its noblest sense, is an organized body that pledges itself to the people to administer the government on a constitutional basis. The people have no interest in parties, except to have them pledged to administer the government for the protection of their rights. The leaders of the masses, brilliant men, great statesmen, may, by ever ignoring the people's rights, still have a brilliant destiny in the rewards of office and the distribution of eighty millions annually; but when those leaders, those statesmen, become untrue to the people, and ask the people to vote for a party that ignores their rights, and dares not acknowledge them, in order to put and keep them in office, they ought to be strung upon a political gallows higher than that ever erected for Haman.

JOHN J. CRITTENDEN

Amendments Proposed in Congress, December 18, 1860

Kentucky senator John J. Crittenden was the political heir to Henry Clay. An experienced statesman, Crittenden served as governor and in the U.S. House of Representatives and the Senate; he was also U.S. Attorney General under the Harrison and Fillmore administrations.

Throughout his years in government, Crittenden aligned himself with the Whig Party, supported Henry Clay, and opposed the Democratic Party led by Andrew Jackson and Martin Van Buren. When the Whigs began to disintegrate, Crittenden joined the Know-Nothings. The rise in sectional tensions encouraged him to help create the Constitutional Union Party, but he refused to accept the party's nomination for the presidency.

Instead, he turned to crafting the following amendments in the hopes of averting civil war. In addition to guaranteeing the legality of slavery in states where it is already established, the amendments protect the interstate slave trade and slavery in the District of Columbia. They also strengthen the Fugitive Slave Act and repudiate the policy of popular sovereignty by reinstating the Missouri Compromise Line in western territories. Crittenden's final proposed amendment makes the others permanent and immune from future revisions.

SOURCE: *Paul Leicester Ford,* The Federalist: A Commentary on the Constitution of the United States by Alexander Hamilton, James Madison and John Jay Edited with Notes, Illustrative Documents and a Copious Index *(New York: Henry Holt and Co., 1898).*

Whereas, serious and alarming dissensions have arisen between the Northern and Southern States, concerning the rights and security of the rights of the slaveholding States, and especially their rights in the common territory of the United States; and whereas it is eminently desirable and proper that these dissensions, which now threaten the very existence of this Union, should be permanently quieted and settled by constitutional provisions, which shall do equal justice to all sections, and thereby restore to the people that peace and good will which ought to prevail between all the citizens of the United States: Therefore,

Resolved by the Senate and House of Representatives of the United States of America in Congress assembled (two-thirds of both Houses concurring), That the following articles be, and are hereby, proposed and submitted as amendments to the Constitution of the United States, which shall be valid to all intents and purposes, as part of said Constitution, when ratified by conventions of three-fourths of the several States:

ARTICLE I

In all the territory of the United States now held, or hereafter acquired, situated north of latitude 36° 30′, slavery or involuntary servitude, except as a punishment for crime, is prohibited while such territory shall remain under territorial government. In all the territory south of said line of latitude, slavery of the African race is hereby recognized as existing, and shall not be interfered with by Congress, but shall be protected as property by all the departments of the territorial government during its continuance. And when any Territory, north or south of said line, within such boundaries as Congress may prescribe, shall contain the population requisite for a member of Congress according to the then Federal ratio of representation of the people of the United States, it shall, if its form of government be republican, be admitted into the Union, on an equal footing with the original States, with or without slavery, as the constitution of such new State may provide.

This is essentially a return to the Missouri Compromise Line, but it extends it all the way to the Pacific Ocean.

ARTICLE II

Congress shall have no power to abolish slavery in places under its exclusive jurisdiction, and situate within the limits of States that permit the holding of slaves.

ARTICLE III

Congress shall have no power to abolish slavery within the District of Columbia, so long as it exists in the adjoining States of Virginia and Maryland, or either, nor without the consent of the inhabitants, nor without just compensation first made to such owners of slaves as do not consent to such abolishment. Nor shall Congress at any time prohibit officers of the Federal Government, or members of Congress, whose duties require them to be in said District, from bringing with them their slaves, and holding them as such, during the time their duties may require them to remain there, and afterward taking them from the District.

This article essentially makes it impossible to abolish slavery in Washington D.C.

ARTICLE IV

Congress shall have no power to prohibit or hinder the transportation of slaves from one State to another, or to a Territory in which slaves are by law permitted to be held, whether that transportation be by land, navigable rivers, or by the sea.

ARTICLE V

That in addition to the provisions of the third paragraph of the second section of the fourth article of the Constitution of the United States,[1] Congress shall have power to provide by law, and it shall be its duty so to provide, that the United States shall pay to the owner who shall apply for it, the full value of his fugitive slave in all cases when the marshal or other officer whose duty it was to arrest said fugitive was prevented

The federal government becomes the guarantor of slaveholders with escaped slaves.

---

1. *This refers to the fugitive slave clause of the Constitution, which reads, "No person held to service or labor in one state, under the laws thereof, escaping into another, shall, in consequence of any law or regulation therein, be discharged from such service or labor, but shall be delivered up on claim of the party to whom such service or labor may be due."*

from so doing by violence or intimidation, or when, after arrest, said fugitive was rescued by force, the owner thereby prevented and obstructed in the pursuit of his remedy for the recovery of his fugitive slave under the said clause of the Constitution and the laws made in pursuance thereof. And in all such cases, when the United States shall pay for such fugitive, they shall have the right, in their own name, to sue the county in which said violence, intimidation, or rescue was committed, and to recover from it, with interest and damages, the amount paid by them for said fugitive slave. And the said county, after it has paid said amount to the United States may, for its indemnity, sue and recover from the wrongdoers or rescuers by whom the owner was prevented from the recovery of his fugitive slave, in like manner as the owner himself might have sued and recovered.

ARTICLE VI

No future amendment of the Constitution shall affect the five preceding articles; nor the third paragraph of the second section of the first article of the Constitution,[2] nor the third paragraph of the second section of the fourth article of said Constitution[3] and no amendment shall be made to the Constitution which shall authorize or give to Congress any power to abolish or interfere with slavery in any of the States by whose laws it is, or may be allowed or permitted.

And whereas, also, besides these causes of dissension embraced in the foregoing amendments proposed to the Constitution of the United States, there are others which come within the jurisdiction of Congress, as far as its power will extend, to remove all just cause for the popular discontent and agitation which now disturb the peace of the country, and threaten the stability of its institutions: Therefore,

1. Resolved by the Senate and House of Representatives of the United States of America in Congress assembled, That the laws now in force for the recovery of fugitive slaves are in strict pursuance of the plain and mandatory provisions of the Constitution, and have been sanctioned as valid and constitutional by the judgment of the Supreme Court of the United States, that the slaveholding States are entitled to the faithful observance and execution of those laws, and that they ought not to be repealed, or so modified or changed as to impair their efficiency; and that laws ought to be made for the punishment of those who attempt by rescue of the slave, or other illegal means, to hinder or defeat the due execution of said laws,

2. That all State laws which conflict with the fugitive slave acts of Congress, or any other constitutional acts of Congress, or which, in their operation, impede, hinder, or delay the free course and due execution of any of said acts, are null and void by the plain provisions of the Constitution of the United States; yet those State laws, void as they are, have given color to practice, and led to consequences which have obstructed the due administration and execution of acts of Congress, and

---

2. *This refers to the three-fifths rate of representation for slaves in the House of Representatives.*

3. *This is another reference to the fugitive slave clause.*

especially the acts for the delivery of fugitive slaves, and have thereby contributed much to the discord and commotion now prevailing. Congress, therefore, in the present perilous juncture, does not deem it improper respectfully and earnestly to recommend the repeal of those laws to the several States which have enacted them, or such legislative corrections or explanations of them as may prevent their being used or perverted to such mischievous purposes.

3. That the act of the 18th of September, 1850, commonly called the fugitive slave law, ought to be so amended as to make the fee of the commissioner, mentioned in the eighth section of the act, equal in amount, in the cases decided by claimant. And to avoid misconstruction, the last clause of the fifth section of said act which authorizes the person holding a warrant for the arrest or detention of a fugitive slave, to summon to his aid the posse comitatus, and which declares it to be the duty of all good citizens to assist him in its execution, ought to be so amended as to expressly limit the authority and duty to cases in which there shall be resistance or danger of resistance or rescue.[4]

4. That the laws for the suppression of the African slave-trade and especially those prohibiting the importation of slaves in the United States, ought to be made effectual, and ought to be thoroughly executed; and all further enactments necessary to those ends ought to be promptly made.

---

4. *These changes remove the parts of the fugitive slave law of 1850 that Northerners found most frustrating, unjust, and invasive. A posse comitatus is a group of citizens called up by a law enforcement official to arrest a criminal.*

STEPHEN F. HALE

"Letter to Governor Beriah Magoffin," December 27, 1860

Stephen F. Hale was appointed commissioner to Kentucky by Governor A. B. Moore and charged with urging his home state to consider secession from the Union. He presented the following letter to the governor in which he praises Kentucky as an original defender of state sovereignty in 1798, outlines the South's complaints regarding the free states, and warns Kentucky that failure to join the movement for secession will be interpreted as weakness by the state's adversaries.

SOURCE: *United States War Department*, The War of the Rebellion: A Compilation of the Official Records of the Union and Confederate Armies, *Series IV, vol. 1, 4–11.*

I have the honor of placing in your hands herewith, a Commission from the Governor of the State of Alabama, accrediting me as a Commissioner from that State to the sovereign State of Kentucky, to consult in reference to the momentous issues now pending between the Northern and Southern States of this Confederacy. Although each State, as a sovereign political community, must

"Confederacy" is a reference to the United States, not the Confederate States of America, which had not yet been formed.

finally determine these grave issues for itself, yet the identity of interest, sympathy, and institutions, prevailing alike in all the slaveholding States, in the opinion of Alabama, renders it proper that there should be a frank and friendly consultation, by each one, with her sister Southern States, touching their common grievances, and the measures necessary to be adopted to protect the interest, honor, and safety of their citizens.

I come, then, in a spirit of fraternity, as the Commissioner on the part of the State of Alabama, to confer with the authorities of this Commonwealth, in reference to the infraction of our Constitutional rights, wrongs done and threatened to be done, as well as the mode and measure of redress proper to be adopted by the sovereign States aggrieved, to preserve their sovereignty, vindicate their rights and protect their citizens. In order to [develop] a clear understanding of the appropriate remedy, it may be proper to consider the rights and duties, both of the State and citizen, under the Federal Compact, as well as the wrongs done and threatened.

I therefore submit, for the consideration of your Excellency, the following propositions, which I hope will command your assent and approval:

1. The people are the source of all political power; and the primary object of all good Governments is to protect the citizen in the enjoyment of life, liberty and property; and whenever any form of Government becomes destructive of these ends, it is the inalienable right, and the duty of the people to alter or abolish it.

2. The equality of all the States of this Confederacy, as well as the equality of rights of all the citizens of the respective States under the Federal Constitution, is a fundamental principle in the scheme of the Federal Government. The Union of these States under the Constitution, was formed "to establish justice, insure domestic tranquility, provide for the common defense, promote the general welfare, and secure the blessings of liberty to her citizens and their posterity;" and when it is perverted to the destruction of the equality of the States, or substantially fails to accomplish these ends, it fails to achieve the purposes of its creation, and ought to be dissolved.

3. The Federal Government results from a Compact entered into between separate sovereign and independent States, called the Constitution of the United States, and Amendments thereto, by which these sovereign States delegated certain specific powers to be used by that Government, for the common defense and

general welfare of all the States and their citizens; and when these powers are abused, or used for the destruction of the rights of any State or its citizens, each State has an equal right to judge for itself, as well of the violations and infractions of that instrument, as of the mode and measure of redress; and if the interest or safety of her citizens demands it, may resume the powers she had delegated, without let or hindrance from the Federal Government, or any other power on earth.

4. Each State is bound in good faith to observe and keep, on her part, all the stipulations and covenants inserted for the benefit of other States in the Constitutional Compact—the only bond of Union by which the several States are bound together; and when persistently violated by one party to the prejudice of her sister States, ceases to be obligatory on the States so aggrieved, and they may rightfully declare the compact broken, the Union thereby formed dissolved, and stand upon their original rights, as sovereign and independent political communities; and further, that each citizen owes his primary allegiance to the State in which he resides, and hence it is the imperative duty of the State to protect him in the enjoyment of all his Constitutional rights, and see to it that they are not denied or withheld from him with impunity, by any other State or Government.

If the foregoing propositions correctly indicate the objects of this Government, the rights and duties of the citizen, as well as the rights, powers and duties of the State and Federal Government under the Constitution, the next inquiry is, what rights have been denied, what wrongs have been done, or threatened to be done, of which the Southern States, or the people of the Southern States, can complain?

At the time of the adoption of the Federal Constitution, African slavery existed in twelve of the thirteen States. Slaves are recognized as property, and as a basis of political power, by the Federal Compact, and special provisions are made by that instrument for their protection as property. Under the influences of climate, and other causes, slavery has been banished from the Northern States, the slaves themselves have been sent to the Southern States, and there sold, and their price gone into the pockets of their former owners at the North. And in the meantime, African Slavery has not only become one of the fixed domestic institutions of the Southern States, but forms an important element of their political power, and constitutes the most valuable species of

> "The Peculiar Institution" was a polite way to refer to slavery.

their property—worth, according to recent estimates, not less than four thousand millions of dollars; forming, in fact, the basis upon which rests the prosperity and wealth of most of these States, and supplying the commerce of the world with its richest freights, and furnishing the manufactories of two continents with the raw material, and their operatives with bread. It is upon this gigantic interest, this peculiar institution of the South, that the Northern States and their people have been waging an unrelenting and fanatical war for the last quarter of a century.

An institution with which is bound up, not only the wealth and prosperity of the Southern people, but their very existence as a political community.

This war has been waged in every way that human ingenuity, urged on by fanaticism, could suggest. They attack us through their literature, in their schools, from the hustings, in their legislative halls, through the public press, and even their courts of justice forget the purity of their judicial ermine, to strike down the rights of the Southern slave-holder, and over-ride every barrier which the Constitution has erected for his protection; and the sacred desk is desecrated to this unholy crusade against our lives, our property, and the Constitutional rights guaranteed to us by the Compact of our Fathers. During all this time the Southern States have freely conceded to the Northern States, and the people of those States, every right secured to them by the Constitution, and an equal interest in the common Territories of the Government; protected the lives and property of their citizens of every kind, when brought within Southern jurisdiction; enforced through their courts, when necessary, every law of Congress passed for the protection of Northern property, and submitted, ever since the foundation of the Government, with scarcely a murmur, to the protection of their shipping, manufacturing and commercial interest, by odious bounties, discriminating tariffs, and unjust navigation-laws, passed by the Federal Government to the prejudice and injury of their own citizens.

The law of Congress for the rendition of fugitive slaves, passed in pursuance of an express provision of the Constitution, remains almost a dead letter upon the Statute Book. A majority of the Northern States, through their legislative enactments, have openly nullified it, and impose heavy fines and penalties upon all persons who aid in enforcing this law; and some of those States declare the Southern slave-holder, who goes within their jurisdiction to assert his legal rights under the Constitution, guilty of a high crime, and affix imprisonment in the penitentiary as the penalty. The Federal officers who attempt to discharge their duties under the law, as well as the owner of the slave, are set upon by mobs, and are fortunate if they escape without serious injury to life or limb; and the State authorities, instead of aiding in the enforcement of this law, refuse the use of their jails, and by every means which unprincipled fanaticism can devise, give countenance to the mob, and aid the fugitive to escape. Thus, there are annually large amounts of property actually stolen away from the Southern States, harbored and protected in Northern States, and by their citizens. And when a requisition is made for the thief by the Governor of a Southern State upon the Executive of a Northern State, in pursuance of the express conditions of the Federal Constitution, he is insultingly told that the felon has committed no crime—and thus the criminal escapes, the property of the citizen is lost, the sovereignty of the State is insulted—and there is no redress, for the Federal Courts have no jurisdiction to award a mandamus to the Governor of a sovereign State, to compel him to do an official Executive act, and Congress, if disposed, under the Constitution has no power to afford a remedy. These are wrongs under which the Southern people have long suffered, and to which they have patiently submitted, in the hope that a returning sense of justice would prompt the people of the Northern States to discharge their Constitutional obligations, and save our common country. Recent events, however, have not justified their hopes; the more daring and restless fanatics have banded themselves together, have put in practice the terrible lessons taught by the timid, by making an armed incursion upon the sovereign State of Virginia, slaughtering her citizens, for the purpose of exciting a servile insurrection among her slave population, and arming them for the destruction of their own masters. During the past summer, the Abolition incendiary has lit up the prairies of Texas, fired the dwellings of the inhabitants, burned down whole towns and laid poison for her citizens—thus literally executing the terrible denunciations of fanaticism against the slave-holder—"Alarm to their sleep, fire to their dwellings, and poison to their food."

The same fell spirit, like an unchained demon, has for years swept over the plains of Kansas, leaving death, desolation and ruin in its track. Nor is this the mere ebullition of a few half-crazy fanatics, as is abundantly apparent from the sympathy manifested all over the North, where, in many places, the tragic death of John Brown, the leader of the raid upon Virginia, who died upon the gallows a condemned felon, is celebrated with public honors, and his name canonized as a martyr to liberty; and many, even of the more conservative papers of the Black Republican school, were accustomed to speak of his murderous attack upon the lives of the unsuspecting citizens of Virginia, in a half-sneering and half-apologetic tone. And what has the Federal Government done in the meantime to protect slave property upon the common Territories of the Union? Whilst a whole squadron of the American Navy is maintained on the coast of Africa, at an enormous expense, to enforce the execution of the laws against the slave trade—and properly, too—and the whole navy is kept afloat to protect the lives and property of American citizens upon the high seas, not a law has been passed by Congress, or an arm raised by the Federal Government, to protect the slave property of citizens from the Southern States upon the soil of Kansas—the common Territory and common property of the citizens of all the States—purchased alike by their common treasure, and held by the Federal Government, as declared by the Supreme Court of the United States, as the trustee for all their citizens; but, upon the contrary, a Territorial Government, created by Congress, and supported out of the common treasury, under the influence and control of Emigrant Aid Societies and Abolition emissaries, is permitted to pass laws excluding and destroying all that species of property within her limits—thus ignoring, on the part of the Federal Government, one of the fundamental principles of all good Governments, the duty to protect the property of the citizen, and wholly refusing to maintain the equal rights of the States and the citizens of the States upon their common Territories.

As the last and crowning act of insult and outrage upon the people of the South, the citizens of the Northern States, by overwhelming majorities, on the 6th day of November last, elected Abraham Lincoln and Hannibal Hamlin,

President and Vice President of the United States. Whilst it may be admitted that the mere election of any man to the Presidency, is not, per se, a sufficient cause for a dissolution of the Union; yet, when the issues upon, and circumstances under which he was elected, are properly appreciated and understood, the question arises whether a due regard to the interest, honor, and safety of their citizens, in view of this and all the other antecedent wrongs and outrages, do not render it the imperative duty of the Southern States to resume the powers they have delegated to the Federal Government, and interpose their sovereignty for the protection of their citizens.

What, then are the circumstances under which, and the issues upon which he was elected? His own declarations, and the current history of the times, but too plainly indicate he was elected by a Northern sectional vote, against the most solemn warnings and protestations of the whole South. He stands forth as the representative of the fanaticism of the North, which, for the last quarter of a century, has been making war upon the South, her property, her civilization, her institutions, and her interests; as the representative of that party which overrides all Constitutional barriers, ignores the obligations of official oaths, and acknowledges allegiance to a higher law than the Constitution, striking down the sovereignty and equality of the States, and resting its claims to popular favor upon the one dogma, the Equality of the Races, white and black.

It was upon this acknowledgment of allegiance to a higher law, that Mr. Seward rested his claim to the Presidency, in a speech made by him in Boston, before the election. He is the exponent, if not the author, of the doctrine of the Irrepressible Conflict between freedom and slavery, and proposes that the opponents of slavery shall arrest its further *expansion, and by Congressional Legislation exclude it from the common Territories of the Federal Government, and place it where the public mind shall rest in the belief that it is in the course of ultimate extinction.*

He claims for free negroes the right of suffrage, and an equal voice in the Government—in a word, all the rights of citizenship, although the Federal Constitution, as construed by the highest judicial tribunal in the world, does not recognize Africans imported into this country as slaves, or their descendants, whether free or slaves, as citizens.

These were the issues presented in the last Presidential canvass, and upon these the American people passed at the ballot-box.

Upon the principles then announced by Mr. Lincoln and his leading friends, we are bound to expect his administration to be conducted. Hence it is, that in high places, among the Republican party, the election of Mr. Lincoln is hailed, not simply as a change of Administration, but as the inauguration of new principles, and a new theory of Government, and even as the downfall of slavery. Therefore it is that the election of Mr. Lincoln cannot be regarded otherwise than a solemn declaration, on the part of a great majority of the Northern people, of hostility to the South, her property and her institutions—nothing less than an open declaration of war—for the triumph of this new theory of Government destroys the property of the South, lays waste her fields, and inaugurates all the horrors of a San Domingo servile insurrection, consigning her citizens to assassinations, and her wives and daughters to pollution and violation, to gratify the lust of half-civilized Africans. Especially is this true in the cotton-growing States, where, in many localities, the slave outnumbers the white population ten to one.

If the policy of the Republicans is carried out, according to the programme indicated by the leaders of the party, and the South submits, degradation and ruin must overwhelm alike all classes of citizens in the Southern States. The slave-holder and non-slave-holder must ultimately share the same fate—all be degraded to a position of equality with free negroes, stand side by side with them at the polls, and fraternize in all the social relations of life; or else there will be an eternal war of races, desolating the land with blood, and utterly wasting and destroying all the resources of the country.

Who can look upon such a picture without a shudder? What Southern man, be he slave-holder or non-slave-holder, can without indignation and horror contemplate the triumph of negro equality, and see his own sons and daughters, in the not distant future, associating with free negroes upon terms of political and social equality, and the white man stripped, by the Heaven-daring hand of fanaticism of that title to superiority over the black race which God himself has bestowed? In the Northern States, where free negroes are so few as to form no appreciable part of the community, in spite of all the legislation for their protection, they still remain a degraded caste, excluded by the ban of society from social association with all but the lowest and most degraded of the white race. But in the South, where in many places the African race largely predominates, and, as a consequence, the two races would be continually pressing together, amalgamation, or the extermination of the one or the other, would be inevitable. Can Southern men submit to such degradation and ruin? God forbid that they should.

But, it is said, there are many Constitutional, conservative men at the North, who sympathize with and battle for us. That is true; but they are utterly powerless, as the late Presidential election unequivocally shows, to breast the tide of fanaticism that threatens to roll over and crush us. With them it is a question of principle, and we award to them all honor for their loyalty to the Constitution of our Fathers. But their defeat is not their ruin. With us it is a question of self-preservation—our lives, our property, the safety of our homes and our hearthstones—all that men hold dear on earth, is involved in the issue. If we triumph, vindicate our rights and maintain our institutions, a bright and joyous future lies before us. We can clothe the world with our staple, give wings to her commerce, and supply with bread the starving operative in other lands, and at the same time preserve an institution that has done more to civilize and Christianize the heathen than all human agencies beside—an institution alike beneficial to both races, ameliorating the moral, physical and intellectual condition of the one, and giving wealth and happiness to the other. If we fail, the light of our civilization goes down in blood, our wives and our little ones will be driven from their homes by the light of our own dwellings. The dark pall of barbarism must soon gather over our sunny land, and the scenes of West India emancipation, with its attendant horrors and crimes (that monument of British fanaticism and folly), be re-enacted in our own land upon a more gigantic scale.

Then, is it not time we should be up and doing, like men who know their rights and dare maintain them? To whom shall the people of the Southern States look for the protection of their rights, interests and honor? We answer, to their own sons and their respective States. To the States, as we have seen, under our system of Government, is due the primary allegiance of the citizen; and the correlative obligation of protection devolves upon the respective States—a duty from which they cannot escape, and which they dare not neglect without a violation of all the bonds of fealty that hold together the citizen and the sovereign.

The Northern States and their citizens have proved recreant to their obligations under the Federal Constitution; they have violated that Compact, and refused to perform their covenants in that behalf.

The Federal Government has failed to protect the rights and property of the citizens of the South, and is about to pass into the hands of a party pledged for the destruction, not only of their rights and property, but the equality of the States ordained by the Constitution, and the heaven-ordained superiority of the white over the black race. What remains, then, for the Southern States, and the people of these States, if they are loyal to the great principles of civil and religious liberty, sanctified by the sufferings of a seven-year's war, and baptized with the blood of the Revolution? Can they permit the rights of their citizens to be denied and spurned? their property spirited away, their own sovereignty violated, and themselves degraded to the position of mere dependencies, instead of sovereign States? or shall each for itself, judging the infractions of the Constitutional Compact, as well as the mode and measure of redress, declare that the covenants of that sacred instrument, in their behalf, and for the benefit of their citizens, have been willfully, deliberately, continuously and persistently broken and violated by the other parties to the compact, and that they and their citizens are therefore absolved from all further obligations to keep and perform the covenants thereof, resume the powers delegated to the Federal Government, and, as sovereign States, form other relations for the protection of their citizens and the discharge of the great ends of Government? The Union of these States was one of fraternity as well as equality; but what fraternity now exists between the citizens of the two sections? Various religious associations, powerful in numbers and influence, have been broken asunder, and the sympathies that bound together the people of the several States, at the time of the formation of the Constitution, has ceased to exist, and feelings of bitterness, and even hostility, have sprung up in its place. How can this be reconciled, and a spirit of fraternity established? Will the people of the North cease to make war upon the institution of Slavery, and award to it the protection guaranteed by the Constitution? The accumulated wrongs of many years, the late action of the members in Congress in refusing every measure of justice to the South, as well as the experience of all the past, answers, *No, never!*

Will the South give up the institution of slavery, and consent that her citizens be stripped of their property, her civilization destroyed, the whole land laid waste by fire and sword? It is impossible; she can not, she will not. Then why attempt any longer to hold together hostile States under the stipulations of a violated Constitution? It is impossible; disunion is inevitable. Why then wait longer for the consummation of a result that must come? Why waste further time in expostulations and appeals to Northern States and their citizens, only to be met, as we have been for years past, by renewed insults and repeated injuries? Will the South be better prepared to meet the emergency when the North shall be strengthened by the admission of the new territories of Kansas, Nebraska, Washington, Jefferson, Nevada, Idaho, Chippewa, and Arizonia [*sic*], as non-slaveholding States, as we are warned from high sources will be done within the next four years, under the administration of Mr. Lincoln? Can the true men at the North ever make a more powerful or successful rally for the preservation of our rights and the Constitution, than they did in the last Presidential contest? There is nothing to inspire a hope that they can.

Shall we wait until our enemies shall possess themselves of all the powers of the Government? until Abolition Judges are on the Supreme Court bench, Abolition Collectors at every port, and Abolition Postmasters in every town, secret mail agents traversing the whole land, and a subsidized Press established in our midst to demoralize the people? Will we be stronger then, or better prepared to meet the struggle, if a struggle must come? No, verily! When that time shall come, well may our adversaries laugh at our folly, and deride our impotence. The deliberate judgment of Alabama, as indicated by the Joint Resolutions of her General Assembly, approved February 24, 1860, is, that prudence, patriotism, and loyalty to all the great principles of civil liberty incorporated in our Constitution, and consecrated by the memories of the past, demand that the Southern States should now resume their delegated powers, maintain the rights, interests and honor of their citizens, and vindicate their own sovereignty. And she most earnestly, but respectfully, invites her sister sovereign State, Kentucky, who so gallantly vindicated the sovereignty of the States in 1798, to the consideration of these grave and vital questions, hoping she may concur with the State of Alabama in the conclusions to which she has been driven by the impending dangers that now surround the Southern States. But if, on mature deliberation, she dissents on any point from the conclusions to which the State of Alabama has arrived, on behalf of that State I most respectfully ask a declaration by this venerable Commonwealth of her conclusions and position on all the issues discussed in this communication; and Alabama most respectfully urges upon the people and authorities of Kentucky the startling truth that *submission or acquiescence on the part of the Southern States, at this perilous hour, will enable Black Republicanism to redeem all its nefarious pledges, and accomplish its flagitious ends;* and that hesitation or delay in their action will be misconceived and misconstrued by their adversaries, and ascribed, not to that elevated patriotism that would sacrifice all but their honor to save the Union of their Fathers, but to division and dissension among themselves, and their consequent weakness; that prompt, bold and decided action is demanded alike by prudence, patriotism and the safety of their citizens.

Permit me, in conclusion, on behalf of the State of Alabama, to express my high gratification, at the cordial manner in which I have been received, as her Commissioner, by the authorities of the State of Kentucky, as well as the profound personal gratification which, as a son of Kentucky, born and reared within her borders, I feel, at the manner in which I, as the Commissioner from the State of my adoption, have been received and treated by the authorities of the State of my birth. Please accept assurances of the high consideration and esteem of,

Your obedient servant, &c.,

S.F. Hale,

Commissioner from the State of Alabama.

JAMES HENLEY THORNWELL

"A Southern Christian View of Slavery," December 4, 1861

One of the many bonds between the North and the South that was broken by the Civil War was religious unity. On May 16, 1861, the Presbyterian Assembly met in Philadelphia. Only a minority of Southern presbyteries were represented. When a Northern clergyman called for an oath of allegiance to the federal government, the Southern clergymen defected. On December 4th, Presbyterian clergymen of the South met in Augusta, Georgia, to establish the General Assembly of the Presbyterian Church in the Confederate States of America. The Assembly adopted this statement drafted by James Henley Thornwell, a prominent South Carolina Presbyterian clergyman, that justified the church's secession from the parent church.

A political moderate and opponent of the church's participation in secular affairs such as slavery prior to 1860, Thornwell became a champion of the Confederacy and one of the strongest advocates of slavery in the South. Thornwell delivered this statement as a speech on December 4, 1861, months after the game takes place; despite this anachronism, however, it perfectly distills his position and is therefore included here. This excerpt from the speech deals with the slavery question.

SOURCE: The Annals of America: 1858–1865, The Crisis of the Union *(Chicago: Encyclopædia Britannica, 1968), 298–303, available at www.teachingamericanhistory.org/library/index.asp?document=1124.*

The antagonism of Northern and Southern sentiment on the subject of slavery lies at the root of all the difficulties which have resulted in the dismemberment of the federal Union, and involved us in the horrors of an unnatural war.

The Presbyterian Church in the United States has been enabled by the Divine Grace to pursue, for the most part, an eminently conservative, because a thoroughly scriptural, policy in relation to this delicate question. It has planted itself upon the word of God and utterly refused to make slaveholding a sin or nonslaveholding a term of communion. But though both sections are agreed as to this general principle, it is not to be disguised that the North exercises a deep and settled antipathy to slavery itself, while the South is equally zealous in its defense. Recent events can have no other effect than to confirm the antipathy on the one hand and strengthen the attachment on the other.

The Northern section of the church stands in the awkward predicament of maintaining, in one breath, that slavery is an evil which ought to be abolished and of asserting, in the next, that it is not a sin to be visited by exclusion from communion of the saints. The consequence is that it plays partly into the hands of Abolitionists and partly into the hands of slaveholders and weakens its influence with both. It occupies the position of a prevaricating witness whom neither party will trust. It would be better, therefore, for the moral power of the Northern section of the church to get entirely quit of the subject.

At the same time, it is intuitively obvious that the Southern section of the church, while even partially under the control of those who are hostile to slavery, can never have free and unimpeded access to the slave population. Its ministers and elders will always be liable to some degree of suspicion. In the present circumstances, Northern alliance would be absolutely fatal. It would utterly preclude the church from a wide and commanding field of usefulness.

This is too dear a price to be paid for a nominal union. We cannot afford to give up these millions of souls and consign them, so far as our efforts are concerned, to hopeless perdition for the sake of preserving an outward unity which, after all, is an empty shadow. If we would gird ourselves heartily and in earnest for the work which God has set before us, we must have the control of our ecclesiastical affairs and declare ourselves separate and independent.

And here we may venture to lay before the Christian world our views as a church upon the subject of slavery. We beg a candid hearing.

In the first place, we would have it distinctly understood that, in our ecclesiastical Capacity, we are neither friends nor the foes of slavery, that is to say, we have no commission either to propagate or abolish it. The policy of its existence or nonexistence is a question which exclusively belongs to the state. We have no right, as a church, to enjoin it as a duty or to condemn it as a sin. Our business is with the duties which spring from the relation; the duties of the masters, on the one hand, and of the slaves, on the other. These duties we are to proclaim and to enforce with spiritual sanctions. The social, civil, political problems connected with this great subject transcend our sphere, as God had not entrusted His church the organization of society, the construction of governments, nor the allotment of individuals to their various stations. The church has as much right to preach to the monarchies of Europe and the despotism of Asia the doctrines of republican equality as to preach to the governments of the South the extirpation of slavery. This position is impregnable unless it can be shown that slavery is a sin. Upon every other hypothesis, it is so clearly a question for the state that the proposition would never for a moment have been doubted had there not been a foregone conclusion in relation to its moral character. Is slavery, then, a sin?

In answering this question, as a church, let it be distinctly borne in mind that the only rule of judgment is the written word of God. The church knows nothing of the intuitions of reason or the deductions of philosophy, except those reproduced in the Sacred Canon. She has a positive constitution in the Holy Scriptures and has no right to utter a single syllable upon any subject except as the Lord puts words in her mouth. She is founded, in other words, upon express *revelation*. Her creed is an authoritative testimony of God and not a speculation, and what she proclaims, she must proclaim with the infallible certitude of faith and not with the hesitating assent of an opinion. The question, then, is brought within a narrow compass: Do the Scriptures directly or indirectly condemn slavery as a sin? If they do not, the dispute is ended, for the church, without forfeiting her character, dares not go beyond them.

Now, we venture to assert that if men had drawn their conclusions upon this subject only from the Bible, it would no more have entered into any human head to denounce slavery as a sin than to denounce monarchy, aristocracy, or poverty. The truth is, men have listened to what they falsely considered as primitive intuitions, or as necessary deductions from primitive cognitions, and then have gone to the Bible to confirm the crotchets of their vain philosophy. They have gone there determined to find a particular result, and the consequence is that they leave with having made, instead of having interpreted, Scripture. Slavery is no new thing. It has not only existed for ages in the world but it has existed, under every dispensation of the covenant of grace, in the Church of God.

Indeed, the first organization of the church as a visible society, separate and distinct from the unbelieving world, was inaugurated in the family of a slaveholder. Among the very first persons to whom the seal of circumcision was affixed were the slaves of the father of the faithful, some born in his house and others bought with his money. Slavery again reappears under the Law. God sanctions it in the first table of the Decalogue, and Moses treats it as an institution to be regulated, not abolished; legitimated and not condemned. We come down to the age of the New Testament, and we find it again in the churches founded by the apostles under the plenary inspiration of the Holy Ghost. These facts are utterly amazing, if slavery is the enormous sin which its enemies represent it to be. It will not do to say that the Scriptures have treated it only in a general, incidental way, without any clear implication as to its moral character. Moses surely made it the subject of express and positive legislation, and the apostles are equally explicit in inculcating the duties which spring from both sides of the relation. They treat slaves as bound to obey and inculcate obedience as an office of religion—a thing wholly self-contradictory if the authority exercised over them were unlawful and iniquitous.

But what puts this subject in a still clearer light is the manner in which it is sought to extort from the Scriptures a contrary testimony. The notion of direct and explicit condemnation is given up. The attempt is to show that the genius and spirit of Christianity are opposed to it—that its great cardinal principles of virtue are utterly against it. Much stress is laid upon the Golden Rule and upon the general denunciations of tyranny and oppression. To all this we reply that no principle is clearer than that a case positively excepted cannot be included under a general rule.

Let us concede, for a moment, that the law of love, and the condemnation of tyranny and oppression seem logically to involve, as a result, the condemnation of slavery; yet, if slavery is afterwards expressly mentioned and treated as a lawful relation, it obviously follows, unless Scripture is to be interpreted as inconsistent with itself, that slavery is, by necessary implication, excepted. The Jewish law forbad, as a general rule, the marriage of a man with his brother's wife. The same law expressly enjoined the same marriage in a given case. The given case was, therefore, an exception, and not to be treated as a violation of the general rule. The law of love has always been the law of God. It was enunciated by Moses almost as clearly as it was enunciated by Jesus Christ. Yet, notwithstanding this law, Moses and the apostles alike sanctioned the relation of slavery.

The conclusion is inevitable, either that the law is not opposed to it or that slavery is an excepted case. To say that the prohibition of tyranny and oppression include slavery is to beg the whole question. Tyranny and oppression involve either the unjust usurpation or the unlawful exercise of power. It is the unlawfulness, either in its principle or measure, which constitutes the core of the sin. Slavery must, therefore, be proved to be unlawful before it can be referred to any such category. The master may, indeed, abuse his power, but he oppresses, not simply as a master but as a wicked master.

But apart from all this, the law of love is simply the inculcation of universal equity. It implies nothing as to the existence of various ranks and graduations in society. The interpretation which makes it repudiate slavery would make it equally repudiate all social, civil, and political inequalities. Its meaning is not that we should conform ourselves to the arbitrary expectations of others but that we should render unto them precisely the same measure which, if we were in their circumstance, it would be reasonable and just in us to demand at their hands. It condemns slavery, therefore, only upon the supposition that slavery is a sinful relation—that is, he who extracts the prohibition of slavery from the Golden Rule begs the very point in dispute.

We cannot prosecute the argument in detail, but we have said enough, we think, to vindicate the position of the Southern church. We have assumed no new attitude. We stand exactly where the Church of God has always stood—from Abraham to Moses, from Moses to Christ, from Christ to the reformers, and from the reformers to ourselves. We stand upon the foundation of the prophets and apostles, Jesus Christ himself being the chief cornerstone. Shall we be excluded from the fellowship of our brethren in other lands because we dare not depart from the charter of our faith? Shall we be branded with the stigma of reproach because we cannot consent to corrupt the word of God to suit the intentions of an infidel philosophy? Shall our names be cast out as evil and the finger of scorn pointed at us because we utterly refuse to break our communion with Abraham, Isaac and Jacob, with Moses, David and Isaiah, with apostles, prophets, and martyrs, with all who have gone to glory from slaveholding countries and from a slaveholding church, without ever having dreamed that they were living in mortal sin by conniving at slavery in the midst of them? If so, we shall take consolation in the cheering consciousness that the Master has accepted us.

We may be denounced, despised, and cast out of the synagogues of our brethren. But while they are wrangling about the distinctions of men according to the flesh, we shall go forward in our divine work and confidently anticipate that, in the great day, as the consequence of our humble labors, we shall meet millions of glorified spirits who have come up from the bondage of earth to a nobler freedom than human philosophy ever dreamed of. Others, if they please, may spend their time in declaiming on the tyranny of earthly masters; it will be our aim to resist the real tyrants which oppress the soul—sin and Satan. These are the foes against whom we shall find it employment enough to wage a successful war. And to this holy war is the purpose of our church to devote itself with redoubled energy. We feel that the souls of our slaves are a solemn trust, and we shall strive to present them faultless and complete before the presence of God.

Indeed, as we contemplate their condition in the Southern states, and contrast it with that of their fathers before them and that of their brethren in the present day in their native land, we cannot but accept it as a gracious providence that they have been brought in such numbers to our shores and redeemed from the bondage of barbarism and sin. Slavery to them has certainly been overruled for the greatest good. It has been a link in the wondrous chain of providence, through which many sons and daughters have been made heirs of the heavenly inheritance. The providential result is, of course, no justification if the thing is intrinsically wrong; but it is certainly a matter of devout thanksgiving, and no obscure intimation of the will and purpose of God and of the consequent duty of the church. We cannot forbear to say, however, that the general operation of the system is kindly and benevolent; it is a real and effective discipline, and, without it, we are profoundly persuaded that the African race in the midst of us can never be elevated in the scale of being. As long as that race, in its comparative degradation, coexists, side by side with the white, bondage is its normal condition.

As to the endless declamation about human rights, we have only to say that human rights are not a fixed but fluctuating quantity. Their sum is not the same in any two nations on the globe. The rights of Englishmen are one thing, the rights of Frenchmen, another. There is a minimum without which a man cannot be responsible; there is a maximum which expresses the highest degree of civilization and of Christian culture. The education of the species consists in its ascent along this line. As you go up, the number of rights increases, but the number of individuals who possess them diminishes. As you come down the line, rights are diminished, but the individuals are multiplied. It is just the opposite of the predicamental scale of the logicians. There, comprehension diminishes as you ascend and extension increases, and comprehension increases as you descend and extension diminishes.

Now, when it is said that slavery is inconsistent with human rights, we crave to understand what point in this line is the slave conceived to occupy. There are, no doubt, many rights which belong to other men—to Englishmen, to Frenchmen, to his masters, for example—which are denied to him. But is he fit to possess them? Has God qualified him to meet the responsibilities which their possession necessarily implies? His place in the scale is determined by his competency to fulfill its duties. There are other rights which he certainly possesses, without which he could neither be human nor accountable. Before slavery can be charged with doing him injustice, it must be shown that the minimum which falls to his lot at the bottom of the line is out of proportion to his capacity and culture—a thing which can never be done by abstract speculation.

The truth is, the education of the human race for liberty and virtue is a vast providential scheme, and God assigns to every man, by a wise and holy degree, the precise place he is to occupy in the great moral school of humanity. The scholars are distributed into classes according to their competency and progress. For God is in history.

To avoid suspicion of a conscious weakness of our cause, when contemplated from the side of pure speculation, we may advert for a moment to those pretended intuitions which stamp the reprobation of humanity upon this ancient and hoary institution. We admit that there are primitive principles in morals which lie at the root of human consciousness. But the question is, how are we to distinguish them? The subjective feeling of certainty is no adequate criterion, as that is equally felt in reference to crotchets and hereditary prejudices. The very point is to know when this certainty indicates a primitive cognition and when it does not. There must, therefore, be some eternal test, and whatever cannot abide that test has no authority as a primary truth. That test is an inward necessity of thought, which in all minds at the proper stage of maturity is absolutely universal.

Whatever is universal is natural. We are willing that slavery should be tried by this standard. We are willing to abide by the testimony of the race, and if man, as man, has everywhere condemned it—if all human laws have prohibited it as crime—if it stands in the same category with malice, murder, and theft, then we are willing, in the name of humanity, to renounce it, and to renounce it forever. But what if the overwhelming majority of mankind have approved it? What if philosophers and statesmen have justified it, and the laws of all nations acknowledged it; what then becomes of these luminous institutions? They are an *ignis fatuus*,[1] mistaken for a star.

We have now, brethren, in a brief compass, for the nature of this address admits only of an outline, opened to you our whole hearts upon this delicate and vexed subject. We have concealed nothing. We have sought to conciliate no sympathy by appeals to your charity. We have tried our cause by the word of God; and though protesting against its authority to judge in a question concerning the duty of the church, we have not refused to appear at the tribunal of reason.

Are we not right, in view of all the preceding considerations, in remitting the social, civil, and political problems connected with slavery to the state? It is not a subject, save in the moral duties which spring from it, which lies beyond the province of the church? Have we any right to make it an element in judging of Christian character? Are we not treading in the footsteps of the flock? Are we not acting as Christ and His apostles have acted before us? Is it not enough for us to pray and labor, in our lot, that all men may be saved without meddling as a church with the technical distinction of their civil life?

We leave the matter with you. We offer you the right hand of fellowship. It is for you to accept it or reject it. We have done our duty. We can do no more. Truth is more precious than union, and if you cast us out as sinners, the breach of charity is not with us as long as we walk according to the light of the written word.

---

1. Ignis fatuus: *a will-o'-the-wisp.*

SELECTED BIBLIOGRAPHY

Secession, in General

Abrahamson, James L. *The Men of Secession and Civil War, 1859–1861.* Wilmington, Delaware: Scholarly Resources, 2000.

Freehling, William. *The Road to Disunion, Volume I: Secessionists at Bay, 1776–1854.* New York: Oxford University Press, 1990.

Freehling, William. *The Road to Disunion, Volume II: Secessionists Triumphant.* New York: Oxford University Press, 2007.

Varon, Elizabeth R. *Disunion!: The Coming of the American Civil War, 1789–1859.* Chapel Hill: University of North Carolina Press, 2010.

Secession, in Kentucky

Boyd, John A. "Intimidation, Conspiracy, Provocation & Intrigue: The Militias of Kentucky, 1859-1861." *Army History* (Fall 2008): 6–17.

Coulter, E. M. *Civil War and Readjustment in Kentucky.* Charlotte: University of North Carolina Press, 1926.

Crofts, Daniel. *Reluctant Confederates: Upper South Unionists in the Secession Crisis.* Chapel Hill: University of North Carolina Press, 1989.

Mackey, Thomas C. "Not a Pariah, but a Keystone: Kentucky and Secession." In Kent T. Dollar, Larry H. Whiteaker, and W. Calvin Dickinson, eds., *Sister States, Enemy States: The Civil War in Kentucky and Tennessee,* pp. 25–45. Lexington: University Press of Kentucky, 2009.

Porter, David. "The Kentucky Press and the Election of 1860." *The Filson Club History Quarterly* 46, no. 1 (1972): 49–52.

Speed, Thomas. *The Union Cause in Kentucky, 1860–1865.* New York: G. P. Putnam's Sons, 1907.

Slavery, in General

Berlin, Ira. *Generations of Captivity: A History of African-American Slaves.* Cambridge: Harvard University Press, 2003.

Deyle, Steven. *Carry Me Back: The Domestic Slave Trade in American Life.* New York and Oxford: Oxford University Press, 2005.

Stewart, James Brewer. *Abolitionist Politics and the Coming of the Civil War.* Amherst: University of Massachusetts Press, 2008.

Slavery, in Kentucky

Bogart, Pen. "'Sold for My Account': The Early Slave Trade between Kentucky and the Lower Mississippi Valley." *Ohio Valley History: The Journal of the Cincinnati Historical Society* 2, no. 1 (January 2002): 3–16.

Harlow, Luke E. "Neither Slavery nor Abolitionism: James M. Pendleton and the Problem of Christian Conservative Antislavery in 1840s Kentucky." *Slavery and Abolition* 27, no. 3 (December 2006): 367–89.

Harlow, Luke E. "Religion, Race, and Robert J. Breckinridge: The Ideology of an Antislavery Slaveholder, 1830–1860." *Ohio Valley History: The Journal of the Cincinnati Historical Society* 6, no. 3 (2006): 1–24.

Harlow, Luke E. *Religion, Race, and the Making of Confederate Kentucky, 1830–1880.* New York: Cambridge University Press, 2014.

Harrison, Lowell H. *The Antislavery Movement in Kentucky.* Lexington: University Press of Kentucky, 1978.

Harrold, Stanley. "Violence and Nonviolence in Kentucky Abolitionism." *The Journal of Southern History* 57, no. 1 (February 1991): 15–38.

Lee, Jacob F. "Between Two Fires: Cassius M. Clay, Slavery, and Antislavery in the Kentucky Borderlands." *Ohio Valley History: The Journal of the Cincinnati Historical Society* 6, no. 3 (2006): 50–70.

Tallant, Harold D. *Evil Necessity: Slavery and Political Culture in Antebellum Kentucky* (Lexington: University Press of Kentucky, 2003.

Religion

Carwardine, Richard. "Methodists, Politics, and the Coming of the Civil War." *Church History* 69, no. 3 (September 2000): 578–610.

Chrisman, Richard A. "'In the Light of Eternity': The Southern Methodist Church in Illinois." *Methodist History* 37, no. 1 (1998): 37–47.

Daly, John P. *When Slavery Was Called Freedom: Evangelicalism, Proslavery, and the Causes of the Civil War.* Lexington: University Press of Kentucky, 2004.

Howard, Victor B. *The Evangelical War against Slavery and Caste: The Life and Times of John G. Fee.* Selinsgrove: Susquehanna University Press, 1996.

Najar, Monica. "'Meddling with Emancipation': Baptists, Authority, and the Rift over Slavery in the Upper South." *Journal of the Early Republic* 25 (Summer 2005): 157–86.

Padgett, Chris. "Evangelicals Divided: Abolitions and the Plan of Union's Demise in Ohio's Western Reserve." In John R. McKivigan and Mitchell Snay, eds., *Religion and the Antebellum Debate over Slavery*, pp. 249–72. Athens: University of Georgia Press, 1998.

Padgett, Chris. "Hearing the Antislavery Rank-and-File: The Wesleyan Methodist Schism of 1843." *Journal of the Early Republic* 12, no. 1 (Spring 1992): 63–84.

Snay, Mitchell. *Gospel of Disunion: Religion and Separatism in the American South.* Chapel Hill: University of North Carolina Press, 1997.

Antebellum Politics, in General

Etcheson, Nicole. *Bleeding Kansas: Contested Liberty in the Civil War Era.* Lawrence: University Press of Kansas, 2004.

Gienapp, William E. "Nativism and the Creation of a Republican Majority in the North before the Civil War." *The Journal of American History* 72, no. 3 (December 1985): 529–59.

Green, Don. "Constitutional Unionists: The Party that Tried to Stop Lincoln and Save the Union." *Historian* 69, no. 2 (2007): 231–53.

Holt, Michael. *The Rise and Fall of the American Whig Party: Jacksonian Politics and the Onset of the Civil War.* New York: Oxford University Press, 2003.

Antebellum Kentucky

Connelley, William Elsey, and E. M. Coulter. *History of Kentucky.* Chicago and New York: The American Historical Society, 1922.

Harrison, Lowell Hayes, and James C. Klotter. *A New History of Kentucky.* Lexington: University Press of Kentucky, 1997.

Hopkins, James F. *A History of the Hemp Industry in Kentucky.* Lexington: University Press of Kentucky, 1998 [1951].

NOTES

Part Two: Historical Background

1. Thomas C. Mackey, "Not a Pariah, but a Keystone: Kentucky and Secession," in *Sister States, Enemy States: The Civil War in Kentucky and Tennessee*, eds. Kent T. Dollar, Larry H. Whiteaker, and W. Calvin Dickinson (Lexington: University Press of Kentucky), 25–6.

2. K. R. Constantine Gutzman, "The Virginia and Kentucky Resolutions Reconsidered: 'An Appeal to the Real Laws of Our Country,'" *Journal of Southern History* 66, no. 3 (August 2000): 477.

3. "Virginia Resolutions of 1798, Pronouncing the Alien and Sedition Laws to be Unconstitutional, and Defining the Rights of the States," in *The Debates in the Several State Conventions, on the Adoption of the Federal Constitution, as Recommended by the General Convention at Philadelphia, in 1787, Together with the Journal of the Federal Convention, Luther Martin's Letter, Yates's Minutes, Congressional Opinions, Virginia and Kentucky Resolutions of '98–'99, and Other Illustrations of the Constitution, in Four Volumes*, vol. 4, ed. Jonathan Elliot (Washington: Printed for the Editor, 1836,) 529.

4. Ibid., 428.

5. Ibid., 540. Emphasis in the original.

6. Ibid., 534. The Kentucky legislature bristled at such criticism and in November 1799 offered even more explicit assertions of states' rights in the face of what it called "censure and columniation." It was resolved that "the several states who formed [the Constitution], being sovereign and independent, have the unquestionable right to judge of the infraction [of the limits of federal power]; and, *That a nullification, by those sovereignties, of all unauthorized acts done under color of that instrument, is the rightful remedy*" (emphasis in original). See Ibid., 545.

7. Ibid., 534.

8. John C. Calhoun, *A Disquisition on Government and Selections from the Discourse*, ed. C. Gordon Post (Indianapolis.: Hackett, 1995[1953]), xvii–xviii.

9. Ibid., xviii.

10. Ibid., xix.

11. Brian Steele, "Thomas Jefferson, Coercion, and the Limits of Harmonious Union," *Journal of Southern History* VXXIV, no. 4 (November 2008): 425, 425n4; Calhoun, *A Disquisition on Government*, xvii–xviii.

12. James F. Hopkins, *A History of the Hemp Industry in Kentucky* (Lexington: University Press of Kentucky, 1998[1951]), 4, 80–1.

13. Ira Berlin, *Generations of Captivity: A History of African-American Slaves* (Cambridge, MA: Harvard University Press, 2003), 104.

14. Ibid., Table I: Slave Population of the American Colonies and the United States, 1680–1860, 273.

15. Steven Deyle, *Carry Me Back: The Domestic Slave Trade in American Life* (New York and Oxford: Oxford University Press, 2005), 36–42, 87–93.

16. Berlin, *Generations of Captivity*, 168; Deyle, *Carry Me Back*, 95–6.

17. Berlin, *Generations of Captivity*, 169, 161; Deyle, *Carry Me Back*, 289.

18. Pen Bogart, "'Sold for My Account': The Early Slave Trade Between Kentucky and the Lower Mississippi Valley," *Ohio Valley History: The Journal of the Cincinnati Historical Society* 2, no. 1 (January 2002): 12. Throughout this time, however, the slave population grew in number even as it declined as a proportion of the whole.

19. Berlin, *Generations of Captivity*, 273. Also see: John P. Daly, *When Slavery Was Called Freedom: Evangelicalism, Proslavery, and the Causes of the Civil War* (Lexington: University Press of Kentucky, 2004), 1–2.

20. Richard Carwardine, "Methodists, Politics, and the Coming of the Civil War," *Church History* 69, no. 3 (September 2000): 584–5.

21. Elizabeth R. Varon, *Disunion!: The Coming of the American Civil War, 1789–1859* (Chapel Hill: University of North Carolina Press, 2010), 96–8; James Brewer Stewart, *Abolitionist Politics and the Coming of the Civil War* (Amherst: University of Massachusetts Press, 2008), 13.

22. Mitchell Snay, *Gospel of Disunion: Religion and Separatism in the American South* (Chapel Hill: University of North Carolina Press, 1997), 6; Jacob F. Lee, "Between Two Fires: Cassius M. Clay, Slavery, and Antislavery in the Kentucky Borderlands," *Ohio Valley History* 6, no. 3 (2006): 50; Luke E. Harlow, "Neither Slavery nor Abolitionism: James M. Pendleton and the Problem of Christian Conservative Antislavery in 1840s Kentucky," *Slavery and Abolition* 27, no. 3 (December 2006): 368.

23. Berlin, *Generations of Captivity*, 162.

24. Lowell Hayes Harrison and James C. Klotter, *A New History of Kentucky* (Lexington: University Press of Kentucky, 1997), 168.

25. Bogart, "'Sold for My Account,'" 3–4; T. D. Clark, "The Slave Trade between Kentucky and the Cotton Kingdom," *Mississippi Valley Historical Review* 21, no. 3 (December 1934), 337.

26. Harold D. Tallant, *Evil Necessity: Slavery and Political Culture in Antebellum Kentucky* (Lexington: University Press of Kentucky, 2003), 9; E. M. Coulter, *Civil War and Readjustment in Kentucky* (Charlotte: University of North Carolina Press, 1926), 739, 743; Clark, "The Slave Trade," 331.

27. Monica Najar, "'Meddling with Emancipation': Baptists, Authority, and the Rift over Slavery in the Upper South," *Journal of the Early Republic* 25 (Summer 2005): 158–9.

28. *The Kentucky Encyclopaedia*, s.v. "James Gillespie Birney," 82; Samuel J. May, *Some Recollections of Our Antislavery Conflict* (Boston: Fields, Osgood, & Co., 1869), 204–5, quotation from 210.

29. Victor B. Howard, *The Evangelical War against Slavery and Caste: The Life and Times of John G. Fee* (Selinsgrove: Susquehanna University Press, 1996), 14, 16–17, 23; Stanley Harrold, "Violence and Nonviolence in Kentucky Abolitionism," *Journal of Southern History* 57, no. 1 (February 1991), 18; John G. Fee, *Autobiography of John G. Fee, Berea, Kentucky* (Chicago: National Christian Association, 1891), 11–12.

30. Clay quoted in William Elsey Connelley and E. M. Coulter, *History of Kentucky*, vol. 2 (Chicago and New York: The American Historical Society, 1922), 796. Pendleton quoted in Harlow, "Neither Slavery nor Abolitionism," 369.

31. Luke E. Harlow, "Religion, Race, and Robert J. Breckinridge: The Ideology of an Antislavery Slaveholder, 1830–1860," *Ohio Valley History* 6, no. 3 (2006): 3, 8–9. Also see: Harlow, "Neither Slavery nor Abolitionism," 369.

32. Lee, "Between Two Fires," 54.

33. Cassius M. Clay, *The Life of Cassius Marcellus Clay: Memoirs, Writings, and Speeches Showing His Conduct in the Overthrow of American Slavery, the Salvation of the Union, and the Restoration of the Autonomy of the States*, vol. 1 (Cincinnati: J. Fletcher Brennan & Co., 1886), 56–7.

34. Lee, "Between Two Fires," 60–1.

35. Connelley and Coulter, *History of Kentucky*, 802–3, 812; Clay, *The Life of Cassius Marcellus Clay*, 107–8. Clay brought suit against the leaders of the mob for inciting a riot; a jury found them not guilty.

36. Lowell H. Harrison, *The Antislavery Movement in Kentucky* (Lexington: University Press of Kentucky, 1978), 45–8; Harlow, "Religion, Race, and Robert J. Breckinridge" 16; Connelley and Coulter, *History of Kentucky*, 817.

37. Edward Ayers, *In the Presence of Mine Enemies: War in the Heart of America, 1859–1863* (New York: W. W. Norton, 2004), xix.

38. Chris Padgett, "Hearing the Antislavery Rank-and-File: The Wesleyan Methodist Schism of

1843," *Journal of the Early Republic* 12, no. 1 (Spring 1992): 68; Charles Grandison Finney, *Lectures on Revivals of Religion* (New York: Leavitt, Lord & Co., 1835), 278–9.

39. Richard A. Chrisman, "'In the Light of Eternity': The Southern Methodist Church in Illinois," *Methodist History* 37, no. 1 (1998): 37; Varon, *Disunion!*, 178; Alexander Gross, *A History of the Methodist Church, South, in the United States* (New York: The Christian Literature Co., 1907), 42.

40. Garry Wills, *Head and Heart: American Christianities* (New York: Penguin, 2007), 310–11; Bill J. Leonard, *Baptists in America* (New York: Columbia University Press, 2007), 99.

41. Stewart, *Abolitionist Politics*, 7, 17.

42. William Goodell, *Slavery and Anti-Slavery: A History of the Great Struggle in Both Hemispheres; With a View of the Slavery Question in the United States*, 3rd ed. (New York: William Goodell, 1855), 470–1; Jonathan H. Earle, *Jacksonian Antislavery and the Politics of Free Soil, 1824–1854* (Chapel Hill: University of North Carolina Press, 2004), 144. Immediatist quotation in Stewart, *Abolitionist Politics*, 17.

43. Varon, *Disunion!*, 145.

44. Ibid., 184.

45. Manisha Sinha, *The Counterrevolution of Slavery: Politics and Ideology in Antebellum South Carolina* (Chapel Hill: University of North Carolina Press, 2000), 71.

46. William Freehling, *The Road to Disunion, Volume I: Secessionists at Bay, 1776–1854* (New York: Oxford University Press, 1990), 476.

47. Ibid., 456, 476; Christopher Clark, *Social Change in America: From the Revolution through the Civil War* (Chicago: Ivan R. Dee, 2006), 202–9.

48. Freehling, *The Road to Disunion, Volume I*, 490.

49. Michael Holt, *The Rise and Fall of the American Whig Party: Jacksonian Politics and the Onset of the Civil War* (New York: Oxford University Press, 2003), 464. Southern Whigs, though not exactly enthusiastic about their president's actions, nonetheless found the hullabaloo from Southern Democrats bewildering.

50. Freehling, *The Road to Disunion, Volume I*, 480–2.

51. Varon, *Disunion!*, 223–4.

52. The new Fugitive Slave Act made it a federal offense for any person or state to refuse to extradite accused runaways to the South; though moderates (including Henry Clay) had attempted to include a jury trial as the next stage after extradition, this element failed. The law also set up commissioners in each state to hear the case for extradition; moreover, the commissioner was empowered to call a posse into existence to hunt for runaways; failure to serve when called resulted in stiff fines. See Freehling, *The Road to Disunion, Volume I*, 501.

53. John Caldwell Calhoun, *The Papers of John C. Calhoun*, vol. 27, eds. Robert Lee Meriwether and Clyde Norman Wilson (Columbia: University of South Carolina Press, 2003), 189.

54. Ibid., 210.

55. Paul Finkelman, "*Prigg v. Pennsylvania* and Northern State Courts: Anti-Slavery Use of a Pro-Slavery Decision," *Civil War History* 25, no. 1 (1979): 6–8, 10, 13–14, 21; Varon, *Disunion!*, 158–9; Thomas D. Morris, *Free Men All: The Personal Liberty Laws of the North, 1780–1861* (Baltimore: Johns Hopkins University Press, 1974), 94–5, 104–5; Eric Plaag, "'Let the Constitution Perish': *Prigg v. Pennsylvania*, Joseph Story, and the Flawed Doctrine of Historical Necessity," *Slavery and Abolition* 25, no. 3 (December 2004): 77.

56. Quoted in Connelley and Coulter, *History of Kentucky*, 839.

57. Freehling, *The Road to Disunion, Volume I*, 503.

58. Connelley and Coulter, *History of Kentucky*, 809–17. Historian Marion Lucas breaks this down by decade. In the 1850s there were ninety-six confirmed runaways from Kentucky; see Marion B. Lucas, *From Slavery to Segregation, 1760–1891*, vol. 1 of *A History of Blacks in Kentucky* (Frankfort: Kentucky Historical Society, 1992), 57–62.

59. Ibid., 15.

60. Ibid., 16–17.

61. "Appeal of the Independent Democrats in Congress to the People of the United States," January 19,

1854, in *The Library of Original Sources, Volume 9: 1833–1865*, ed. Oliver Joseph Thatcher (New York and Chicago: University Research Extension, 1907), 151–2. Emphasis added.

62. Nicole Etcheson, *Bleeding Kansas: Contested Liberty in the Civil War Era* (Lawrence: University Press of Kansas, 2004), 20.

63. Holt, *The Rise and Fall of the American Whig Party*, 805.

64. Varon, *Disunion!*, 257.

65. Etcheson, *Bleeding Kansas*, 22–5.

66. Varon, *Disunion!*, 257–9; William E. Gienapp, "Nativism and the Creation of a Republican Majority in the North before the Civil War," *Journal of American History* 72, no. 3 (December 1985): 531.

67. Connelley and Coulter, *History of Kentucky*, 845–7, quotation on 845.

68. "Speech of Senator Seward," *New York Times*, May 27, 1854; Etcheson, *Bleeding Kansas*, 29.

69. Etcheson, *Bleeding Kansas*, 29–33.

70. Varon, *Disunion!*, 261–2; Etcheson, *Bleeding Kansas*, 110–11.

71. Varon, *Disunion!*, 269; James L. Abrahamson, *The Men of Secession and Civil War, 1859–1861* (Wilmington, DE: Scholarly Resources, 2000). Both Brooks and Keitt were returned to Congress in the next election.

72. Varon, *Disunion!*, 269–71.

73. William Cullen Bryant, *Power for Sanity: Selected Editorials of William Cullen Bryant, 1829–1861* (New York: Fordham University Press, 1994), 290.

74. Gienapp, "Nativism and the Creation of a Republican Majority," 539, 541–2.

75. Etcheson, *Bleeding Kansas*, 129.

76. Connelley and Coulter, *History of Kentucky*, 849.

77. "Portion of Speech at Republican Banquet in Chicago, Illinois," in Connelley and Coulter, *History of Kentucky*, 386.

78. William Freehling, *The Road to Disunion, Volume II: Secessionists Triumphant* (New York: Oxford University Press, 2007), 116–18.

79. Ibid., 121. Freehling notes that despite his argument in the case, Taney himself had manumitted his own slaves.

80. Text of *Dred Scott v. John F. A. Sanford* (March 6, 1857), *60 U.S. 393*, Missouri State Archives-St. Louis, December 10, 1855, 17–18.

81. Ibid., 38.

82. Ibid., 56–7.

83. *DeBow's Review: Agricultural, Commercial, Industrial Progress and Resources* 22, no. 4 (April 1857): 403.

84. Kenneth M. Stampp, *America in 1857: A Nation on the Brink* (New York: Oxford University Press, 1992), 100–1.

85. Ibid., 101.

86. Varon, *Disunion!*, 303.

87. Ibid., 304.

88. Ibid., 103–4.

89. Etcheson, *Bleeding Kansas*, 150–9.

90. Ibid., 160–1; Varon, *Disunion!*, 313–14.

91. "Freedom in Kansas: Speech of William H. Seward in the Senate of the United States, March 3, 1858" (Washington, D.C.: Buell & Blanchard, 1858), quotations on 10, 12, and 14.

92. "Speech on the Admission of Kansas, Under the Lecompton Constitution, Delivered in the Senate of the United States, March 4, 1858," in *Selections from the Letters and Speeches of the Hon. James H. Hammond* (New York: John F. Trow & Co., 1866), 308–10, quotation on 310.

93. Ibid., 317.

94. Ibid., 319.

95. Harold Holzer, ed., *The Lincoln-Douglas Debates: The First Complete, Unexpurgated Text* (Fordham, NY: Fordham University Press, 2004), 348.

96. Varon, *Disunion!*, 316–17.

97. The letter also offered $50,000 for "Fred Douglass, but regarding him head and shoulders above these Traitors, will permit him to remain where he now is." See Frederick W. Seward, *Seward at Washington as Senator and Secretary of State: A Memoir of His Life, with Selections from His Letters, 1846–1861*

(New York: Derby and Miller, 1891), 440. Emphasis in the original. Also see Varon, *Disunion!*, 330–1.

98. Luke E. Harlow, *Religion, Race, and the Making of Confederate Kentucky, 1830–1880* (New York: Cambridge University Press, 2014), 111.

99. Abrahamson, *The Men of Secession*, 58–9; Austin L. Venable, "The Conflict between the Douglas and Yancey Forces in the Charleston Convention," *Journal of Southern History* 8, no. 2 (May 1942): 235–8. Free states delegates supported the platform 154 to 30; southern delegates opposed it 108 to 11. See James M. McPherson, *Battle Cry of Freedom: The Civil War Era* (Oxford and New York: Oxford University Press, 1988), 215.

100. Abrahamson, *The Men of Secession*, 60; McPherson, *Battle Cry of Freedom*, 215.

101. McPherson, *Battle Cry of Freedom*, 215–16; Horace Greeley, *The American Conflict: A History of the Great Rebellion in the United States of America, 1860–'64: Its Causes, Incidents, and Results, Intended to Exhibit Especially Its Moral and Political Phases with the Drift and Progress of American Opinion Respecting Human Slavery from 1776 to 1864*, vol. 1 (Hartford, CT: O. D. Case & Company, 1864), 317–18.

102. Greeley, *The American Conflict*, 319.

103. McPherson, *Battle Cry of Freedom*, 217.

104. Greeley, *The American Conflict*, 320.

105. Don Green, "Constitutional Unionists: The Party that Tried to Stop Lincoln and Save the Union," *Historian* 69, no. 2 (2007): 233. Quotation from Greeley, *The American Conflict*, 319.

106. Daniel Crofts, *Reluctant Confederates: Upper South Unionists in the Secession Crisis* (Chapel Hill: University of North Carolina Press, 1989), 76; Green, "Constitutional Unionists," 234, 236.

107. Lewis Collins, *History of Kentucky: Embracing… Incidents of Pioneer Life and Nearly Five Hundred Biographical Sketches of Distinguished Pioneers, Soldier, Statesmen, Jurists, Lawyers* (Baltimore: Genealogical Publishing Co., 1998), 82–3; *Acts of the General Assembly of the Commonwealth of Kentucky*, vol. 1 (Frankfort: J. B. Major, 1860), 128–31.

108. *Acts of the General Assembly*, 120; Thomas Speed, *The Union Cause in Kentucky, 1860–1865* (New York: G.P. Putnam's Sons, 1907), 126–7. Speed writes that there were forty-five fully equipped companies in place by January 1861; Coulter and Connelley put the number at sixty-five in "early 1861" (*History of Kentucky*, 885).

109. *Acts of the General Assembly*, 128–31.

110. David Porter, "The Kentucky Press and the Election of 1860," *The Filson Club History Quarterly* 46, no. 1 (1972): 50–1; Charles Yonkers, "The Civil War Transformation of George W. Smith: How a Western Kentucky Farmer Evolved from Unionist Whig to Pro-Southern Democrat," *The Register of the Kentucky Historical Society* 103, no. 4 (2005): 667.

111. Crofts, *Reluctant Confederates*, 79–80, 90–4.

112. The other four were Delaware, Maryland, Missouri, and Virginia.

113. Quoted in Crofts, *Reluctant Confederates*, 89.

114. Mrs. Chapman Coleman, *The Life of John J. Crittenden: With Selections from His Correspondence and Speeches*, vol. 2 (New York: J. B. Lippincott & Co., 1871), 220.

Part Three: The Game

1. Kentucky Constitution of 1850, XIII§2, XIII§9.

2. Ibid., XIII§3.

3. Ibid., X§1. The process of legal manumission was clarified earlier in 1860. For details, see pp. 143–44.

4. Kentucky Constitution of 1850, II§37.

5. Ibid., VIII§15. However, the constitution makes a provision for people who are physically unable to speak: they may vote by ballot.

6. Ibid., II§29.

7. Ibid., III§22.

8. E. M. Coulter, *Civil War and Readjustment in Kentucky* (Charlotte: University of North Carolina Press, 1926), 48; Richard G. Stone Jr., *A Brittle Sword: The Kentucky Militia, 1776–1912* (Lexington: University Press of Kentucky, 1977), 63.

9. Kentucky Constitution of 1850, XIII§25–26.

10. Ibid., VIII§1. In VIII§8, the constitution adds that taking this oath forbids future challenges.

Part Four: Roles and Factions

1. Kentucky Constitution of 1850, III§12.

2. Ibid., III§8, VII§2.

3. Ibid., III§16.

4. Richard G. Stone Jr., *A Brittle Sword: The Kentucky Militia, 1776–1912* (Lexington: University Press of Kentucky, 1977), 61–3.

ACKNOWLEDGMENTS

Many thanks to all of the undergraduate testers in our courses. Andrew Zepeda deserves special thanks for convincing us to move the description of certain rules to the instructor's guide.

Also thanks to the participants in the 2010, 2012, and 2016 Reacting to the Past Summer Institutes at Barnard College. Roland Machold and Amy Tyson provided particularly detailed feedback on these tests, which helped to clarify the intellectual focus of the game.

Special thanks to Gretchen McKay, Jeff Ostler, Eric Cannon, Ruth Truss, Patrick Kirkwood, and Kathleen Donohue, who were among the first instructors to use the game in the field. Their thoughtful questions about game mechanics greatly improved the clarity of the game book and the accompanying instructor's guide. Betsy Powers and Kathy Donohue also deserve special thanks for voicing their frustrations with the old militia mechanics, which were overly complicated. As a result of their travails, the militia system is now much simpler. If it works well in your game, it is due to their struggles. Ed Conner deserves a special shout-out for staging an early version of the game in the old state capitol in Frankfort on the sesquicentennial of the secession winter.

The final draft of the game book greatly benefitted from close readings by Christine Lambert and Jace Weaver. They pointed out a number of inconsistencies, complications, and overlong passages. Readings and tests of the game by Paul Fessler, Cynthia Krutsinger, Scott Giltner, Jeff Fortney, Ian Binnington, John Moser, Jeff Ostler, and Emily Hess were quite useful too. They (and their students) picked up on a number of small but important oversights. Everything is much smoother and more efficient as a result.

Bill Offutt deserves a paragraph of his own for his comments and suggestions that informed the game throughout its development and shaped its evolution.

Participants in the editorial and production process at W. W. Norton as overseen by Scott Sugarman did an excellent job of putting the finishing touches on the game. Peer reviews by Jay Case, Michael Connolly, Ely Janis, Matthew Norman, and Tamara Venit-Shelton provided helpful clarifying edits.

Finally, thanks to Mark Carnes, Dana Johnson, Jenn Worth, John Burney, and the rest of the Reacting Consortium for awarding us a development grant to move the game forward.

9 781469 670713